D0252503

A BRIEF HISTORY OF EDUCATION

A BRIEF HISTORY OF EDUCATION

A Handbook of Information on Greek, Roman, Medieval, Renaissance, and Modern Educational Practice

by

FRANCESCO CORDASCO
Professor of Education
Montclair State College

1976

LITTLEFIELD, ADAMS & CO.
Totowa, New Jersey

First Edition, 1963

Second Edition, 1970

Revised Edition, 1976

Library of Congress Cataloging in Publication Data

Cordasco, Francesco, 1920-
A Brief History of Education

(A Littlefield, Adams Quality Paperback No. 67)
Includes bibliographies.
1. Education—History—Outlines, syllabi, etc.
I. Titlc.
LA14.C72 1976 370'.9 75-26956
ISBN 0-8226-0067-6

PRINTED IN THE UNITED STATES OF AMERICA

FOR

WILLIAM W. BRICKMAN

Scholar, Colleague, Friend

The needs of the student of the history of education are to acquire a sufficient body of fact concerning the educational practices of the past; to develop an ability to interpret that experience in order to guide his own practice; to exercise his judgment in estimating the relations existing between various theories and corresponding practices; and, above all, to obtain a conception of the meaning, nature, process, and purpose of education that will lift him above the narrow prejudices, the restricted outlook, the foibles, and the petty trials of the average schoolroom, and afford him the fundamentals of an everlasting faith as broad as human nature and as deep as the life of the race.

Paul Monroe, *A Textbook in the History of Education* (1905)

PREFACE

THIS text is intended primarily for those students who are taking courses in the history of education, introduction to education, or courses in education that require some basic historical framework to which educational theory and curriculum development must be related. As a *review manual* it is nonspecialized, and major attention has been given to the important figures in the history of educational thought; to so-called "schools" in which certain tendencies and theoretical commitments may be discerned; to the developments within certain countries, themselves essentially representative of the progress of Western European thought; and to the history of curriculum. The text is not intended as a comprehensive history of education, but rather as a guide to the readings in educational history which the beginning student will usually have been assigned. As a guide, it should give the student the historical background he needs and further furnish him with a brief but reasonably complete discussion of those ideas and developments that make his readings and more extended study meaningful. For the most part, biographical data has been kept at a minimum or not noted at all, and adequate (if very selective) documentary references have been supplied to allow the student both the encouragement and the bibliographical aids he may need for further study. All too often, a *review manual* is either a skeletal outline or a biographical digest without any scholarly underpinning, and without real assistance to the student. I have tried to make this text more than an outline or a collection of notes, and I have adapted the materials to those needs that I have discerned in my classes in the history of educational thought.

I have had the invaluable assistance of many friends and colleagues in the preparation of this manual, and I am certain that much of what is good derives from their sage and knowledgeable counsel. Gratitude is extended to Professor William W. Brickman of the University of Pennsylvania with whom I initially discussed the manual's design and who would have joined me in this venture but for the pressing commitments of a busy agenda; to Dr. Leonard Covello, former educational consultant of the Migration Division, Commonwealth of Puerto Rico; to Dr. George Turner, Professor Virginia Voigt, and Dean John H. Callan of the School of Education, Seton Hall University; to Mr. Louis Romano and other graduate students at New York University, the City University of New York, and Seton Hall University, where much of the material of the manual had its origin. I welcome suggestions on the text's improvement, and am alone responsible for its deficiencies.

Permission has been given by the Macmillan Company to reproduce the valuable chronological plates from Paul Monroe's *A Brief Course in the History of Education* (New York, 1907), and this is gratefully acknowledged.

In this revised edition, bibliographical references have been updated and many new entries have been provided. I am grateful to Professor John E. Talbott of Princeton University whose essay on "The History of Education" (from *Daedalus*) furnishes a perceptive introduction to the historical study of education which (as he correctly observes) has come "to be seen not only as an end in itself but as a promising and hitherto neglected avenue of approach to an extremely broad range of problems." New materials have been added to Part V (American Education) by providing a skeletal overview of crucial educational issues of the last decade; and in Part VI (Recent European Educational History), some further notices of developments bring the account down to the present.

In keeping with its original design, the manual has been kept nonspecialized, but the updating of sources does provide the means for extended and more detailed study. I have also made some revisions which have been suggested by teachers and students who have used the *Handbook* over the years, and who have been generous in their praise and recommendations.

F. C.

CONTENTS

PREFACE vii

THE HISTORY OF EDUCATION xi

GENERAL BIBLIOGRAPHICAL NOTE xxix

PART I: EDUCATION IN CLASSICAL ANTIQUITY 1

Chapter I: Greek Education 3

Chapter II: Roman Education 13

PART II: THE MEDIEVAL WORLD 21

Chapter III: Education during the Early Middle Ages 23

Chapter IV: Education in the Late Middle Ages 31

PART III: TRANSITION TO THE MODERN ERA: THE RENAISSANCE AND REFORMATION 39

Chapter V: The Renaissance and Humanistic Education 41

Chapter VI: The Reformation and Educational Theory 49

PART IV: THE MODERN ERA: (1600–1900) 59

Chapter VII: Realism in Education: the 17th Century 61

Chapter VIII: Naturalism in Education: the 18th Century 77

Chapter IX: Nationalism and Science in Education: the 19th Century 93

PART V: AMERICAN EDUCATION 107

Chapter X: The Colonial Period (1607–1787) 109

Chapter XI: The National Period (1787–1900) 115

Chapter XII: The Twentieth Century 135

PART VI: RECENT EUROPEAN DEVELOPMENTS 151

Chapter XIII: Recent European Educational History 153

INDEX 163

JOHN E. TALBOTT

THE HISTORY OF EDUCATION*

HISTORIANS HAVE begun to stake new claims in the history of education. Over the past decade a number of pioneering books and articles have appeared on subjects whose long neglect now seems quite remarkable—from the Spanish universities under the Habsburgs to childrearing practices in colonial America. Despite the great diversity of themes and problems with which these studies are concerned, they share a similarity of approach. Nearly all seek, to use Bernard Bailyn's phrase, "to see education in its elaborate, intricate involvements with the rest of society."[1] This approach has opened new perspectives in a field historians had long ignored.

Not that the history of education has been neglected. The bibliography in the field is enormous. But it is lopsided, mainly concerned with "house history" and the ideas of pedagogical reformers. Countless histories of individual schools and universities have been published, describing aims, organization, faculty, curricula, finances, student life, and so forth; histories of pedagogical ideas have surveyed the views of leading theorists from Plato through Dewey. To be sure, great monuments of historical scholarship stand forth in the field; such studies as Hastings Rashdall's *The Universities of Europe in the Middle Ages* and Werner W. Jaeger's *Paideia* are not likely soon to be surpassed.

But to the contemporary historian much of the older literature seems inadequate—impressive in bulk but insubstantial, seldom addressed to the sorts of questions with which historical scholarship is now concerned. A good share of the institutional history has been the work of antiquaries and devoted alumni, who uncovered much valuable information but rarely sought to interpret it. With the professionalization of schoolteaching and the establishment of teachers' colleges educational history became nearly a separate discipline, isolated from the mainstream of historical study. The educationists

* Reprinted by permission of *Daedalus,* Journal of The American Academy of Arts and Sciences, Boston, Massachusetts. Winter, 1971, *Historical Studies Today.*

who founded and sustained these institutions sought to give prospective schoolteachers a historical sense of mission, certainly a not unworthy aim. But in the hands of some of them educational history became a weapon against adversaries living and dead, a vindication of their own ideas and efforts in the struggle for public schooling; in the hands of others it became a whiggish chronicle, a quick guided tour of the past in search of the antecedents of contemporary educational institutions.

If historians were frequently heard to lament the inadequacies of traditional approaches to the history of education, they were slow to do anything about them. Only after the Second World War, when educational issues began to loom larger in the public consciousness, did they turn in any numbers to the subject. The deepening crisis in education, charted in issues of this journal, from the neutral-sounding "The Contemporary University: U.S.A." of 1964, to "The Embattled University" of 1970, is likely to accelerate this trend.

Trends in the professional study of history also encouraged the new interest. Chief among these, perhaps, was what might be called an increasing concern for the interrelatedness of past experience, brought on by the pervasive influence of social history, the emphasis on interdisciplinary approaches to the past, and the collapse of the internal boundaries that once delineated "areas" of historical study. Historians began to recognize that education touches upon nearly all aspects of a particular society. The historical study of education came to be seen not only as an end in itself but as a promising and hitherto neglected avenue of approach to an extremely broad range of problems.

New approaches to the history of education differ from the old primarily in the attention now being given to the interplay between education and society. But this is a very great difference indeed. What was once a narrow specialty is now seen to have such broad ramifications that it has become hopelessly ill-defined. For if the role of education in the historical process is to be understood, attention must be paid to the external influences that shape the educational arrangements a society has made; to the ways in which these external influences impinge upon each other at the same time they are acting upon education; and to the ways in which education itself influences the society. The social composition of an elite educational institution, for example, is the consequence of the interaction of economic factors, of patterns of social stratification, of the conscious political decisions of the established authorities, and so forth.

It is one thing, however, to recognize all the influences that need to be taken into account in the study of a particular problem in the history of education. It is quite another thing to determine the relative weight that is to be assigned each of them, especially over long periods of time. Research is at an early stage, and has not moved far beyond an enumeration of influences. In some important areas, such as the study of literacy in pre- and early industrial societies, the collection of raw data has scarcely begun; only recently have statistics long available in manuscript form been published and useful manuscript sources rescued from neglect.[2] In advanced industrial societies, where statistics on literacy abound, nearly the entire adult population is formally literate. But these figures conceal the functional illiteracy that is one of the consequences of technological change, and about which very little is now known. The questions that need to be asked in the new educational history are only beginning to be clarified. Conceptual models for dealing with these questions have yet to be devised; the methodological controversies that have enlivened more developed areas of study have yet to take place.

Thus the history of education is an area of study whose potentialities are only beginning to be exploited and the inchoate state in which it now exists is precisely what makes it attractive. So varied are the purposes now brought to the history of education, so patchy is the present state of knowledge, that the field does not lend itself to systematic treatment. Nevertheless, an idea of present concerns and problems can be conveyed by tugging at a few strands in the network of relationships that bind education to society.

I

Conventional histories of education are filled with generalizations about relationships between education and social structure. It has been a common practice, for example, to attach a class label to an educational institution, which is then held to respond to the "needs" or "demands" of a particular social class. Who determines these needs, or whether, if such needs exist, the institution in fact responds to them, is left unclear. Moreover, such static descriptive statements, based on implicit assumptions about how the class system works, explain very little about the dynamics of the interaction between education and the structure of society. Nor do they allow for the possibility that cultural values and styles of education once presumably moored to a particular social class may drift loose from that class and become the common property of an entire society—in which case they are not particularly amenable to class analysis except in its crudest forms. It is hard to see how describing an American university education as "middle class" explains very much about either the American university or American society. To be sure, education and social class have been, and continue to be, intimately connected. But the complexity of the historical connections between them has only begun to receive the carefully nuanced analysis it requires.[3] One would expect to find a large number of aristocrats' sons in an institution labeled "aristocratic." But one would also find some people who were not the sons of aristocrats. Who were they? Furthermore, one might also find aristocrats' sons in fairly large numbers in institutions not traditionally associated with the aristocracy. What were they doing there? Detailed research has only recently begun on who actually received the education a particular society has offered, how this has changed, and what the causes and consequences of change have been.[4]

With more attention being paid to who actually got educated, historians are now beginning to see that relationships between education and social structure have often been different from what the providers of education intended. It is roughly true that, until very recently, the structure of education in most European countries had the effect of reinforcing class distinctions and reducing the flow of social mobility—and was often intentionally designed to do so. Different social classes received different kinds of education in different schools; the upper levels of education were the preserve of the upper classes, a means of maintaining their children in established social positions and of bolstering their own political and social authority. But attempts to make patterns of education conform to the pattern of society have often been frustrated, both by forces the established authorities have been unable to control and by changes in other sectors of society which they have promoted themselves. One example of the latter is an expansion of job opportunities. Lawrence Stone has shown that in early modern England, economic growth and the proliferation of the bureaucracy of the state triggered an educational expansion: "So great was the boom . . . that all classes above a certain level took their part,"[5]—a consequence not entirely welcome to the ruling class of a highly stratified society. Other forces, of which demographic change is one, need to be identified and assessed.[6]

Patterns of social stratification affect the structure of education. But educational arrangements also turn back upon the structure of society and exert their own influences upon it: the relationship between education and social stratification is a two-way street. This process can be seen at work in the history of European secondary education. Elitist patterns that took shape during the sixteenth and seventeenth centuries, when the hereditary ruling classes sent their sons to secondary schools in increasing numbers, persisted well into modern times. Recent studies of the English public school have addressed themselves to some of the consequences of this persistence. Among the most important and far-reaching of these consequences was the preservation of the values and attitudes—and therefore the social ascendancy—of the aristocracy, in a fully industrialized and formally democratic society.[7]

Research into who actually got educated will lend a good deal more precision to statements about the historical role of education in the promotion of social mobility and in the maintenance of established social positions. Until recently, these have possessed all the rigor of the notorious generalizations about the rising middle classes. Such research should shed light on changes and continuities in the recruitment of elites, matters of particular concern to social and political historians. What has been the role of education in this process, in the long movement away from a society in which status was based on birth to a society in which status is increasingly based on achievement? What have been the social and political consequences of the paradoxical principle of the career open to talent, which holds that everyone should have an equal chance to become unequal? To what extent were traditional elites able to adjust themselves to the pressures for meritocratic standards of recruitment which emerged from the economic and political revolutions of the eighteenth century? To what extent did the implementation of such standards truly open the way for new men? For the upper levels of education, which prepared their clientele for elite positions, abundant evidence is available on the social origins of students over long periods of time. University matriculation registers, for example, are waiting to be tapped.

But it is not enough simply to describe with greater precision the role of education in the promotion of social mobility (or in the maintenance of established social positions). It also needs to be asked what the consequences of this form of mobility have been, what it has meant to the individuals who experienced it and the societies in which they lived. Such qualitative questions may be exceedingly difficult to answer.

The education of the lower classes presents the historian with equally difficult problems. What influences have primary schools exerted on the values and attitudes of their clientele? Recent studies of elite institutions offer persuasive evidence of the ways in which education acts upon social structure through the medium of values and attitudes. But for lower levels of education, the kinds of literary evidence that permit one to generalize about the gentlemanly life-style of the public school, or the bourgeois ethos of the lycée, rarely exist. So far, historical studies of the impact of popular education on values and attitudes have been mainly concerned with such public issues as the promotion of nationalism and nation building—as in the case of the Third French Republic, whose founders quite consciously undertook a sweeping reform and extension of a state-supported system of primary education in order to provide a new regime with republicans. Comparatively little is known about the role of the school in shaping attitudes toward more ostensibly private matters, such as sex, or toward such divisive questions as social class. Analysis of the content of textbooks would at least suggest what attitudes the authorities sought to inculcate, though the degree to which they succeeded is quite another question.[8]

Attention to the social consequences that educational arrangements have produced, apart from what their designers intended, should help put to rest the largely speculative leaps of the kind which assume an exact correspondence between the structure of a society and the structure of its education. Indeed, given the extraordinarily high incidence of anachronistic features that educational arrangements exhibit (such as the persistence of classical studies in the West), it is hard to see how such a direct correspondence could ever have been drawn. Instead, historical relationships between education and social structure, as one sociologist has perceptively remarked, "are various, involve structural discontinuities and are singularly lacking in symmetry."[9]

Nevertheless, the sons of the rich are usually better educated (or spend more time in school) than the sons of the poor. As soon as education began to confer social, economic, or political benefits, the question of who should be educated became a source of bitter controversy. Some of the involvements of education in politics have received considerable attention: the intervention of the state in the provision of popular education has been one traditional area of concern. State intervention followed on centuries of debate about the wisdom of providing widespread education; seldom has a question been agonized over so long and settled so swiftly. The arguments for and against popular education, the activities of certain reform groups, the legislative aspects of reform, the church-state struggle, have all been treated in a number of studies. These questions fall within the traditional preoccupations of political history. But a vast amount of territory remains to be explored, and older interpretations need to be reexamined.

Older studies, for example, regarded the extension of popular education as an aspect of the process of democratization, a necessary consequence of the implications of liberal political philosophy. More recent work has held that the decisive motive in the drive for public schooling was social control of the lower classes in an industrializing and urbanizing society.[10]

But both interpretations are mainly concerned with the attitudes of the upper-class proponents of widespread schooling; they stress the intentions of the reformers, not the consequences of the reforms. Very little is known about the attitudes toward education of the people whom the upper classes quarreled over. Popular education needs to be studied "from below." and several works have opened the way. E. P. Thompson, for example, has shown how an eagerness for learning and an enthusiasm for the printed word were important elements in the radical culture of the English working class.[11] Inquiry is now moving beyond the confines of the politically-conscious elements of that class. What were the attitudes toward education of the unskilled and illiterate laborers who poured into the factories with their wives and children in the early stages of industrialization? Literary evidence is likely to yield very few answers; such evidence as does exist is likely to be testimony from men who were not themselves workers. An investigation of this kind must rely on indirect evidence: census records, school attendance records, the reports of factory inspectors, and so forth; new methods must be added to those already devised for dealing with the inarticulate.

Traditional governing elites, from their point of view, at least, had reason to fear the possible consequences of widespread literacy. To be sure, there existed conservative arguments in support of popular instruction. In Protestant countries, Christian duty seemed to require that the people be enabled to read the Bible; the idea that popular literacy was one more means of teaching the lowly respect for their betters and resignation to their lot bolstered the moral and religious arguments in its favor. But once people had been taught to read, it was nearly impossible to control what they read, without resort to the extraordinary measures which only twentieth-century dictatorships have been willing, or able, to undertake. Events of our own times provide abundant evidence that education can influence political behavior and the structure of politics in ways that the established authorities by no means intend. This aspect of the relationship between politics and education offers many promising lines of historical inquiry.

In recent studies of revolution, for example, attention has been given to the conditions which produce that ubiquitous revolutionary figure, the alienated intellectual. An oversupply of overeducated and underemployed men seems to be a common plight of countries in the early stages of development.[12] These conditions existed in both seventeenth-century England and eighteenth-century France. In both countries an expansion of enrollments at the upper levels of education produced too many educated men seeking too few places, frustrated in their ambitions and ready to turn against a society that had no use for their talents. All that was needed to create an extremely dangerous situation for the established authorities was an ideology which enabled personal grievances to be elevated into opposition to the regime: Puritanism in the case of England; a radical version of the Enlightenment in the case of France.[13]

If historians have begun to hammer out answers to important questions concerning the relationship between education and politics, in the equally significant area of education's links with the economy they are just beginning their work. Economists since Adam Smith have been interested in the relationship of education to the economy, and particularly to economic development; in the last decade the economics of education has become a vigorous subdiscipline. But historians have their own contribution to make, especially since the vexing question of the ways in which education has influenced economic growth demands historical treatment. As David McClelland has put it, "Did increases in educational investment precede rapid rates of economic growth, or were rapid increases in wealth followed by increased spending on education? Or did both occur together? These are the critical questions of social dynamics that cry out for an answer."[14] Historians are just starting to attempt to break the vicious circle in which such questions have been enclosed.

Take, for example, the problem of literacy—a topic which itself is only beginning to be investigated systematically. R. S. Schofield has remarked, "Today literacy is considered to be a necessary precondition for economic development; but the historian might well ask himself whether this was so in England at the end of the eighteenth century."[15] It would be plausible to argue that the relatively high rate of literacy that had long prevailed in England had much to do with that country's becoming the first industrial power. But on closer examination it is far from clear how literacy and schooling have contributed to rapid growth, especially in the early stages. In the first decades of industrialization, the factory system put no premium on even low-level intellectual skills. Whatever relationships existed between widespread literacy and early industrial development must have been quite roundabout. In one of the best treatments of this problem, Ronald Dore has shown that what was actually learned in school mattered less than the discipline involved in learning anything at all:

> But what does widespread literacy do for a developing country? At the very least it constitutes a training in being trained. The man who has in childhood submitted to some process of disciplined and conscious learning is more likely to respond to further training, be it in a conscript army, in a factory, or at lectures arranged by his village agricultural association. And such training can be more precise and efficient, and more nationally standardized, if the written word can be used to supplement the spoken.[16]

Directing his attention to a higher level of training, David Landes has recently argued that the links between technical and scientific education on the one hand and economic development on the other are much more direct than the links between literacy and development.[17] Certainly, the prima facie evidence in the classic comparison between the sluggishness of the British and the explosiveness of the German economies in the late nineteenth century, when industrial processes came increasingly to depend upon scientific innovation, would appear to support Landes's case: German scientific education was undoubtedly superior to British, and German entrepreneurs were more willing to hire and to heed the advice of graduates of scientific and technical institutes than were their British counterparts. But too little is now known about scientific education in the industrial age; historians of science have so far given more attention to the early modern period. When work in progress on scientific education in later times appears, it may well complicate, even if it does not substantially modify, the picture Landes presents.[18]

Such studies, which define education as a process that takes place in specialized institutions, are likely to remain at the center of attention in historical writing. Nevertheless, any definition of education must be broad enough to include learning experiences which take place outside the framework of formal institutions, particularly within the family, whose role in the educational process remains of primary importance. But historical research on the family is now at a rudimentary stage. Very little is known, for example, about the ways in which responsibility for education after the earliest years of childhood shifted over a period of centuries, from the family to specialized institutions, such as the apprenticeship system and schools. Nor have we discovered much about the interaction between changes in the structure of the family and changes in the structure of education, or about how these changes have differed from class to class and among various levels of education. Did changes in family structure make formal educational institutions increasingly important agencies of socialization, or did pressures outside the family, from government or from social and religious institutions, provide the impetus for this shift in educational responsibilities? What have been the social and psychological consequences of these changes? How has submission to the discipline of the school altered the experience of childhood and affected patterns of adult behavior? Only in the last decade have such questions begun to receive the attention they deserve.[19]

II

If the exploration of "the involvements of education with the rest of society" is the new credo, it is a credo not without its own ambiguities and difficulties. The phrase can be interpreted in a variety of ways. It has been employed in a specific critical sense, to suggest the inadequacies of the history of education, old style, without meaning to lay down a program for the new. It has been used superficially, to dress up straightforward descriptions of educational institutions hardly different from older institutional histories.

More significantly, the phrase also lends itself to a quasi-functionalist interpretation which may distort the role of education in the historical process. This interpretation assumes that everything which may be identified with education responds to or fulfills the needs of society; that the structure of an educational system is merely a reflection of the class structure; that the pace of change in education is roughly equal to, indeed responds to, the pace of other changes in the larger society. First of all, it is never easy to decide what constitutes "society," the abstract entity to which education responds. Moreover, the functionalist view runs afoul of empirical evidence which suggests that the pace of change in education has often been widely at variance with the pace of social change. And this view is hard-pressed to allow for the anomalies and anachronisms so frequently found in educational systems. The relationship between change in an educational system and changes in the society of which it is a part is certainly one of the most important and least understood problems confronting the historian of education. An explanatory model which could be applied to this relationship would be an extremely useful tool, but for all its compelling simplicity—indeed, because of it—the functionalist approach is inadequate.[20]

The new credo may also be interpreted too broadly. An undiscriminating concern with relationships between education and society can lead to an emphasis on certain aspects of the role of education in the historical process at the expense of others. If the historical study of education is too preoccupied with relationships and interconnections, it may slight certain problems internal to the process of education itself, problems which may not be very satisfactorily explained in terms of external influences. Along with our attempts to understand how the larger society influences education, perhaps we need to understand the ways it does not.

For this very reason the study of educational institutions remains important—but what is needed is institutional history in a new key. The new studies should indeed take into account the larger social context in which educational institutions are located, but their viewpoints should be from the inside looking out. Only in this way are we likely to understand such matters as the consequences of educational reform as opposed to the intentions of reformers, or such significant topics in intellectual history as the influence which institutional settings exercise on patterns of thought and intellectual creativity.

Sheldon Rothblatt has attacked some of the foregoing problems in his recent book on nineteenth-century Cambridge, an important example of the new institutional history.[21] He argues that two historiographical traditions can be traced in the writing of English university history. The Whig interpretation assumed that university history could be written as an extension of political history: the ancient universities were seen as pliant tools of the Georgian

Establishment. Unable and unwilling to respond to the challenge of industrialism, Oxbridge was forced into the modern world only by pressure administered from the outside, in the form of investigations by royal commissions. Of course the Whig version applauded these nineteenth-century changes. A second historiographical tradition, the class-conflict interpretation, holds that "the function of the university is to serve whichever social class is in power." This view reverses the Whig judgment: it does not regard the nineteenth-century reforms as progressive but as merely the transfer of control of the universities from one class to another. Whatever their respective merits, Rothblatt argues, both the Whig and the class-conflict versions have assumed much too close a fit between society's wishes and the response of educational institutions to them. Especially in a pluralistic society, "it is entirely possible that the university and society will be in subtle and complex states of disagreement as well as agreement with one another, that the direction of university change may not be completely obvious, that surprises will occur."[22] Rothblatt elaborates this thesis by showing how the reform of Cambridge, though quickened by external pressures, sprang largely from within the university, from the reformulation of donnish traditions which had very little to do with either the presumed needs of an industrial society or the "demands" of a rising middle class, and which in fact set itself against them.

The new institutional history is valuable not only as an illustration of the dangers in interpreting the new credo too broadly. There are other good reasons for maintaining institutional history amid the central concerns of the history of education. Despite the wealth of old-style studies of institutions, little is known about most of the problems with which contemporary historians are now engaged. Modeled on the constitutional history that dominated nineteenth-century scholarship, the older studies were preoccupied with formal structures; contemporary historical writing, on the other hand, might be characterized as mainly concerned with processes, with relationships of power and influence and social interaction that may have been widely at variance with the dictates of formal institutional structures. There are many histories of individual American universities, for example, but there is not even a handful of trans-institutional, comparative studies of the caliber of Laurence R. Veysey's *The Emergence of the American University*.[23] The standard history of the French universities, published at the end of the nineteenth century, is surely not the last word that can be written on the subject.[24] And the histories of many other important educational institutions remain to be written.

Moreover, the study of universities is an ideal theater for historians interested in problems of the *longue durée*. For universities are one of the oldest forms of corporate organization in the West. Few institutions have been at once so fragile and so durable; few have been altered so radically, both internally and in their relationship to the larger society, adding new purposes, allowing others to lapse, and managing to maintain some of those for which they were originally founded. And perhaps because their existence and purpose presuppose an acute sense of the past, universities are rich repositories of information about themselves.

No scholar working alone can expect to take full advantage of these vast sources, nor can he exploit on his own that unique opportunity for the investigation of long-term problems offered by the university as a subject of study. The new institutional history demands collaborative efforts which will press into service the methods of several disciplines as well as the computer.

One such project, under the direction of Allan Bullock and T. H. Aston, is concerned with the social history of Oxford University from earliest times to the present. Another collaborative study, a statistical survey of universities in the West, is under way at the Shelby Cullom Davis Center for Historical Studies of Princeton University. A major goal of the project is to explore the cyclical patterns of expanding and contracting enrollments in Western universities, a phenomenon whose causes are not understood. Universities in England, Spain, and Germany exhibited similar patterns of rising enrollments in the sixteenth and early seventeenth centuries, of rapid decline beginning in the mid-seventeenth century, and of stagnation throughout the eighteenth. English and German enrollments again rose sharply in the nineteenth century. Was there a general decline in university matriculation throughout the West between about 1650 and 1800? If so, what were its causes, and what were its social, cultural, economic, and political consequences? Why did expansion resume in the nineteenth century? How did these cycles affect the pace and character of modernization in the West?

The Davis Center project is also concerned with two other problems: one, patterns in the relationship of university education to social mobility and to recruitment for professional, political, and administrative elites; two, the role of universities as transmitters of culture. The latter problem will consider education both as an intellectual and a socializing process and will ask how the structure, composition, and intellectual activities of the faculty changed over time—how and why the university was eventually able to become the critic of society as well as its servant.

Such collaborative enterprises can make significant contributions to our knowledge of the internal history of universities. But each study will eventually have to face the general problem with which much of this essay has been concerned: the establishment of cause-and-effect relationships between changes in education and changes in other sectors of society. This task, though the most difficult, may also prove the most rewarding.

III

Why has the history of education undergone such extreme change in recent years? The resurgence of interest is in part a consequence of the troubled state of contemporary education. New questions shaped by the dilemmas of our own times require new approaches to the past. The older historiography was found inadequate both because it was too narrow and inward-looking, and because it was ignorant of some essential facts concerning education itself. Long untouched by the great changes that have overtaken historical research in this century, the history of education became one of the last refuges of the Whig interpretation. So long as its practitioners were mainly concerned with searching the past for the antecedents of their own contemporary institutions, they could believe that education in the West had followed an upward linear progression. We now find this view hard to accept. We know, for example, that periods in which formal instruction was fairly widespread have been followed by periods in which it was restricted to small groups. The older historiography could neither accommodate such findings nor answer the questions they raise. Their exploration requires new modes of analysis. To pursue our example, it is clear that any satisfactory explanation of these expansions and contractions will have to take into account changes in demographic patterns and in the family, in the economy, the social structure, and the political system, in beliefs about the nature and purpose of human life. And it will also have to be recognized that education has turned back upon these influences in subtle and complex ways, working changes on its own.

Such a task is clearly beyond the old-style historian of education and the old-style historiography. But the demands of the task will not be satisfied by a new historiography of education as such. It may be doubted whether education, a process so deeply entangled in the life of an entire society, deserves to be called an "area of study" at all. Surely there can be little justification for making education a particular genre of historical scholarship. The history of education touches upon all the varieties of history. It is a task for the generalist, who must bring to the study of education a thorough knowledge of the society of which it is a part.

REFERENCES

1. Bernard Bailyn, *Education in the Forming of American Society: Needs and Opportunities for Research* (Chapel Hill: University of North Carolina Press, 1960), p. 14. I am grateful to my friends and colleagues in the Shelby Cullom Davis Center for Historical Studies of Princeton University, whose comments in a seminar on The University in Society provided suggestions for this essay. They are: Robert Church, Richard Kagan, Tom Laqueur, Sheldon Rothblatt, Henry Smith II, and Lawrence Stone.

2. See, for example, Michel Fleury and Pierre Valmary, "Les progrès de l'instruction élémentaire de Louis XIV à Napoléon III, d'après l'enquête de Louis Maggiolo, 1877-1879," *Population,* 12 (1957), 71-92.

3. For a brilliant example of the analyses now going on see Pierre Bourdieu and Jean-Claude Passeron, *Les héritiers: les étudiants et la culture* (Paris: Editions de Minuit, 1964).

4. For a pioneer effort see J. H. Hexter, "The Education of the Aristocracy in the Renaissance," *Reappraisals in History* (New York: Harper and Row, 1961), pp. 45-70, an earlier version of which appeared in the *Journal of Modern History* (March 1950); also Hester Jenkins and D. Caradog Jones, "Social Class of Cambridge University Alumni of the 18th and 19th Centuries," *British Journal of Sociology,* 1 (1950), 93-116.

5. Lawrence Stone, "The Educational Revolution in England, 1560-1640," *Past and Present,* no. 28 (July 1964), 68.

6. See, for example, François de Dainville, "Effectifs des collèges et scolarité aux XVIIe et XVIIIe siècles dans le nord-est de la France," *Population,* 10 (1955), 455-488; "Collèges et fréquentation scolaire au XVIIe siècle," *Population,* 12 (1957), 467-494; Frank Musgrove, "Population Changes and the Status of the Young in England Since the 18th Century," *Sociological Review,* 11 (1963), 69-93.

7. See, for example, David Ward, "The Public Schools and Industry in Britain after 1870," *Journal of Contemporary History,* 2, no. 3 (1967), 37-52; two studies by Rupert Wilkinson, *Gentlemanly Power: British Leader-*

ship and the Public School Tradition (New York: Oxford University Press, 1964), and with T. J. H. Bishop, *Winchester and the Public School Elite* (London: Faber, 1967). On the French lycée see John E. Talbott, *The Politics of Educational Reform in France, 1918-1940* (Princeton: Princeton University Press, 1969); Paul Gerbod, *La condition universitaire en France au XIXe siècle* (Paris: Presses universitaires de France, 1965).

8. For an early and still useful discussion of the role of primary education in the promotion of nationalism see Carleton J. H. Hayes, *France, A Nation of Patriots* (New York: Columbia University Press, 1930); also Charles E. Merriam, *The Making of Citizens: A Comparative Study of Methods of Civic Training* (Chicago: University of Chicago Press, 1931); for recent work see, for instance, Pierre Nora, "Ernest Lavisse, son rôle dans la formation du sentiment national," *Revue historique*, 228 (July-September 1962), 73-106; Jacques and Mona Ozouf, "Le thème du patriotisme dans les manuels primaires," *Le Mouvement Social*, no. 49 (October-November 1964), 5-32.

9. Donald G. MacCrae, "The Culture of a Generation: Students and Others," *Journal of Contemporary History*, 2, no. 3 (1967), 3.

10. For an early suggestion that the American common school may not have been the spearhead of democracy, see the essay in intellectual history of Merle Curti, *The Social Ideas of American Educators* (New York: C. Scribner's Sons, 1935); more recently, Michael Katz has expressed a similar view from the perspective of social history in *The Irony of Early School Reform: Educational Innovation in Mid-Nineteenth Century Massachusetts* (Cambridge, Mass.: Harvard University Press, 1968).

11. E. P. Thompson, *The Making of the English Working Class* (New York: Vintage, 1963), especially pp. 711-745; also Georges Duveau, *La pensée ouvrière sur l'éducation pendant la Seconde République et le Second Empire* (Paris: Domat-Montchrestien, 1948); R. K. Webb, *The British Working-Class Reader, 1790-1848* (London: Allen and Unwin, 1955); R. D. Altick, *The English Common Reader* (Chicago: University of Chicago Press, 1957); J. F. C. Harrison, *Learning and Living, 1790-1960: A Study in the History of the English Adult Education Movement* (London: Routledge and Kegan Paul, 1961).

12. Edward Shils, "Intellectuals in the Political Development of the New States," *World Politics*, 12 (April 1960), 329-368.

13. See Lawrence Stone, "The Educational Revolution in England, 1540-1640," *Past and Present*, no. 28 (July 1964), 41-80. In a more recent essay Stone has concluded: "More and more it looks as if this educational expansion was a necessary—but not sufficient—reason for the peculiar and ultimately radical course the revolution took." "The Causes of the English Revolution," in Robert Forster and Jack P. Greene, eds., *Preconditions of Revolution in Early Modern Europe* (Baltimore: Johns Hopkins University Press, 1970); Mark H. Curtis, "The Alienated Intellectuals of Early Stuart England," *Past and Present*, no. 23 (November 1962), 25-43; J. H. Elliot, "Revolu-

tion and Continuity in Early Modern Europe," *Past and Present,* no. 42 (February 1969), 35-56; Robert Darnton, "Social Tensions in the Intelligentsia of Pre-Revolutionary France," paper read at the annual meeting of the American Historical Association, December 1969. On the importance of a similar phenomenon in nineteenth-century Spain see Raymond Carr, *Spain, 1806-1939* (Oxford: Oxford University Press, 1966), p. 167; on nineteenth-century Germany see Lenore O'Boyle, "The Democratic Left in Germany, 1848," *Journal of Modern History,* 33 (1961), 374-383; John R. Gillis, "Aristocracy and Bureaucracy in Nineteenth-Century Prussia," *Past and Present,* no. 41 (December 1968), 105-129.

14. David C. McClelland, "Does Education Accelerate Economic Growth?" *Economic Development and Cultural Change,* 14, no. 3 (April 1966), 259.

15. R. S. Schofield, "The Measurement of Literacy in Pre-Industrial England," in Jack Goody, ed., *Literacy in Traditional Societies* (Cambridge, Eng.: Cambridge University Press, 1969), p. 312 and n: "The necessity of literacy as a pre-condition for economic growth is a persistent theme running through many UNESCO publications . . . These measures [established by UNESCO] are very general and throw no light at all on the question of why literacy should be considered essential to economic growth." See also Lawrence Stone, "Literacy and Education in England, 1640-1900," *Past and Present,* no. 42 (February 1969), 69-139; Carlo M. Cipolla, *Literacy and Development in the West* (Baltimore: Penguin, 1969).

16. Ronald P. Dore, *Education in Tokugawa Japan* (Berkeley: University of California Press, 1965), p. 292.

17. David Landes, *The Unbound Prometheus: Technological Change and Industrial Development in Western Europe from 1750 to the Present* (Cambridge, Eng.: Cambridge University Press, 1969), pp. 343-348.

18. One of the few studies of nineteenth-century scientific education is D. S. L. Cardwell, *The Organisation of Science in England* (Melbourne: Heinemann, 1957). On literature on scientific education see Thomas G. Kuhn, "The History of Science," *International Encyclopedia of the Social Sciences,* XIV, 78. John H. Weiss is writing a Harvard University doctoral dissertation on scientific education in nineteenth-century France; Steven Turner is preparing a Princeton University dissertation on scientific education in Germany.

19. For a brief discussion of some of these problems, see Stone, "Literacy and Education in England, 1640-1900," pp. 93-95; Bailyn, *Education in the Forming of American Society,* pp. 75-78. One of the boldest and most widely-heralded inquiries into these questions to have appeared in recent years is Philippe Ariès, *Centuries of Childhood: A Social History of Family Life* (New York: Knopf, 1962). The idea of childhood as a distinct phase of life, Ariès argues, is an invention of the late Middle Ages, when changes in the family and a new concern for education led to the removal of the child from the adult society in which he had formerly been free to roam. This practice, at first limited to the upper classes, gradually permeated the rest

of society. Though Ariès has perhaps done more than anyone to stimulate interest in the historical study of the family, the argument of his book, despite—or because of—his ingenious use of iconographical evidence, is not entirely convincing. For a study that owes much to Ariès but has a great deal more to say about education see Georges Snyders, *La pédagogie en France aux XVIIe et XVIIIe siècles* (Paris: Presses Universitaires de France, 1965). Important historical work on the family is now beginning to appear in the United States, pursuing lines of inquiry established by Edmund S. Morgan and Bernard Bailyn. See, for example, John Demos, *A Little Commonwealth: Family Life in Plymouth Colony* (New York: Oxford University Press, 1970); Philip J. Greven, Jr., *Four Generations: Population, Land, and Family in Colonial Andover, Massachusetts* (Ithaca: Cornell University Press, 1970). Demos has more to say about education. For England see, among the articles of Frank Musgrove, "The Decline of the Educative Family," *Universities Quarterly*, 14 (September 1960), 377-406.

20. For an interesting discussion of functionalism see Olive Banks, *The Sociology of Education* (London: Schocken, 1968). See also Gillian Sutherland, "The Study of the History of Education," *History*, 54 (February 1969), 53-54.

21. Sheldon Rothblatt, *The Revolution of the Dons: Cambridge and Society in Victorian England* (New York: Basic Books, 1968).

22. *Ibid.*, pp. 17-26.

23. Laurence R. Veysey, *The Emergence of the American University* (Chicago: University of Chicago Press, 1965). Veysey follows ground broken by Richard Hofstadter and Walter P. Metzger in *The Development of Academic Freedom in the United States* (New York: Columbia University Press, 1955), which is about much else besides academic freedom. Veysey's study of the movement to redefine the purpose and structure of American higher education in the post-Civil War era also shows how much can be missed by assuming too close a fit between a society's needs and the response of educational institutions to these needs. "During the early years of the American university movement, until about 1890," he contends, "academic efforts burgeoned largely in spite of the public, not as the result of popular acclaim . . . Academic and popular aspirations seemed rarely to meet" (p. 16).

24. Louis Liard, *L'enseignement supérieur en France, 1789-1889*, 2 vols. (Paris, 1888-1894).

SOURCE COLLECTIONS AND GENERAL HISTORIES OF EDUCATION

I. *Sources:* Many illustrative excerpts from the theorists and from the documents of educational history are available in:

Baskin, Wade, ed. *Classics in Education.* New York, 1966.

Binder, Frederick M., ed. *Education in the History of Western Civilization: Selected Readings.* New York, 1970.

Cohen, Alan, and Norman Garner, eds. *Readings in the History of Educational Thought.* London, 1967.

Cubberley, E. P., ed. *Readings in the History of Education.* New York, 1920.

Fraser, Stewart E., and William W. Brickman, eds. *A History of International and Comparative Education: Nineteenth Century Documents.* Glenview, Ill., 1968.

Hart, J. K., ed. *Creative Moments in Education.* New York, 1931.

Monroe, Paul, ed. *Source Book of the History of Education for the Greek & Roman Period.* New York, 1921.

Nash, Paul, ed. *Models of Man: Explorations in the Western Educational Tradition.* New York, 1968.

Norton, A. O., ed. *Readings in the History of Education.* Harvard University Press, 1909.

Sylvester, D. W., ed. *Educational Documents, 800–1816.* New York, 1970.

Ulich, Robert, ed. *Three Thousand Years of Educational Wisdom, Selections from Great Documents,* 2nd ed. Harvard University Press, 1971.

II. *General Histories of Education:* A list of selected general histories of education in English which may be consulted includes:

Adamson, J. W. *Pioneers of Modern Education.* New York, 1905.

———. *A Short History of Education.* New York, 1920.

Beck, Robert H. *A Social History of Education.* Englewood Cliffs, N.J., 1965.

Bowen, James. *A History of Western Education*, 3 vols. New York, 1972–1975.

Boyd, William. *History of Western Education*, 7th ed. London, 1965.

Brubacher, John S. *A History of the Problems of Education*, 2nd ed. New York, 1966.

Butts, R. Freeman. *The Education of the West.* New York, 1973.

Cole, Luella. *A History of Education: Socrates to Montessori.* New York, 1950.

Cole, Percival R. *History of Educational Thought.* New York, 1931.

Compayré, G. *History of Pedagogy.* New York, 1885.

Cubberley, Ellwood P. *The History of Education.* Boston, 1920.

Davidson, T. *History of Education.* New York, 1900.

Duggan, Stephen. *Students' Textbook in the History of Education*, 3rd ed. New York, 1936.

Eby, Frederick. *The Development of Modern Education*, 2nd ed. New York, 1952.

———, and Charles F. Arrowood. *The History and Philosophy of Education: Ancient and Medieval.* New York, 1940.

Frost, S. E., Jr. *Historical and Philosophical Foundations of Western Education*, 2nd ed. Columbus, 1973.

Good, Harry B., and James D. Teller. *A History of Western Education*, 3rd ed. New York, 1969.

Graves, Frank P. *A History of Education Before the Middle Ages.* New York, 1909.

———. *A History of Education During the Middle Ages.* New York, 1910.

———. *Great Educators of Three Centuries.* New York, 1912.

———. *A History of Education in Modern Times.* New York, 1913.

Gutek, Gerald L. *A History of Western Educational Experience.* New York, 1972.

Kandel, Isaac L. *History of Secondary Education: A Study of the Development of Liberal Education.* Boston, 1930.

Kane, William T., S. J. *An Essay Toward a History of Education*, rev. ed. Chicago, 1954.

Knight, Edgar W. *Twenty Centuries of Education.* Boston, 1940.

Lucas, Christopher J. *Our Western Educational Heritage.* New York, 1972.

Marique, Pierre J. *History of Christian Education*, 3 vols. New York, 1924–1932.

McCormick, Patrick J., and Francis P. Cassidy. *History of Education.* Washington, D.C., 1953.

Medlin, William K. *The History of Educational Ideas in the West.* New York, 1964.

Messenger, J. F. *Interpretive History of Education.* New York, 1931.

Meyer, Adolphe E. *An Educational History of the Western World*, 2nd ed. New York, 1972.

Monroe, Paul. *Textbook in the History of Education.* New York, 1905.

Moore, E. C. *The Story of Instruction*, 2 vols. New York, 1936–1938.

Mulhern, James. *A History of Education*, 2nd ed. New York, 1959.

Myer, Frederick. *A History of Educational Thought*, 2nd ed. Columbus, 1966.

Nash, Paul, ed. *History and Education: The Educational Uses of the Past.* New York, 1970.

———, Andreas M. Kazamias, and Henry J. Perkinson. *The Educated Man: Studies in the History of Educational Thought.* New York, 1965.

Painter, F. V. N. *History of Education.* New York, 1897.

Parker, S. C. *The History of Modern Elementary Education.* New York, 1912. (Rep., Littlefield, 1970)

———. *The Story of Education for All.* Calcutta, 1960.

Pollard, Hugh M. *Pioneers of Popular Education.* New York, 1957.

Pounds, Ralph L. *The Development of Education in Western Culture.* New York, 1968.

Power, Edward J. *Evolution of Educational Doctrine: Major Educational Theorists of the Western World.* New York, 1970.

———. *Main Currents in the History of Education*, 2nd ed. New York, 1970.

Quick, R. H. *Essays on Educational Reformers*. New York, 1897. (Rep., Littlefield, 1970)

Rusk, R. R. *Doctrines of Great Educators*, 4th ed. London, 1969.

Thut, I. N. *The Story of Education*. New York, 1957.

Ulich, Robert. *History of Educational Thought*, rev. ed. New York, 1968.

Weimer, Hermann. *Concise History of Education: From Solon to Pestalozzi*. New York, 1962.

Wilds, Elmer H., and Kenneth V. Lottich. *The Foundations of Modern Education*, rev. ed. New York, 1971.

Wise, John E. *The History of Education*. New York, 1964.

III. *Encyclopedias:* Lee C. Deighton, ed., *The Encyclopedia of Education*, 10 vols., New York, 1971, deals primarily with American education with some notices of international education, comparative education and foreign systems. Edward Blishen, ed., *Encyclopedia of Education*, New York, 1970, a British work, is useful. A wealth of information on educators, educational institutions, theories, and related subjects will be found in Paul Monroe, ed., *A Cyclopedia of Education*, 5 vols., New York, 1911–1913; although old, this is the only general educational encyclopedia in English and is invaluable. It has been reissued (Detroit, 5 vols., 1968) with a new introductory essay by W. W. Brickman, F. Cordasco, and T. H. Richardson. A cogent review of educational research for the decade preceding publication in all areas of education will be found in *An Encyclopedia of Educational Research*, 4th ed., New York, 1970 (1st ed., 1940; 2nd ed., 1950; 3rd ed., 1960). An excellent adjunct to the study of the history of education is William W. Brickman, *Guide to Research in Educational History*, New York, 1949, which has been reissued with some additions (Norwood, Pa., 1974). Two old but very useful bibliographies are Will S. Monroe, *Bibliography of Education* (New York, 1897; reissued, Detroit, 1968), and G. Stanley Hall and John Mansfield, *Hints Toward A Select and Descriptive Bibliography of Education* (Boston, 1886; reissued, Detroit, 1973). Generally useful, if limited to American education, is Francesco Cordasco and William W. Brickman, eds., *A Bibliography of American Educational History: An Annotated and Classified Guide*, New York, 1975.

Part I

EDUCATION IN CLASSICAL ANTIQUITY

Chronological Survey of Greek Education

Political Events	Poets, Dramatists, Orators, etc.	Philosophers, Sophists	Writings Possessing Direct Educational Significance	Educational Events
First Olympiad 776 Dominance of Sparta . 750-600 Messenian Wars . 743-668 Laws of Draco 629 Laws of Solon 594 The Pisistratids . . 560-510 Laws of Clisthenes . 509 Persian Wars . 500-479 Athenian supremacy 479-431 Confederacy of Delos 477-450 B.C.	Homer flourished c. 900 or 850 Hesiod . . c. 700 Terpander . c. 676 Sappho . . c. 612 Thespis . . c. 536 Simonides 556-468 Pindar c. 522-c. 443 Æschylus 525-456	Thales . c. 624-548 Anaximander c. 611-547 Anaximenes c. 588-524 Pythagoras c. 580-500 Heraclitus c. 525-475 Anaxagoras c. 500-428 Zeno, the Eleatic fl. c. 460-440	*Iliad* . . . c. 850 Laws of Lycurgus c. 850 or 800	Parental duty in education in Solon's Laws . 594 Origin of the drama c. 556
Age of Pericles 459-431 Peloponnesian War . . 431-404 Sicilian expedition . . 415-413 Spartan supremacy 404-371 Retreat of the Ten Thousand . 399 Theban supremacy 371-362 Philip of Macedon . . 359-336 The Sacred Wars . 346-338 338 B.C. Battle of Chaeronea	Sophocles 495-405 Euripides 480-406 Phidias . 488-432 Herodotus c. 484-c. 425 Thucydides 471-400 Aristophanes 450-385 (Old comedy) Xenophon 434-359 Menander 344-292 (New comedy) Demosthenes 384-322	Gorgias . c. 485-380 Protagoras c. 480-411 Prodicus . fl. c. 435 Socrates . 469-399 Antisthenes 422-371 Plato . . 420-348 Isocrates . 436-338 Aristotle . 384-322	Thucydides' *Pericles' Oration* 431 Aristophanes' *Clouds* . 423 Plato's *Protagoras* Plato's *Republic* c. 395 Plato's *Laws* c. 350 Xenophon's *Economics* c. 380 Xenophon's *Memorabilia* . c. 380 Xenophon's *Cyropedeia* . c. 380 Isocrates' *Against the Sophists* 390 Isocrates' *Exchange of Estates* . 354	Protagoras teaches at Athens . 445 Trial of Socrates 399 Isocrates establishes a school at Athens . 392 Founding of the Academy 386 Founding of the Lyceum 335
Macedonian supremacy 338 Alexander the Great . 336-323 Battle of Issus 333 Alexandria founded . 330 Ptolemy I (Soter) 322-285 First invasion of Greece by Gauls . 279 Ptolemy III (Euergetes) . 247-222 Agis (Sparta) r. 244-240 Cleomenes (Sparta) r. 236-222 Destruction of Corinth — Greece a Roman province . 146 Egypt a Roman province 30 A.D.	Theocritus . b. 324 Polybius c. 205-c. 123 Strabo c. 63 B.C.-c. 24 A.D.	Epicurus . 341-270 Zeno . . c. 350-260 Chrysippus 280-207 Pyrrhon . . c. 330	Aristotle's *Politics* c. 330	Museum at Alexandria founded 280 Euclid systematizes geometry c. 250
	Plutarch c. 46-120 A.D. Lucian c. 125-c. 192 A.D.	Philo of Judea 20 B.C. 40 A.D.	Plutarch's *Training of Children* c. 100 A.D Lucian's *Teacher of Orators*, *Anacharses*, etc. Gregory of Nazianzus' *Panegyric* 379	Imperial support for the University of Athens A.D. 69-79 University of Athens suppressed A.D. 529

Chapter I

GREEK EDUCATION

Historical background. The people who called themselves Hellenes came into the Greek peninsula sometime soon after 2,000 B.C. They were united by language, religion, and a common civilization, but there was no Greek government or nation. The settlements on the mainland were separated by steep valleys and tall mountains. Each large settlement formed a polis, or city-state. The Doric Age (*ca.* 1200 B.C.) began with the movement of primitive tribes called Dorians from northern Greece into the Peloponnesus. Migrations forced Hellenic peoples in Peloponnesus to cross the Aegean Sea to Asia Minor where they established Greek colonies. The chief Dorian tribe, the Spartans, developed the city-state of Sparta into one of two great powers of Greece; in this period the city-state of Athens in Attica took form. The Doric Age lasted several hundred years. The struggle of the Greek city-states and the Persian Empire culminated in 479 B.C. with a Greek victory at Plataea. Rivalry between Sparta and Athens caused the Peloponnesian War, with the final defeat of Athens in 404 B.C. Spartan leadership passed to Thebes in 371 B.C. Greece was finally overrun by Macedon and made part of its empire in 338 B.C. The period of Hellenistic civilization ended with the Roman conquest of Greece in 146 B.C.[1]

[1] J. C. Stobart, *The Glory That Was Greece: A Survey of Hellenic Culture and Civilization,* 3rd ed., New York, 1962.

Periods of Greek education. The division of Greek education is into the Old and the New Greek periods, with the division point at the Periclean Age (459–431 B.C.). The Old Greek period is divided into (1) the Homeric Age; (2) the historic period, including both Spartan and Athenian types. In the Old Greek education the emphasis was on the social and institutional rather than on the individualistic aspect of education. The New Greek period includes (1) a period of transition in the educational, religious, and moral ideas following the Age of Pericles; (2) a period from the Macedonian conquest until Greek civilization is thoroughly incorporated with Roman life. By the time of the end of the New Greek period, the philosophical schools had been formed and were finally organized into the University of Athens.

The education of the Homeric period was best exemplified in the great epic poems, *The Iliad* and *The Odyssey* (*ca.* 900–800 B.C.). It included the two fold ideal of the man of action and the man of wisdom, typified by Achilles and Odysseus. Both ideals were to be attained by each free Greek. Bravery was to be tempered by reverence; the primary virtue of the man of wisdom was good practical judgment.

The Old Greek education of the historic period was determined, in its character and its organization, by the dominant social institution, the polis, or city-state. The city-state was the outgrowth of the tribe and council of the Homeric period, and furnished the basis and ideals of education.

1. **Spartan education** was typical of the Old Greek education in its most pronounced form. Definite formulation of this system of education was consolidated in the constitution of Lycurgus (*ca.* 850–800 B.C.). It resulted in a socialistic state with governmental control of education with emphasis upon the educational function of various social institutions.

a) **The aim of Spartan education** was an extreme paternalistic education, which sought the complete submergence of the individual in the citizen with attributes of courage, complete obedience, and physical perfection.

b) **The organization of Spartan education.** A general superintendent (*paedonomus*) and assistants were in charge of education. The first seven years of the child were spent with its mother; afterwards as wards of the state they were instructed by elder males; from eighteen to twenty they were classed as Irens, and at thirty were classed as warriors completely devoted to the state.

c) **The content of Spartan education** was dominantly physical and moral with very little that was intellectual or aesthetic. Plutarch says, "All the rest of their education was calculated to make them subject to command, to endure labor, to fight, and to conquer." Emphasis on gymnastics made for military resourcefulness. Music and religious dances were used to develop the same quality. Approval or disapproval of the elders was a constant source of discipline. Every Spartan adult was a teacher, and every Spartan boy had a tutor. Women were educated as men, with the purpose of training mothers of warriors.

2. **Athenian education** had little in common with that of Sparta, save in the simplicity of aim and in the means adopted for training. Even in these two general aspects there was wide divergence.

a) **The organization of Athenian education.** While Sparta destroyed the family, Athens preserved it and placed upon it the burden of responsibility for education. All schools were private schools. The state provided only for education between the ages of sixteen and twenty, almost wholly a direct preparation for military service. Until the age of seven, the training of a child was in the hands of its family. For the next eight or nine years, the Athenian boy attended two public schools—the music school, and the *palaestra* (gymnastic school). At about age sixteen, he discontinued all literary and musical instruction to attend the gymnasium, where for two years hc prepared for the life of an Athenian citizen; the last two years (*ephebic* or cadet education) were under the direct control of state officials.

b) **The content of Athenian education.** Reading, writing, and the literary element of education were included in the work of the music school. Heavy emphasis in palaestra and formal education of the ephebic period was given to gymnastics. Music was understood to mean poetry, drama, history, oratory, and the sciences, as well as music in the more limited sense.

The New Greek education—Transitional period. The Old Greek education culminated in the brilliant Age of Pericles, but this period of fruition was also one of transition. The life of the period made greater demands on the individual and offered greater opportunities. Placement of greater emphasis on the individual, and not on the citizen, led to the New Greek education. Many transitional forces induced change, among which may be numbered (1) political changes; (2) literary development; (3) introspective psychology and philosophy; (4) greater freedom for the individual.

1. **The Sophists.** Agencies of the new education were teachers known as Sophists, peripatetic professors-at-large, who increased in numbers following the Age of Pericles. The Sophists were unorganized and represented no common opinion, but they laid great stress on rhetoric, and were skeptical of old Athenian beliefs and traditions; their educational aims were chiefly utilitarian, and Plato reports one of the Sophists, Protagoras (481–411 B.C.), as saying of an ambitious Athenian youth, "If he comes to me, he will learn that which he comes to learn." The moral teachings of the Sophists placed an unprecedented emphasis on individuality. Consequently, there arose against the Sophists a violent opposition by all the conservatives and those concerned with the most worthy traits of old Greek life. Both in content and method, education was graphically changed by the Sophists, who both modified the old Greek education and contributed to the new. The former home training became milder, intellectual instruction supplanted the process of forming moral habits, a knowledge content was added to gymnastics and music, and the gymnasium tended to substitute beauty for strength. The destructive tendencies and criticism of the Sophists aroused Socrates, and so the movement of Plato and Aristotle was made possible.

2. **The Greek Educational theorists.** The occasion for the work of the theorists was the conflict between the New

Greek education and the Old. They held the ideals as well as the process of the Old Greek education to be wholly inadequate; but they rejected the negative attitude of the Sophists and believed that some general moral bonds must be furnished.

a) **Socrates** (469–399 B.C.) first stated the problem of conflict between the Old and the New Greek education, between social and individual interests, and somewhat vaguely suggested the principles of solution. Although he left no writings, Socrates is studied in the writings of Xenophon and Plato. He accepted as his starting point the basal principle of the Sophists, "Man is the measure of all things," but added that the first obligation of man is to know himself. As opposed to the purely individualistic basis of opinion, he held that knowledge possessed universal validity, and from this arrived at the fundamental principle, "Knowledge is virtue." The Socratic Method is a process of obtaining a concept or definition inductively by conversation on moral and philosophic problems. Socrates' method can be studied in the *Dialogues* of Plato (e.g., *Apology, Euthyphro, Lysis, Protagoras, Republic*) and in Xenophon's *Memorabilia.* The contributions of Socrates to education are: (a) knowledge is obtained objectively by conversation, and subjectively by the reflection and classification of one's experiences; (b) knowledge has a moral and therefore universal value; (c) education has for its immediate object the development of the power of thought, not the imparting of knowledge.[2]

b) **Plato** (420–348 B.C.) agreed with Socrates that the great need of the time was the formulation of a new moral bond in life to replace the ancient ideals of old Greek society rejected by the new individualism. In his ideal schemes of education, he formulated an aristocratic government of socialistic nature. *The Republic* is Plato's exposition of an ideal society. There were three classes in this society: the philosophical (to rule); the soldier (to protect); the artisan (to obey and support the first two). The education outlined in *The Republic* is similar to that of the Athens of Plato's day. The substance is formed of gymnastics and music for

2 See further R. W. Livingstone, *Portrait of Socrates,* Oxford University Press, 1938.

children and youth; higher education is divided into two phases: scientific and philosophic. The scientific extends from age twenty to thirty and includes arithmetic, geometry, music, and astronomy. The philosophic extends over a period of five years devoted to study of dialectic, i.e., philosophy. The value of Plato's educational writings is in the principles formulated, which suggest that it is the function of education to determine what each individual is most fitted by nature to do, and then to prepare him for this service. This is the formulation of the Greek ideal of a liberal education. Plato allows for the education of women, and gives one of the earliest defenses of women's education. The practical influence of Plato is to be seen in the formation of the philosophical schools of Athens; in the direction he gave these schools; in the determination of a curriculum that remained influential for centuries; and in the final formulation of the Greek idea of a liberal education. Essentially, this last consisted in discarding the practical value of all the subjects of study as subordinate to that which they possess as mental disciplines.[3]

c) **Aristotle** (384–322 B.C.). Aristotle's ideas on education appear in *The Ethics* and *The Politics*. The first describes how the individual should discipline himself in life; the second describes the social and economic conditions in society most favorable for achieving this purpose. Aristotle viewed education as an important branch of practical political science and the means of securing the well-being and well-doing of the citizens of the community. The ultimate function of the state is educational, and the perfection of society depends upon the perfection of its members. The method of the education of Aristotle is objective and scientific, as opposed to the philosophical plan of Plato; the educational scheme is composed of elements drawn chiefly from Athenian education and is similar to that of Plato. The child until six should be trained by the parent; beyond this period education should be controlled by the government. *The Politics*, which is a fragment, says nothing about higher education, although from his other writings we can

[3] See further Richard L. Nettleship, *Lectures on the Republic of Plato*, London, 1936.

infer that higher education would include mathematics, physics, and astronomy. Theoretical or intellectual education is followed with practical education in citizenship. The influence of Aristotle was profound; through scholasticism his work became the basis of all studies and of all educational institutions during the Middle Ages.

The Cosmopolitan period of Greek education. Two general characteristics are educational features of this period, extending to the period of the dominance of Christianity: (1) the spread of Greek culture; (2) fusion with Roman education.[4]

1. **Spread of Greek culture.** Through the military and administrative genius of Alexander the Great, the habits and customs of all the East were influenced by Greece. As culture became universal and education individual, new types of educational institutions came into existence. By the latter part of the fourth century B.C., the work of the Sophists resulted in the formation of two types of schools, the rhetorical and the philosophical. The rhetorical schools prepared for the practical activities of life by training in oratory and the new knowledge of the times. A leader in the formation of rhetorical schools was Isocrates (393–338 B.C.); just as Socrates formed a transition from the early Sophists to the philosophical schools whose primary interest lay in speculative questions of metaphysical or ethical import, Plato, Aristotle, and other philosophers gathered students around them that were soon organized into schools (e.g., Zeno and the Stoics; Epicurus and the Epicureans). Eventually, Platonism, Stoicism, and Epicureanism adapted themselves to Roman ideals of life. The philosophical schools became as formal and artificial as the work of the early Sophists, and represented an educational decline.

2. **The Universities** of the Greek world grew out of the rhetorical and philosophical schools. **The University of Athens** represented a combination of three such schools: the Academy; the Peripatetic school (Aristotle's); and the Stoic. Its head was elected by the Athenian senate. In many

[4] W. W. Tarn, *Hellenistic Civilization,* 3rd ed., Cleveland, 1961.

ways, it had the elaborate structure of a modern university and it continued to function until suppressed by Justinian in 529 A.D. The **University of Alexandria,** during the early Christian centuries, surpassed Athens as the intellectual center of the world. In Alexandria, the Aristotelian method of investigation was employed, and many early scientific theories were formulated (e.g., Archimedes, Euclid, Ptolemaic theory of the universe).[5] With the fall of Alexandria to Islamic power in 640 A.D., all university activity ceased, even though some interest was transferred to the Arabs to be revived later at Baghdad and the Moorish intellectual centers of Spain.

3. **Fusion with Roman education.** After the Roman Conquest of 146 B.C., Greek civilization in general was rapidly appropriated by the Roman conquerors, and Greek education extended its boundaries without changing its character. In a sense, Roman education is but one aspect of the cosmopolitan education of Greece.

[5] For science in ancient times, see S. F. Mason, *A History of the Sciences,* London, 1953.

Part II

THE MEDIEVAL WORLD

Historical background. Generally, the period is divided into "The Early Middle Ages" (sixth to eleventh centuries) and "The Late Middle Ages" (eleventh to thirteenth centuries.) Although necessarily arbitrary, the divisions suggest that order and stability were being established in the later period.

Early Middle Ages. The seat of the Roman Empire was shifted, beginning in the fourth century, from Rome to Constantinople. The center of political authority moved northward to Frankish kingdoms, which had been consolidated under the leadership of Merovingian kings. The important political leaders included Charles Martel, Pepin, and Charlemagne (r. 771–814); in the ninth century internal strife split the Empire, which was further weakened by invasions. Stability was restored by Otto I (962), as head of the Holy Roman Empire. The rise of Islam in the early seventh century eventually had great influence on Europe (Mohammed, d. 632).

Late Middle Ages. This period was marked by centuries of struggle between the papacy and the emperors, e.g., the struggle between Pope Innocent III and Frederick II. Some centralized political power existed in France and England, but very little in Italy or Germany. Important French kings included Louis IX and Philip IV; English kings included William the Conqueror (Norman invasion) and King John (*Magna Carta,* 1215). The dominant institution of feudalism was based on class distinction and gained strength as Charlemagne's empire broke up. In the later centuries, there was some growth in commerce and towns, with merchant and craft guilds assuming particular importance.

POLITICAL EVENTS	WRITERS, SCHOOLMEN, ETC.	CHURCHMEN AND ECCLESIASTICAL EVENTS	EDUCATIONAL WRITINGS	EDUCATIONAL EVENTS
"Fall" of Rome . . . 476 Odoacer . . . 476 Theodoric . . 493 Tothila . 541–542 Justinian . . 527 The empire reunited . . 565 Arab conquest of Spain . . 714 Karl Martel defeats Saracens . . 732 Carolingian line 752 End of Lombard kingdom . . 774 Charlemagne 772–814 800 A.D.	Boethius *c.* 480–524 Cassiodorus *c.* 480–575 Gregory of Tours *c.* 538–594 Isidore of Seville *c.* 570–636 Venerable Bede . . 673–735 Alcuin . . 735–804 Paulus Diaconus 725–797	St. Benedict 480–543 Franks converted . . 496 Gregory I *c.* 540–604 Mohammed *b.* 572 Columban . 540–615 Hegira of Mohammed . 622 Conference at Whitby . . 664 Boniface converts the Germans 721–754 Last council recognized by Eastern and Western churches . . 787 Leo III . 795–817	Benedict's *Rules* Boethius, *Consolations*, *Translations of Aristotle*. Cassiodorus, *Institutes of Sacred Literature* Gregory of Tours, *Chron.* Isidore, *Etymologies* Bede, *Chron.* Alcuin, *On Seven Liberal Arts*, etc.	Monte Cassino founded . . 529 Cassiodorus founds monastery . 540 Christian era first used for dating . . . 526 St. Gall founded 614 Reichenau f. . 724 Fulda founded . 744 Alcuin called to Frankland . 781 Karl's *Capitularies* on ed. 787 *et seq.* Alcuin, Abbot of Tours . 794–804
Carolingian Empire founded . . 800 Charles the Bald . 840–877 Treaty Verdun 843 Alfred . 871–901 Henry of Saxony 919–936 Otho . . 936–973 Holy Roman Empire founded 962 Otho III . 996–1002 Caliphate of Cordova 929–1031 Capetian line . 987 Norman conq. 1066 Canossa . . 1077 1100 A.D.	Einhard . 770–840 Rabanus Maurus . 776–856 John Scotus 810 875 Walafred Strabo . 809–849 Avicenna 980–1037 Anselm . 1033–1109 Roscellinus *c.* 1050–1121 William of Champeaux *d.* 1121	Conversion of Saxons . . . 804 Separation of Eastern and Western churches . . 822 Clugny founded 910 First Crusade 1095 Sylvester II (Gerbert) 999–1003 Cistercians founded . 1098 Knights of St. John founded . 1099	Rabanus Maurus, *Education of the Clergy* Walafred Strabo, *Biography* Anselm and Roscellinus begin scholastic controversy	Division of Monastic Schools into interns and externs . . 817 Hirschau founded . . 830 Oath of Strassburg, earliest form of German and French language . . 841 Salerno . fl. *c.* 1050 Anselm, Abbot of Canterbury 1093–1109
Consular government in Italian cities . fl. 1100 Arnold of Brescia 1100–1155 Frederick Barbarossa 1152–1190 Henry II of England 1154–84 Philip II of France 1180–1223 Treaty of Constance 1183 Fall of Constantinople to Crusaders 1204 Frederick II 1208–1250 Magna Charta 1215 End of Hohenstaufen line 1254 Louis IX of France 1226–70 Latin Empire in East falls . 1261 Hapsburg line begins . . 1273 Model Parliament 1295 1300 A.D.	Bernard . *d.* 1153 Abelard 1079–1142 Hugo St. Victor *c.* 1097–1142 Richard St. Victor *d.* 1173 John of Salisbury . 1110–1180 Peter of Blois 1135–1204 Albertus Magnus 1193–1280 Walter Map *c.* 1140–1210 Averroës 1126–1198 Alex. Hales *d.* 1245 Grosseteste 1175–1253 Bonaventura 1221–1274 Th Aquinas 1221–74 Walter von der Vogelweide fl. 1230 Alexander de Villedieu . . *d.* 1240 Vincent de Beauvais *d.* 1264 Roger Bacon 1214–1294 Raymond Lull 1235–1315	Knights Templars founded . 1119 Second Crusade 1147 Murder of à Becket . 1170 Innocent III 1198–1216 Peter the Venerable *d.* 1156 Albigensian Crusade . 1208 Franciscans founded . 1210 Dominicans founded . 1215 Crusade of St. Louis . 1270 Christians expelled from Palestine . 1291 Boniface 1294–1303	Abelard, *Sic et Non*, etc. Hugo of St. Victor, *On Instruction* John of Salisbury, *Metalogicus* Walter Map, *Latin Students' Songs* Alexander de Villedieu, *Grammar*	Irnerius at Bologna . 1113 Trans. from Arabic under Raymond of Toledo 1130–1150 U. of Paris . *c.* 1160 Aristotle's *Physics* proscribed at Paris . . 1210 *Metaphysics* proscribed . 1215 Frederick II sends trans of Aris. to Bol and Paris 1220 Niebelungenlied *c.* 1220 Epic poetry in Ger. and France *c.* 1200–1250 Dominicans at Paris . . 1217 Franciscans at Paris . . 1230 U. of Padua . 1222 U. of Naples . 1224 U. of Salamanca 1243 U. Col. Oxford 1249 Peterhouse, Cambridge 1284 Aristotle again stud. at Paris . 1255

Chapter II

ROMAN EDUCATION

Historical background. In government, Rome represents the change from a monarchic city-state to a republican city-state, and finally back to an absolute, despotic, and imperialistic monarchy. The early monarchy extends down to 509 B.C. Slowly, the form of government became a republic, the first period of which continued until about 264 B.C. Rome was plundered by the Gauls in 390 B.C., and fought the Samnite Wars (343–290 B.C.), and the war with Pyrrhus (281–272 B.C.). During the second period of the Republic (down to 133 B.C.), Rome expanded outside Italy, destroyed Corinth and Carthage (146 B.C.); the third period of the Republic (to 27 B.C.) included the work of the Gracchi (133–122 B.C.), of Sulla as dictator (82–79 B.C.), and of Cicero as Consul (63 B.C.). Gaul was conquered in 58–50 B.C., and the battle of Actium fought in 31 B.C. The outcome of this battle removed European civilization from the influence of the Orient, and made Egypt a province of Rome. The imperial period began with the rule of Augustus (27 B.C. to 14 A.D.), and continued down to 476 A.D., when the Empire in the West came to an end. From 325 A.D., when Constantine called together the Council of Nicaea, Christianity assumed greater and wider power.

Periods of Roman education. Roman education falls into two great periods. The first of these is that in which its ideals and practices were purely Roman; the second is that in which Greek influence became more and more prominent, and Roman education became a composite or cosmopolitan entity. The dominance of Greek educational practice did not become complete until near the end of the Republic (31 B.C.); Cicero's *On Oratory* (55 B.C.) was the first Roman exposition of the Greek educational method and ideal, and this date might conveniently divide the two periods.

Early Roman education. This period extended from 776 to *ca.* 250 B.C. The home was practically the only agency of education that remained largely moral, with severe discipline and rigorous ideals. *The Laws of Twelve Tablets* (adopted 451–450 B.C.) remained the basis of Roman society for a thousand years; not unlike the laws of Lycurgus, they embodied ideals that gave education definite aims. During the latter part of this period, the elementary schools supplied the rudiments of reading and writing. These schools were known as *ludi* (*ludus*—play, sport), a name that suggests they were supplementary, not essential to the real education of Roman youth. The rearing of the child was in the hands of the mother; the training of the boy, largely reserved to the father.

Period of introduction of Greek schools. This period extends from the middle of the third century to the middle of the first century. The period coincides with a period of national expansion throughout Italy. By the beginning of the period, elementary schools (*ludi*) were well established and known as schools of *literators* and *grammatists.* The translation of the *Odyssey* into Latin by Livius Andronicus (284–204 B.C.) allowed the introduction of the book into the schools, giving them a greater literary content than they had up to this time. Translation of other Greek works followed rapidly, and a change in education was effected largely in the introduction of the Greek grammar school, different from the *ludus* in form and superior to it. Many Greek teachers allowed the development of Greek grammatical and rhetorical schools, and subsequent introduction of the Latin rhetorical school supplemented the work of the Greek rhetorical school and gave it greater scope. The influence of these schools, however, was not great until the imperial period.

Hellenized Roman education extended from *ca.* 50 B.C. to 200 A.D. The general appropriation of Greek culture by Romans was by adoption of Greek educational institutions.

1. **The school of the literator (Ludimagister).** Even during this period this school attempted to give little more than the rudiments of reading and writing and calculation. When the boy had mastered the art of reading ordinary prose, he was transferred to the higher school.

2. **The school of the grammaticus** became a highly formalized educational institution with a definite method, curriculum, and public support. Such schools were of two types: one concerned itself with teaching Greek language, and the other, Latin. The Latin grammar school was of particular importance and was found in every part of the Empire. It remained the most persistent institution of Roman civilization until it was overthrown by the invasions from the north. The master in such schools was called a *literatus* or a *grammaticus,* and grammar was understood to include both linguistic study and the critical study of literature, which was defined to include the work of historians and scientific writers as well as poets; to some extent, the grammar schools included work in mathematics, music, and rudimentary dialectics, but the gymnastics and dancing of the Greek schools were never introduced. Gymnastics, if taught at all, was taught only in connection with military training. Through training in declamation, the work of the grammar schools merged with that of the rhetorical school, which, in a sense, was the culmination of a practical literary education.

3. **The school of the rhetor.** This was similar to the schools of the Sophists, and furnished a direct preparation for the life of affairs at Rome through training in oratory. Those who attended these schools were prepared for public careers, and during the late imperial period, these schools produced most of the members of the senatorial class. The rhetorical training of boys began at about age fifteen, or when the boy laid aside the *toga praetexta* and entered man-

hood. If intended for a public career, he entered the rhetorical school to supplement the training he had received in the grammar school, and the length of the training depended on his abilities, interests, and the schools he attended. Most of the curriculum consisted of declamation and debate, but it would be a mistake to assume that the curriculum was narrow and rigid, since the rhetorical schools included much more than exercise in debate. To the Roman, the skill of the orator represented the many ways in which the educated man could make his training and knowledge effective in the service of his fellow citizens.[1]

4. **Libraries and universities.** The higher education of Rome was largely an imitation of that of Greece. Many libraries were taken as spoils in the conquest of Greece, e.g., that library brought back to Rome by Paulus Aemilius in 167 B.C. Sulla and other military conquerors brought back others. The University of Rome had its origin in the library founded by Vespasian (69–79 A.D.), which, subsidized by Hadrian (117–138 A.D.) and later emperors, developed into an educational institution of higher studies known as the Athenaeum. Typically Roman, the work of the university was practical, more attention being given to medicine and law than to philosophy or creative speculation. However, the university idea did not spread beyond Rome, and libraries were almost unknown in the provinces.

5. **Support of schools by the Empire.** The spread of grammar schools during imperial times was very wide and scarcely one provincial town was without its school, but only in a limited sense did an imperial school system exist. No government supervision existed; no law forced their establishment. Yet several factors suggested the existence of what constituted a school system. Antoninus Pius (138–161 A.D.) conferred upon a limited number of grammarians, rhetoricians, and philosophers in the provinces many of the privileges of the senatorial class. Constantine (306–337 A.D.) extended these privileges; in an unusual move, Gratian (367–383 A.D.) gave money from the imperial treasury for the support of local schools, and in 376 A.D., he established a

[1] Raymond F. Howes, ed., *Historical Studies of Rhetoric and Rhetoricians*, Cornell University Press, 1961.

salary schedule for teachers throughout the Empire. Julian (361–363 A.D.) required the certification of teachers, and in 425 A.D., Theodosius and Valentinian made the imperial government the sole authority for the establishment of schools and, in substance, prohibited the founding of private schools.

6. **Educational writers of Imperial Rome.** Many references to educational practices are to be found throughout Latin literature, e.g., Horace, Martial, Juvenal, Seneca, Suetonius, Pliny the Younger, Marcus Aurelius. In a few works is found a scientific and theoretical discussion of education. Of these, the works of Cicero, Tacitus, and Quintilian are the most important.

a) **Cicero** (106–43 B.C.). His most important educational work is *De Oratore*. This advocated a broad general education as the background for success in private and public life; the conception of "humanities," the studies proper to humanity, was Cicero's most important contribution to education. All of the humanities were to be focused upon the art of leadership in public affairs.

b) **Tacitus** (50–117 A.D.). In the *Dialogus de Oratoribus,* Tacitus contrasted the rhetorical education of Cicero's time with that of his own, which he found artificial and formal. He advocated a liberal education that promoted the needs of public life and warned against artificiality and formalism in school work.

c) **Quintilian** (35–95 A.D) was the most prominent Roman writer on education, with his theory expounded in the *De Institutione Oratoria,* a work in twelve books giving the principles for training the orator. For Quintilian, the orator was not merely the man who could speak eloquently; he was also *vir bonus dicendi peritus* (the virtuous man skilled in speaking), the citizen who employed all his skill in the service of the state.

The Institutes of Oratory. Book I describes the kind of education given to children prior to the study of rhetoric. It stresses individual differences, recognizes that most boys are capable of improvement, and puts emphasis on memory and moral admonition. In learning to read, the child is to start with Greek because it acted as a foundation for Latin.

Public education is preferred to private education, stressing the modern idea that school is a society in which children learn from one another, as well as from the teacher. Books II-XII give detailed descriptions of advanced education suited to civic needs. Beyond elementary education, boys must attend a grammar school, which trains in grammar and composition and requires extensive reading. Book X contains a list of "great books," which form the basis of a liberal education. For the most advanced training of the orator, a thorough study of composition, declamation, prose authors, the theory of rhetoric, is prescribed. The work of Quintilian was rediscovered in the Renaissance (translated in 1411), and it became one of the source books for the humanistic theorists of education.[2]

The decline of Roman education. In form, Roman education continued through the centuries until the end of Roman imperial power in the West; but in spirit, it had already begun to decline shortly after the opening of the Christian era. The education of the Christian church gradually replaced Roman education, whose main characteristic had been its practical recognition of the needs of political and institutional life. More and more, in the centuries of decline, Roman education was limited to the upper class, reflecting the privileges of favor and class distinction. These centuries were, however, not without many minor writers, some of whom are important in the history of education. In the fourth century, with the return to paganism under the Emperor Julian (361–363 A.D.), a revival in classical culture and the schools occurred. Donatus (*ca.* 400) in the West and Priscian (*ca.* 500) in the East wrote textbooks on grammar that remained the basis of study until the sixteenth century. As Roman life tended to become corrupt and the government despotic, the early individualism of the Romans was lost, and the dominant education lost any vital connection with the life of the times. A new education, furnished by the early Christian Church, gradually replaced the old.

[2] C. E. Little, ed., *The Institutio Oratoria of Marcus Fabius Quintilianus,* with an English Summary and a Concordance, George Peabody College for Teachers, 1951.

The structure of Roman education persisted, even with the loss of social balance, but artificially, formally, and unrealistically.

Selected References

Part I: Education in Classical Antiquity

Readings in most of the educational theory of the period may be most conveniently found in Paul Monroe, *Source Book in the History of Education for the Greek and Roman Period*, New York, 1921.

Adamson, J. E. *The Theory of Education in Plato's Republic.* London, 1903.

Barclay, William. *Educational Ideals in the Ancient World.* London, 1959.

Beck, A. G. *Greek Education, 450–350 B.C.* London, 1964.

Bolgar, R. R. *The Classical Heritage and Its Beneficiaries.* New York, 1964.

Burnet, John. *Aristotle on Education.* Harvard University Press, 1928.

Capes, W. W. *University Life in Ancient Athens.* New York, 1922.

Castle, E. B. *Ancient Education and Today.* Baltimore, 1961.

Chambliss, J. J., ed. *Nobility, Tragedy, and Naturalism: Education in Ancient Greece.* Minneapolis, 1971.

Clark, Donald L. *Rhetoric in Graeco-Roman Education.* New York, 1957.

Clarke, M. L. *Higher Education in the Ancient World.* Albuquerque, New Mexico, 1971.

Cole, P. R. *Later Roman Education.* New York, 1909.

Davidson, Thomas. *Aristotle and Ancient Educational Ideals.* New York, 1901.

———. *Education of the Greek People.* New York, 1904.

Dobson, John F. *Ancient Education and Its Meaning to Us.* New York, 1932.

Drever, James. *Greek Education: Its Practices and Principles.* New York, 1912.

Forbes, Clarence A. *Greek Physical Education.* New York, 1929.

Freeman, Kenneth J. *Schools of Hellas*, 3rd ed. New York, 1922.
Gwynn, Aubrey. *Roman Education from Cicero to Quintilian.* New York, 1926.
Highet, Gilbert. *The Classical Tradition.* New York, 1949.
Hobhouse, W. *The Theory and Practice of Ancient Education.* New York, 1910.
Jaeger, Werner W. *Paideia: The Ideals of Greek Culture.* New York, 1945.
Lane, Fred. *Elementary Greek Education.* Syracuse, New York, 1895.
Laurie, S. S. *Historical Survey of Pre-Christian Education.* New York, 1895.
Lodge, Rupert C. *Plato's Theory of Education.* New York, 1948.
Mahaffy, J. P. *Old Greek Education.* New York, 1881.
Marrou, H. I. *A History of Education in Antiquity.* New York, 1964.
Nettleship, Richard L. *The Theory of Education in the Republic of Plato.* Chicago, 1906.
Rounds, Dorothy, ed. *Articles in Festschriften on Antiquity: An Index.* Harvard University Press, 1962.
Smail, W. M. *Quintilian on Education.* New York, 1938.
Smith, William A. *Ancient Education.* New York, 1955.
Van Hook, LaRue. *Greek Life and Thought.* New York, 1937.
Walden, John W. H. *The Universities of Ancient Greece.* New York, 1909.
Westaway, Katherine M. *The Educational Theory of Plutarch.* London, 1922.
Wilkins, A. S. *National Education in Greece in the Fourth Century, B.C.* New York, 1911.
Woody, Thomas. *Life and Education in Early Societies.* New York, 1949.

Chronological Survey of Roman and Early Christian Education

Political Events and Personages	Poets, Dramatists, Historians, etc.	Philosophers, Moralists, Church Fathers, etc.	Writings Possessing Educational Significance	Educational Events
Traditional founding of city . . . 753 Kings . . 753–509 Decemvirs . . 451 Censors . . . 444 Italian Wars 343–272				Laws of Twelve Tables . . . 451 First mention of Ludus . . . 449
300 B.C. Punic Wars 264–146 Death of Cato . 148 Conquest of Greece . . . 146 Reforms of the Gracchi . 132–121 Social War . 91–89 War of Marius and Sulla . . 89–79 First Triumvirate 59 Cæsar's conquests . 58–52	Andronicus c. 284–c. 204 Nævius c. 264–194 Plautus 254–184 Ennius . 239–169 Cato . 234–148 Terence 189–159 Lucretius 97–53 Varro . 116–27 Cicero . 106–53 Nepos . 99–54 Sallust . 86–34		Latinized *Odyssey* . c. 250 Plautus, *Bacchides* 189 Cato, *de Agricultura*, earliest work in Latin prose . c. 175–150 Varro, *Disciplinarum libri novem* c. 43 Cicero, *de Oratore* . 55	Andronicus reaches Rome . . . 272 Spurius Carvilius founds school . 260 First Latin play at Rome . . 240 Paulus Æmilius brings Greek library to Rome 167 Crates est. first gram. school and teaches Greek . . . 167 Greek rhetoricians expelled . . 161 First private library . . c. 150 Censors expel Latin rhetoricians . 92
55 B.C. Conspiracy of Catiline . . . 52 War of Cæsar and Pompey . 49–48 Death of Cæsar . 44 Second Triumvirate . 43 Reign of Augustus 31 B.C.–14 A.D. Tiberius r. 14–37 A.D. Nero . . r. 54–68 Vespasian r. 69–79 Trajan . r. 98–117 Hadrian r. 117–138 Antonines r. 138–180 Public sale of Empire . . . 193 Roman citizenship conferred on all free provincials . . 212 Absolute monarchy of Diocletian 284–305 Constantine r. 306–337	Cæsar . 100–44 Virgil . 70–19 Horace . . 68–8 Sallust . 86–34 Ovid 43 B.C.–18 A.D. Livy 59 B.C.–18 A.D. Pliny, the Elder 23–79 Quintilian 35 A.D.–95 Tacitus c. 55 A.D.–120 Plutarch 46–125 Pliny, the Younger 61–105 Juvenal c. 55–140 Suetonius c. 75–160	Seneca 54 B.C.–39 A.D. Epictetus fl. c. 90 A.D. Marcus Aurelius 121–180 Tertullian c. 150–230 Clement of Alexandria c. 150–c. 215 Cyprian c. 200–255 Origen . 185–254 Plotinus 204–270 Porphyry 233–c. 301	Horace, *Odes and Satires* 35–8 B.C. Tacitus, *de Oratoribus* 79 A.D. Quintilian, *de Oratoria* 96 Martial, *Epigrams* 90–99 Pliny, *Epistles* . 97–108 Juvenal, *Satires* 100–126 Suetonius, *Lives of Rhetoricians* c. 121 Marcus Aurelius, *Meditations* c. 161 Tertullian, *Prescription Against Heresies* Clement, *The Educator*, *Stromata*, etc.	First public library . . . 39 Palatine Library founded . . . 28 First Imperial support of schools c. 75 A.D. Antoninus Pius subsidizes education in the Provinces 138–161 Caracalla destroys foundation of Alexandrian University . . 217 Severus appoints teachers of mathematics at Rome . . . 218 Constantine extends privileges of teachers 321, 326, 333
313 A.D. Toleration of Christianity . 313 Council of Nicæa 325 Julian the Apostate 361–363 Goths invade Empire . . 376 Final div. of Emp. 395 Exposure of infants prohibited . . 374 Last Roman triumph . . 404 Alaric sacks Rome . . . 410 Battle of Chalons 451 Empire combined with the East 476	Eusebius 265–340 Ausonius c. 310–c. 393 Symmachus c. 345–405 Apollonius Sidonius c. 430–480 Martianus Capella fl. c. 500	Basil 331–374 Ambrose 340–397 Gregory of Nyssa c. 343–c. 394 Jerome . 331–420 Chrysostom 344–404 Augustine 354–430	Jerome, *Letters*, to *Læta*, to *Gaudentius*, etc. Donatus, *Grammar* c. 400 Augustine, *Confessions* Capella, *Marriage of Philology and Mercury* Priscian, *Grammar* c. 500	Julian licenses teachers and forbids Christians teaching . . 361 Gratian orders payment of teachers' salaries in provincial capitals and establishes schedule of salaries . . . 376 Death of Hypatia . . 415 All teachers to be licensed . . . 425 Syriac commentaries on Aristotle . 450

Chapter III

EDUCATION DURING THE EARLY MIDDLE AGES

The new educational ideal. Greek and Roman philosophy had offered a solution to the moral problems of man in intellectual speculation; Christianity offered the solution in man's moral nature. Inevitably, this position led to an indifference on the part of the early and medieval Christians to the intellectual and aesthetic features of Greek and Roman education. Generally, the early Christian writers were hostile to Hellenism and Roman learning.[1] Both St. Jerome (331–432), translator of that version of the Bible accepted by the Church for centuries, and St. Augustine (354–430) illustrate this hostility. Tertullian (*ca.* 160–230) denied that a Christian could be a teacher of ancient learning.

Early Christian schools. The early Church turned its attention almost completely to the moral education of its membership, and as probationers awaited full membership in the Church, they were rudimentarily instructed in so-called catechumenal schools. Intellectual and theological activity at Alexandria made it the center of moral training, and the

[1] Werner Jaeger, *Early Christianity and Greek Paideia,* Harvard University Press, 1961.

work of Pantaenus, Clement, Origen, resulted in the growth of so-called catechetical schools, whose purpose again was simple instruction in doctrine and trial of the Christian life. In time such schools were organized by each bishop for the training of the clergy for the churches. This allowed for some system and method, and during the fifth and sixth centuries the Church councils legislated that children destined for the priesthood be placed in such episcopal (bishop) or cathedral schools. After the fall of the Roman Empire in the West, these schools with those of the monasteries were the only remaining ones.

Monasticism. The primary characteristic of monasticism is denial. Monasticism in the East arose from the intimate relation of the new Christianity and the oriental religions; it was transferred to Rome by Athanasius (296–373) and Jerome (340–420). In the West the monks lived in communities rather than insolation as hermits, as was the usual custom in the East. Some of these groups formulated rules. Important among these were the rules of St. Benedict, which he drew up for his community in 529. This Benedictine rule was the first to make recognition of the value of manual labor in education, and it also provided that two hours of each day be devoted to reading. The ideals of monasticism were summed up in the three ideals of chastity, poverty, and obedience. These ideals became, in the larger sense, an educational force of great importance to society as a whole.

Monasticism and literary education. Actually, the monasteries were the sole schools for teaching; they alone offered professional training; they preserved books; they were the only libraries; they produced the only scholars; they were the sole educational institutions of the period. By the tenth century, they developed both inner monastic schools for those intending to take the vows (*oblati*), and outer monastic schools for those not so intending (*externi*). Although instruction in both schools was meager, it provided for reading, writing, music, arithmetic, religious observation, and rules of conduct. In the later centuries the *scriptorium*, or general writing room, was found in most monasteries. Here the monks laboriously copied and preserved many of the manuscripts of antiquity. In this connection the monasteries became the depositories of literature and learning.

The seven liberal arts. The advanced studies that were offered in some of the monastery and cathedral schools came to be known in time as the seven liberal arts, largely as a result of the ecclesiastical and symbolic tendencies of the Middle Ages. The seven liberal arts comprised two divisions:

I. The Trivium: (1) grammar; (2) rhetoric; (3) dialectic
II. The Quadrivium: (4); arithmetic; (5) geometry; (6) astronomy; (7) music

The knowledge contained in these studies represents the amount of secular learning preserved by the Church; and beyond these came ethics, and the greatest of all studies for the Middle Ages, that of theology. The content of the seven liberal arts is wider than was suggested. Geometry included the rudiments of geography; astronomy included physics; grammar included literature; rhetoric included history. Not all of these studies were taught in every monastery or cathedral school. Many of the lesser monasteries offered instruction chiefly in grammar, and only a little of the studies beyond. Others emphasized the Trivium; only a few taught the full range of medieval learning, and these were regarded as the great schools of the period.

Educational writers of the early Middle Ages. The sixth and seventh centuries were periods of transition in the handing down of the scholarly materials of the later imperial period of the Roman Empire; in the eighth and ninth centuries, the level of medieval scholarship rose considerably, culminating in the so-called "Carolingian" (Charlemagne) revival; in the tenth and eleventh centuries, the pace of intellectual activity increased even further. The most important of the educational theorists of the early Middle Ages were the following:

1. **Martianus Capella** (*ca.* 410–427) wrote a treatise entitled *The Marriage of Philology and Mercury*, which was the most widely used textbook on ancient learning used in the first half of the Middle Ages. The seven bridesmaids (or handmaidens) who attend Philology are the Ars Gram-

matica, Ars Dialectica, Ars Rhetorica, Geometrica, Arithmetica, Astronomia, Harmonia; and each as led forward in the ceremony, gives her parentage and expounds the substance of the art typified. Written in Carthage, this text has been called the most successful textbook ever written.[2] In a sense, the book is an encyclopedia of the medieval arts.

2. **Boethius** (*ca.* 480–524) was the most influential of all the writers of the early Middle Ages. His most important work was *The Consolation of Philosophy,* which placed ancient culture in a Christian frame of reference; it summarized ancient ethics and gave to the Middle Ages its best account of ancient philosophy. He also wrote summaries of Aristotle, Plato, and Cicero, and a compendium of the seven liberal arts, to which he helped to give a more permanent form. For centuries Boethius was regarded as a great educational authority, and his texts continued to be used in some universities well into the eighteenth century.

3. **Cassiodorus** (*ca.* 490–585) has been called the father of literary monasticism. His *Introduction to Divine and Human Readings* became an educational syllabus for the monks of the monasteries. The work is divided into two books and was intended to instruct monks in what was to be studied. Book II contains an outline for the seven liberal arts and was used for several centuries as a guide to secular learning. It was largely through the influence of Cassiodorus that the custom of collecting and copying manuscripts became established.

4. **Isidore of Seville** (*ca.* 570–636), one of the most informed men of his time, his *Etymologies,* an encyclopedia or thesaurus that purported to contain all knowledge, was used as a standard reference and text from the seventh through the eleventh centuries. The work is divided into twenty books on a variety of religious and secular topics. As Bishop of Seville, he exercised authority over schools, monasteries, churches, and the clergy. He attempted to improve the education of the clergy.

5. **Charlemagne** (r. 771–814). Although not an educational writer, his *capitularies* on schools have been consid-

[2] P. R. Cole, *Later Roman Education,* New York, 1909, p. 16

ered by some to be the foundations of modern education. These capitularies (letters of advice) called upon ecclesiastical and secular authorities to promote education. In a similar vein, **Alfred the Great** (848-901) stimulated educational practice by the establishment of schools and the encouragement of scholars. Alfred the Great translated into Anglo-Saxon many works, the most important of which was Boethius' *Consolation of Philosophy*.

6. **Alcuin** (735–804) was summoned by Charlemagne in 782 from the cathedral school of York to become master of the palace school at Aachen, where he became chief educational adviser to the great king whose famous capitularies on education he may have written. In 794, Alcuin was made head of the Abbey of Tours, which he made the center of learning in France. His chief educational works are *On Grammar, On Orthography, On Rhetoric, On Dialectics,* all of which are in the catechetical form (question and answer), and of which *On Grammar* is the most important. This treatise is divided into two parts, the first dealing with methods of education and the duties of the student; the second dealing with grammar proper. Power suggests that Alcuin's importance in the history of education is due to: (1) the widespread reform of education initiated by Charlemagne and guided by Alcuin; (2) his texts on education that contributed to an educational consciousness; (3) the cultivation of a closer relationship between liberal learning and spiritual knowledge.[3] The last of these is the most important, in that it demonstrated, in an age of religious dedication, that intellectual training was equally essential for moral betterment.

Minor educational writers. These included **Rabanus Maurus** (776–856), a pupil of Alcuin, whose *Education of the Clergy* is a treatise on the seven liberal arts and covers the entire field of education in his day; **Joannes Scotus Eriginia** (*ca.* 810–875), the most noted successor to Alcuin, who introduced the study of the Greek language and whose work led to the great revival of intellectual interest in the elev-

[3] Edward J. Power, *Main Currents in the History of Education*, New York, 1962, p. 224.

enth and twelfth centuries that was known as scholasticism; **Gerbert** (*ca.* 950–1003), better known as Pope Sylvester II (993–1003), who was a builder of libraries, and who contributed to the integration of secular (liberal) and Christian learning. In addition, note should be made of widely used textbooks of the early Middle Ages that had great influence. These included the grammars of **Donatus** (*ca.* 333–400) and of **Priscian** (*ca.* 500), and the odd work called *The Distychs of Cato* (said to be the work of Cato the Elder, 234–149 B.C.), which was a selection of moral sentiments in versified form, illustrating grammar and rhetoric.

Chronological Table of Educational Development from the Fourteenth to the Seventeenth Century

Political Events and Personages	Literary Men and Scientists	Religious Events and Personages	Educators and Educational Writings	Educational Events
1300. 1339-1453. One Hund. Yrs.' War Edward III of Eng. 1327-1377. 1347. Rienzi. 1347 9. Black Death. 1356 Poitiers. 1356. The Seven Electors established by charter. 1350 1500. Hansa League.	Marco Polo 1234 1324 Dante 1265-1321 Petrarch 1304-1374 Boccaccio 1313 1375 Chaucer 1328 1400	1302. Philip of France triumphs over Boniface. 1312. Suppression of Templars. John Tauler 1290-1361 Wycliffe 1324-1384 1309 1377. Babylonian Captivity. 1387-1417. The Great Schism. 1384. Breth. Com. Life f.	William of Occam 1270-1347 Jean Gerson 1363-1429 Paulus Vergerius 1349-1420	1343. U. Pisa f. 1347. U. Prague f. 1349. U. Florence f. 1362. Use of Eng. est. in law courts. 1365. U. Vienna f. 1384. School at Daventer founded. 1386. U. Heidelberg f. 1387. Winchester f. 1392. U. Erfurt f. 1397-1400. Chrysoloras teaches Gree at Florence.
1400. 1431. Joan of Arc burned. 1453 Fall of Constantinople. 1455 1485. War of Roses. 1474-1509. Ferdinand and Isabella of Spain 1494 Charles VIII of France in Italy. 1498-1515. Italian wars of Louis XI. 1462-1505. Ivan the Great.	Lorenzo Valla 1407-1457. Leonardo Bruni 1369 1444. Pico da Mirandola (1463-1494) and the Platonic Academy. Leonardo da Vinci 1452-1519 Raphael 1485-1520	1414. Council of Constance. 1418. Council of Basle. 1415 John Huss burned. Thomas à Kempis 1380 1472 Savonarola 1452-1498	Vittorino da Feltra 1378 1446 Cosimo de Medici 1389-1446 Wessel 1420-1495 Hegius 1420-1495 Battista Guarino 1434 1460 John Reuchlin 1455-1522 Jacob Wimpfeling 1450-1528 1452. Pope Pius II., *De Liberorum Educatione.* Colet 1456 1519 Linacre 1460-1524 Wm. Lilly 1468-1522	1428. Vitterino establishes school at Mantua. 1440. Eton founde 1455. First book printed. 1458. Greek taugh at Paris. 1460. New learnin at Heidelberg. 1494. First chair o "Poetry" in Europe (at Erfurt 1496. Humanism city schools of Nuremberg.
1500. 1520. Magellan circumnavigates the globe. 1524. Peasants' War. Henry VIII 1509-1547 1533. Reb. of Geneva. Edward VI 1547-1553 Elizabeth 1558 1603 1588 Spanish Armada.	Erasmus 1457-1536 Michael Angelo 1475-1564 Ariosto 1474-1533 Copernicus 1473-1543 Tycho-Brahé 1546-1601 Shakespeare 1564-1616 Kepler 1571-1630	Luther 1483 1546 1517. Luther's Theses. 1521. Diet at Worms. 1535. Suppression of monasteries in England. 1540. Jesuit Order founded. 1538. English Act of Supremacy. 1545-1563. Council of Trent. Zwingli 1484-1531 Knox 1505 1572 Calvin 1509-1564 1542. Inquisition introduced. 1553. Servetus burned. 1555. Peace of Augsburg. 1572. St. Bartholomew's massacre. 1598. Edict of Nantes.	Erasmus 1467-1536 Thomas More 1478-1535 Rabelais 1483-1553 Melanchthon 1497-1560 Trotzendorf 1490-1556 Vives 1492-1540 Sturm 1507-1589 Ascham 1515-1568 Montaigne 1533 1592 Peter Ramus 1515-1572 Michael Neander 1525-1595 1571. Ascham's *Schoolmaster.* 1531. Elyot's *Governour,* first work in Eng on education. Mulcaster 1531-1611 Mulcaster's *Positions* 1581	1502. University Wittemberg founde 1510-1513. Erasm teaches Greek at Cambridge. 1510. St. Paul's f 1519. Erfurt and Leipzig reorganized on humanistic basis 1524. First Prote tant City School 1524. Luther's Address to German Cities. 1526. Melanchth opens gymnasiu at Nuremberg. 1528. Saxony School Plan. 1537. Sturm's School founded. 1540. Jesuit orde 1559. Würtembe School Plan; f sys. of Pub. Sc 1599. Final form Jesuit *Ratio Studiorum.*

Chapter IV

EDUCATION IN THE LATE MIDDLE AGES

Scholasticism or education as an intellectual discipline. Scholasticism was a type of education or intellectual life that flourished from the eleventh to the fifteenth centuries; its greatest importance lies in the origin that it furnished of universities whose work it dominated for three or four centuries. Although it is not characterized by any group of principles or beliefs, its main purpose was to bring reason to the support of religious faith, to strengthen the church by the development of intellectual power. *Credo ut intellegam* (I believe in order that I may understand) was its dominant principle. The educational purposes of scholasticism were: (1) to develop the power of disputation; (2) to systematize knowledge; (3) to give individual mastery of this system of knowledge, now reduced into a logical whole. One of its major interests was the attempted reconciliation between *realism* and *nominalism*. The orthodox Schoolmen accepted Plato's position that views, ideas, concepts, universals were the only reality, and combated the heresy that ideas or universals (Aristotle) are only names and that reality consists only in individual concrete objects. The early Scholastics —**Roscellinus** (d. 1106), **Anselm** (d. 1109), and **Abelard**

(d. 1142)—were primarily concerned with this problem of universals.

The scholastics and their textbooks. The educational content of scholasticism consisted in systematized schemes of learning, with commentaries or glosses. The two most important of these were *The Sententiae* of Peter Lombard (*ca.* 1100–1164) and the *Summa Theologica* of St. Thomas Aquinas (1225–1274). Other Scholastics included Albertus Magnus (1193–1280), who prepared practical books and manuals for the schools; Alexander of Hales (d. 1245), a representative of the mystical tradition in education; Bonaventura (1221–1274), and William of Occam (1280–1347), the last of the Schoolmen. Although Scholasticism produced a large body of scholarly works in law, philosophy, and theology, its educational system had many limitations, among which may be included: (1) its interest in argument, not in the validity of conclusion; (2) its abstract and metaphysical character; (3) its discussion, which possessed no reality, no relation to the world about it.

The origins of the universities. As a result of the interest in dialectic, a number of schools connected with the cathedrals and monasteries came into prominence in the later eleventh and early twelfth centuries. These schools, in time known as universities, represent a reaction to the changed conditions of the times; in a very clear sense, they developed out of the scholastic movement. Many influences combined to produce the universities, no two of which originated under conditions exactly similar. New intellectual interests, particularly those that grew out of the new commercial activity and municipal governments, hastened the development of the universities.

The founding of the universities. Influential schools were not founded and patronized by the church alone, but also by secular authority. German emperors, French kings, and other princes sought to establish universities in their own areas. Greater secular interests prompted educational specialization, and in time, universities came to offer studies in four faculties: arts, law, medicine, and theology. Not all medieval universities offered work in all the faculties, but

study of medicine, Bologna in law, Paris in theology. Important founding dates: University of Naples (including Salerno), 1224; University of Bologna, 1158; University of Paris, 1180; University of Salamanca, 1230; University of Oxford, 1214. By 1500 there were seventy-nine universities in Europe.[1]

Structure and organization of the universities. Features of universities that made them different from previous schools were: (1) democratic government; (2) location in population centers; (3) special privileges. The privileges granted by the charters that founded the universities included those of the clergy which allowed jurisdiction over its members, and (hitherto reserved to the Church) the right to teach. A later development was the right of *cessatio,* that of moving the university if its privileges were infringed. The term university, *universitas,* meant a corporate body of persons, usually a guild; the term *studium generale,* actually synonymous with university in the modern sense, referred to a school with at least a faculty of arts and one in medicine, law, or theology. The so-called university nations were students and masters organized into groups based on national affiliations, the *universitas magistrorum et scholarium.* The nations elected, usually annually, a procurator; each faculty elected a dean; and these representatives elected a rector of the university.

The university degrees. The student (usually age thirteen or fourteen) was obliged, when he appeared at the university, to enroll himself with a master with whom he spent three to seven years. After this period, he gave instruction under the supervision of the master, and with additional study, eventually defended a thesis before the members of the faculty. If successful, he was given his degree, which might be the licentiate, mastership, or doctorate, since these were synonymous terms in the early university period. The baccalaureate was originally formal admission to candidacy for the license. It became defined later as a minor degree.

Influence of the universities. Their greatest influence

1 For a complete list see Hastings Rashdall, *Universities of Europe in the Middle Ages,* 3 vols., new ed., Oxford University Press, 1936.

was political in that they furnished the first example of democratic organization. The university kept alive the spirit of inquiry; educationally, its greatest contribution lay in the numbers of teachers in the Arts that it trained and that it made available to the schools. In the fourteenth and fifteenth centuries, the leadership that emerged in State and Church, in law, in theology, in the infant sciences, actually knew its source and inspiration in the medieval university.

The educational ideals of chivalry. Chivalry began during the latter part of the ninth century, reached its peak during the Crusades in the twelfth century, and disappeared in the sixteenth century. Essentially, it was a system of education for the children of the nobility that included these stages:

Page. To the age of seven or eight, a child was trained at home by his mother; from age seven to fourteen (page-hood), he was educated at court with his instruction supervised by a royal lady. Instruction included religion, music, courtesy, the etiquette of love and honor, with some rudimentary work in reading and writing the vernacular language. By the men he was trained in gymnastics and military skills.

Squire. At fourteen or fifteen, the boy became a squire, in which state he was the personal servant and bodyguard of the lord whom he served.

Knight. At twenty-one, the boy was knighted in an impressive Church ceremonial. He took an oath "to protect the Church, to fight against treachery, to reverence the priesthood, to defend the poor from injustice, to keep peace in his own province, to shed his blood for his brethren, and, if necessary, to lay down his life."[2]

In all of this training there was little of the intellectual. Chivalry performed for the secular life a service identical with that performed by monasticism for the religious life; in a sense, it acted as an ameliorative to the crudities and barbarities of the life of the times. Its educational importance lay in the fact that it was the only education members of the nobility received.

[2] L. F. Salzman, *English Life in the Middle Ages*, Oxford University Press, 1926, p. 190.

Education at the close of the Middle Ages. With the thirteenth century, the intellectual interests and control passed from the monasteries to the schools, which were becoming numerous. This educational world needed only the development of a new spirit, largely evinced in the fifteenth and sixteenth centuries, to become modern. Some forces hastened the process.

The Mendicant Orders. Important Orders were the Franciscans (founded 1212) and the Dominicans (founded 1216), which showed a great interest in education.

The Mohammedan influence. Moslems, sometimes called Arabs, were followers of Mohammed (569–632) who moved their conquering armies westward from Arabia to northern Africa and southern Spain. Eastern learning was carried to Spain, where in Cordova, Granada, Toledo, and Seville, universities were developed and great advances scored in science and mathematics, and in the study of Greek philosophy. This learning made its way to Christian Europe through translations. Important figures include Averroës (1126–1198), who wrote *Commentaries* on Aristotle, and Avicenna (980-1037), who was the greatest name in medicine from 1100 to 1500.[3]

New types of schools. The growing importance of schools brought new types into being, for the most part developing out of the cathedral school. The most important of these were the **Chantry Schools.** A chantry was an endowment for masses, sung by a priest whom the endowment supported. In time it became customary to stipulate that such priests teach the children of the community. The curriculum of such schools was varied and sometimes limited to the very rudiments. Another type, almost completely free from Church control, was the **Guild School.** Often the merchant and craft guilds supported priests for the religious services of their members, and frequently these priests taught school. Ordinarily, these schools were grammar schools, which gave instruction in subjects other than Latin grammar, and quite often in the vernacular. Later, these schools were com-

3 R. W. Southern, *Western Views of Islam in the Middle Ages,* Harvard University Press, 1962.

pletely supported by the municipal government and developed into **Municipal** or **Burgher Schools.** In this way teachers became more and more numerous, although the Church relinquished none of its control. The municipal schools included both secondary and elementary schools and were largely intended for the sons of the commercial class. Although there is some question as to how much influence these schools contributed to the secularization of education that followed, Monroe observes: "Yet it is evident that preparation had been made before the Reformation for the secularization of education that was to follow."[4]

Selected References

Part II: The Medieval World

Abelson, Paul. *The Seven Liberal Arts.* Teachers College, Columbia University, 1906.

Bark, W. C. *Origins of the Medieval World.* Stanford University Press, 1958.

Compayré, J. G. *Abelard and the Origin and Early History of the Universities.* New York, 1893.

Cully, Kendig B., ed. *Basic Writings in Christian Education.* Philadelphia, 1960.

Daly, Lowrie J. *The Medieval University.* New York, 1961.

Dodge, Bayard. *Muslim Education in Medieval Times.* Washington, 1962.

Ellspermann, F. *The Attitude of the Early Christian Fathers Toward Pagan Literature and Learning.* Catholic University of America Press, 1949.

Gabriel, A. L. *Garlandia: Studies in the History of the Medieval University.* South Bend, Indiana, 1969.

Haskins, Charles H. *The Rise of Universities.* New York, 1923.

Huizinga, J. *The Waning of the Middle Ages.* London, 1927.

Kibre, Pearl. *The Nations in the Medieval Universities.* Boston, 1948.

[4] Paul Monroe, *A Brief Course in the History of Education,* New York, 1907, p. 157.

Laurie, S. S. *Rise and Early Constitutions of Universities*. New York, 1903.

Leach, A. F. *Schools of Medieval England*. London, 1915.

Leff, Gordon. *Paris and Oxford Universities in the Thirteenth and Fourteenth Centuries*. New York, 1968.

Mullinger, J. Bass. *The Schools of Charles the Great*. New York, 1911.

Nakosteen, M. *History of Islamic Origins of Western Education, A.D. 800–1350*. University of Colorado Press, 1964.

Paetow, L. J. *Battle of the Seven Liberal Arts*. University of California Press, 1914.

Parry, Albert W. *Education in England in the Middle Ages*. London, 1920.

Poole, R. L. *Illustrations of the History of Medieval Thought*, 2nd ed. New York, 1940.

Rait, Robert S. *Life in the Medieval University*. New York, 1912.

Rashdall, Hastings. *Universities of Europe in the Middle Ages*, new ed., 3 vols. Oxford University Press, 1936.

Schachner, Nathan. *The Medieval Universities*. Philadelphia, 1938.

Sherrill, L. J. *The Rise of Christian Education*. New York, 1944.

Thorndike, Lynn. *University Records and Life in the Middle Ages*. Columbia University Press, 1944.

Waddell, Helen. *The Wandering Scholars*. London, 1927.

Watson, Foster. *The English Grammar Schools to 1660*. New York, 1908.

West, Andrew F. *Alcuin and the Rise of Christian Schools*. New York, 1909.

Wieruszowski, Helen. *The Medieval University*. Princeton, 1966.

Part III

TRANSITION TO THE MODERN ERA: THE RENAISSANCE AND REFORMATION

Historical background. The classical Renaissance of the fifteenth and sixteenth centuries was essentially an intellectual, aesthetic, and social movement. The most important political development of the period was the growth of the centralized authority of the monarchies in France and England, although Italy continued as a number of independent city-states. These centuries are marked by economic expansion, and produced a wealthy group of merchants known as "burghers" or *bourgeoisie*. Frequent revolts of the peasants reflect class structure, and a decline of the Papacy resulted by 1500 in attacks upon the Church from many quarters. Significant dates and events include: the fall of Constantinople to the Turks (1453); the revival of classical learning, called *Humanism;* the invention of printing (1450); geographical discoveries and modern colonization; the beginning of the Reformation (Martin Luther, 1517); the ascendency of Spain (1500–1600); the Tudors and English Reformation (1500–1600); the Huguenot Wars in France (1562–1629); the Thirty Years' War (1618–1648), and the Peace of Westphalia, which settled the question of religious freedom. As Butts notes: "Secular forces had already become strong in the Middle Ages, but the clue to the Renaissance is that secularism began to permeate Renaissance culture to a greater degree."[1]

[1] R. Freeman Butts, *A Cultural History of Western Education*, 2nd ed., New York, 1955, p. 165.

Chapter V

THE RENAISSANCE AND HUMANISTIC EDUCATION

The Renaissance ideal. In the main, the Renaissance was the protest of individualism against authority in the intellectual and social aspects of life. It showed great interest in: (1) the world of the ancient Greeks and Romans; (2) the subjective world of the emotions; (3) the natural world. These three interests were almost unknown in the Middle Ages. These interests led to a more intensive study of Greek and Latin literature, and an unrelenting search for the manuscript remains of this literature; introspective study of the emotional life led to a new creativity in art and literature, and to a new interest in contemporary life, which led to the social and historical sciences; the analytical methods of the Greeks brought the students of the Renaissance to direct observation and experimentation.[2]

The Renaissance in Italy. This extended through the latter half of the fourteenth and all of the fifteenth centuries. A

2 For Renaissance science see Charles Singer, *et al.*, eds., *A History of Technology,* vol. III, "From the Renaissance to the Industrial Revolution," New York, 1960.

connecting link of the medieval and modern worlds is Dante (1264–1321). Important Italian figures include:

1. **Petrarch** (1304–1374). Although little in his writings is educational, his opposition to the restrictions of medievalism, and his insistence on the study of classical literature, suggested a new spirit and content to education. His writings included a biographical compendium, *Lives of Ancient Men.*

2. **Boccaccio** (1313–1375), whose *Decameron,* a collection of prose tales, gave new importance to the vernacular.

3. **Barzizza** (1370–1431), was especially noted for Greek and Latin scholarship.

4. **Chrysoloras** (d. 1415), who was the first teacher of classical Greek in the Western world, taught at the University of Florence and in other Italian cities. Other Greek teachers followed his example.

The Renaissance in the North of Europe. The late Italian Renaissance became formal in its study of literature, and in the educational study degenerated into **"ciceronianism,"** a narrow, stiff, grammatical, and stylistic discipline. In the North, the Renaissance ideal fused with the Reformation movement is best illustrated in Erasmus's effort to remove the common ignorance that was basically the root of the gross evils imputed to the church and to the state. All of the early leaders of the movement in the North were social or religious reformers. In this respect, the movement in the North—while narrow in its rejection of personal development—was much broader in that it heralded social reform and improvement.

Educational significance of the Renaissance. The Renaissance was characterized by two educational features: (1) the revival of the idea of the liberal education; (2) humanism in education.

1. **The revival of the idea of the liberal education** largely inspired the restoration of the idea formulated by the Greeks and adapted by Cicero, Tacitus, and Quintilian. Early Renaissance, following classical models, defined educational aim as the formation of the man who participated in the

activities of the dominant social institutions. The aim was exemplified in *On Noble Character and Liberal Studies* by Paulus Vergerius (1349–1420), in which he said: "We call those studies liberal that are worthy of a free man; those studies by which we attain and practice virtue and wisdom; that education which calls forth, trains, and develops those highest gifts of body and mind, which ennoble men and are rightly judged to rank next in dignity to virtue only." In like vein, most of the educational treatises of the period reaffirmed this aim and discussed the new literary content of education and appropriate methods of study. New elements introduced into education included the physical element (a fusion of the chivalric and literary ideals), an emphasis on practical affairs, and a new regard for the aesthetic, which had largely been excluded from medieval education.

2. **Humanism in education.** Language and literature of ancient Greece and Rome formed the main content of education and were known as *humanities.*[4] At first broadly defined, the humanities by the end of the sixteenth century came to mean the language and literature of the ancient world in a grammatical and linguistic sense, not as a means to the liberal study of what one of the theorists of the early period called, ". . . the pursuits, the activities, proper to mankind."[3] In many ways the term *humanistic education*, despite its original broad, liberally oriented definition, came to mean the narrow linguistic education that dominated European schools from the sixteenth to the middle of the nineteenth century. This narrowing eventually eliminated most of the more desirable elements of the early humanism; both the physical and the social elements were eliminated; the aesthetic prevailed only in the study of rhetoric; and for children, educational work became a drill of the most formal and laborious kind.[4] As Monroe observes: "By the seventeenth century, the study of the humanities was almost as formal and profitless as had been the narrow routine of

3 Battista Guarino, who in 1459 wrote: "Learning and training in virtue are peculiar to man; therefore our forefathers called them 'Humanities,' the pursuits, the activities, proper to mankind."

4 It was this that led Robert H. Quick to charge the Renaissance with "neglect of children." See his *Essays on Educational Reformers*, New York, 1890, pp. 19-21.

scholastic discussion of the fourteenth; Cicero had now become master in place of the dethroned Aristotle."[5] In time, this narrow concept of humanism became known as *Ciceronianism,* which argued that the aim of education was to impart a perfect Latin style, that Cicero and his imitators were the admitted masters of that style, and that all writing and conversation should be in ciceronian phrase. Against this view many Renaissance educators wrote, chief of whom was Erasmus, whose dialogue on *The Ciceronians* is a satire on the absurdity of the ideal.

Renaissance educational theorists. Many of the Renaissance educational theorists were not teachers, although some were. Often a great influence was exercised by treatises on the new learning, whose authors were outside the universities and the schools; often, too, theory tended to be oriented to certain national aims and objectives, e.g., German, French, English.

1. **Vittorino da Feltre** (1378–1446) conducted a school at Mantua for the children of noblemen. He has been called "the first modern schoolmaster." The curriculum of his school gave embodiment to the Greek ideal of a liberal education that became the preparation for a useful life of service to Church and State, for a citizenship based on the best elements in Greek and Roman life. Instruction was in Latin, with little use of the vernacular. He left no writings, and his fame rests solely on his reputation as a schoolmaster. Other Italian theorists include Piccolomini (later Pope Pius II), whose *On the Education of Boys* (1450) had wide influence; Mapheus Vegius, who wrote *On the Education of Boys and Their Moral Culture* and whose approach to the classics was entirely Christian; and Guarino da Verona, who translated Plutarch's *On the Education of Children* (1411).

2. **French humanists and educational theorists.** This group includes Guillaume Budé (1467–1540), whose *On the Education of a Prince* was the first educational treatise to be written in French and presented orthodox humanistic views; Peter Ramus (1515–1574), whose textbooks called

[5] Paul Monroe, *op. cit.*, p. 172.

for a rejection of medieval methods; and François Rabelais (1483–1553) whose *Pantagruel and Gargantua* is world famous and whose humanistic realism had great influence on Montaigne, Locke, and Rousseau.

3. **English humanists and educational theorists.** This group includes Thomas Linacre (1460–1524), William Grocyn (1466–1519), William Latimer (1460–1545), John Colet (1467–1519), Thomas More (1478–1535), Thomas Elyot (1490–1546), Roger Ascham (1515–1568), all of whom were very practical in their approach to education and were concerned with the problems of teaching and learning.[6] Linacre was the author of a Latin grammar and translated Galen's works into Latin; Grocyn was the first man to teach Greek at Oxford; Colet re-established the grammar school at St. Paul's Cathedral Church; More's *Utopia* gave English writing new distinction.

a) **Thomas Elyot's** *The Boke Named the Governour* was the first book on education written in English that endorsed the humanistic education for noblemen, dealing with the training of the rulers of the state in virtue and manners.[7] Elyot also translated Plutarch's *On the Education of Children,* and compiled a Latin-English dictionary which had wide influence.

b) **Roger Ascham** (1515–1568). His *The Schoolmaster* (1571) outlines typical humanistic education, with a thorough discussion of school discipline and the method of "double translation" for the teaching of Greek and Latin.

4. **Early German humanists.** The source of humanism was a community of teachers, scholars, and religious thinkers founded by Gerhard Groot (1340–1384) known as the Brethren of the Common Life,[8] whose primary aim was to bring about reform in the Church. Schools established by the group included classical as well as Christian literature. Important figures include Alexander Hegius (1433–1498),

6 See further Fritz Caspari, *Humanism and Social Order in Tudor England,* Chicago, 1954.

7 Written in 1531, this work went through ten editions in the sixteenth century. Not unlike Baldasarre Casiglione's *Il Cortegiano* (1516), the most popular work of this kind.

8 A. Hyma, *The Brethren of the Common Life,* Grand Rapids, 1950.

who advocated the use of the vernacular; Rudolph Agricola (1443–1485), whose *On the Regulation of Study* had great influence on German education; Jacob Wimpheling (1450–1528), who clarified in his *Adolescentia* the relationship between the classics and moral and religious education; and Jacob Reuchlin (1455–1552), who wrote a Hebrew grammar and dictionary.

5. **Erasmus** (1466–1536) was the most famous of all leaders of the new learning, all of whose work was primarily educational. His influence was exerted through (a) teaching; (b) correspondence; (c) efforts at public enlightenment; (d) editions of Greek classics; (e) textbooks. Two chief educational works are *The Right Method of Instruction* and *The Liberal Education of Boys*, which together form a humanistic theory of education. Central principles in both works include (a) recognition of educational opportunity for the middle class; (b) role of individual differences and talents among children; (c) curriculum remained essentially classical, with little or no provision for use of the vernacular; (d) aim of education was the "good man," refined and informed by the study of classical literature. Erasmus' *Colloquies* (1519) was the most popular text of the time. Primarily a conversational Latin manual, it is typical of Erasmus' textbooks.[9]

Types of humanistic schools. Humanistic educational ideals were first discerned in the universities and the recently founded burgher schools. In founding new schools that were essentially humanistic, Renaissance humanism combined with the Reformation movement, and most of the schools were connected with some form of religious reformation. The narrow humanistic education persisted well into the nineteenth century before any revolt against it was attempted.

1. **The universities.** In the beginning they resisted the new learning, but in time modifications included a broadening of authority; the addition of linguistic study, particularly Greek; the substitution of classical for ecclesiastical Latin. At first successful in the Italian universities (e.g., Pavia,

[9] For translations from some of Erasmus' textbooks, see W. H. Woodward, *Desiderius Erasmus*, Cambridge, 1904. See also P. S. Allen, *Erasmus' Services to Learning*, New York, 1925.

Rome, Padua, Milan, Florence), the movement made its way northward to the universities of Paris, Heidelberg, Erfurt, and Leipzig; it came to Oxford and Cambridge in the early sixteenth century.[10] By the middle of the sixteenth century, humanism at the universities had deteriorated into ciceronianism.

2. **Schools of the court and nobility.** Many new schools were founded under patronage of the nobility because of hostility of monastic and Church schools to new learning. This was especially true of the small Italian states where Vittorino da Feltre's school at Mantua was typically attempting a fusion of humanistic and chivalric education. The German *Fürstenschulen* (schools for princes) were similar to the Italian court schools, but were not as important as the German *Gymnasium*, the typical humanistic school of the North. This type of school, evolved from the burgher and Church schools, substituted classical for medieval Latin, mathematics for philosophy, and in many cases added Greek and Hebrew. The most important of the *Gymnasien* was that organized by John Sturm (1507–1589) at Strassburg in 1537. This school was organized into nine grades based on age and advancement of the pupil; its curriculum was largely chosen from the Latin classics, and its aim was the development of the ability to speak and write the Latin of Cicero, the cultivation of piety and knowledge. No attention was given to the vernacular or to the sciences. Sturm's historical importance lies in the great influence of his school; for all practical purposes it became the prototype of the sixteenth century gymnasium, and with the progress of the Reformation and the organization of state systems of schools, it passed under the control of central governments.[11]

3. **The English public schools.** Public means that they were independent of Church and State and were essentially humanistic schools whose foundation goes back before the

10 At Cambridge it was Erasmus who introduced the new learning between 1510 and 1513. For an account of the introduction of the new learning into England, see J. E. Sandys, *A History of Classical Scholarship*, Cambridge, 1908, vol. II, chap. 15.

11 For a good account of Sturm, see Henry Barnard, *German Teachers and Educators*, Hartford, 1878.

Renaissance, e.g., Winchester (1387), and Eton (1440). The establishment of St. Paul's (1512) begins their importance, since this became the leader in curriculum, method, and purpose, largely as the result of the work of John Colet (1461–1519), and it was here that Lily wrote the *Latin Grammar*,[12] which was used for centuries in the English schools. Other public schools include Westminster, Harrow, Charter-House, Rugby, Shrewsbury, and Merchant Taylor's. All continued a humanistic education, which was not drastically modified until the report of the royal commissioners of investigation in 1864. The grammar school of the American colonies was a transplanted English public school.[13]

[12] William Lily (*ca.* 1468–1522) was headmaster of St. Paul's from 1510 to 1522.

[13] See Part V. One difference between the English public school and its American counterpart was that in America these schools came under colonial or local government control.

Chapter VI

THE REFORMATION AND EDUCATIONAL THEORY

What the Reformation was. It is generally understood t mean the sixteenth century revolt against the Roman Cath olic Church. The immediate impulse was the publication b Martin Luther (1483–1546) in 1517 of ninety-five these that reflected his conviction that salvation comes by fait and not as a result of good works. The fate of the Germa Reformation was determined when the movement becam economic and political. The Peasants' War (1525), sup pressed by rulers and opposed by Luther, led to Anabaptism In various states of Germany, as in Scandinavia and Eng land, churches under national aegis declared themselves in dependent as national churches. The great means of Prote tant influence was book and pamphlet publication, circulate by the newly invented printing press. Within the Empire, th Lutheran princes forced Charles V to concede to them th right to establish their religion in their states (Peace of Aug burg, 1555); later Calvinistic princes obtained the same rig (Peace of Westphalia, 1648). The principal period of Refo mation growth was between 1520 and 1550, after which th Catholic Reform movement got under way. From Genev the doctrine of John Calvin (1509–1564) spread to Fran (Huguenots), Scotland (Presbyterians), Netherlands and son parts of Germany (Reformed Church). On the continent Calvinists were distinguished from Lutherans by the term *Reformed*. Among the lower classes the most radical form of protestantism was Anabaptism. The Church of England retained its episcopacy, reformed its liturgy, and set up its Calvinizing Thirty-nine Articles.[1]

Influence of the Reformation on education. The Reformation at first continued the best educational influence of the Renaissance. However, liberalism of thought and emphasis of reason (which had been proclaimed as the doctrine of the Reformation contained inherently in the right of liberty of conscience and the duty of interpreting the Scriptures according to one's reason) found little realization in the education of the time as organized in the schools or as expressed in educational theory.

1. **Formalism in its results.** Education largely became dominated by a formalism growing out of the theological groups (Lutheran, Calvinistic, Anabaptist) and the interest in the conflicts among themselves, further intensified by the Roman Catholic Counter Reformation. The dominance of this new formalism and the religious wars explain the low ebb of educational affairs in post-Reformation times. Although particularly evident in the universities, the formalism also appeared in the lower schools, where it was characterized by memorization, repetition, abstract logical activities, and little if any interest in content.

2. **Humanistic content.** Reformation educators largely accepted the humanistic curriculum, but with a new and heavy religious emphasis. Catechisms, creeds, and church services were memorized. The Scriptures were used as a text, furnishing the basis for Latin and Greek instruction. The entire aim of education was an exposition of Christian literature and doctrine.[2]

[1] Wilhelm Pauck, *The Heritage of the Reformation*, New York, 1951; also, Preserved Smith, *The Age of the Reformation*, New York, 1930.

[2] In the curriculum which the humanist John Sturm organized for his school at Strassburg, the vernacular was used only as a vehicle for learning the Lutheran Catechism, otherwise the curriculum allowed for reading the Scriptures in the original Greek, and also in Latin. See Henry C. Barnard, *op. cit.*, p. 195.

3. **Institutional effects.** Perhaps the great educational influence of the Reformation was its insistence on a program of universal education to implement its doctrine that the eternal welfare of every individual depended on his application of his reason to the revelation contained in the Scriptures. This idea did promote the establishment of a system of schools, controlled and partly supported by the state, although its full development and completion awaited the emergence of other political ideas. The demand that the individual be able to read the Scriptures in some form presented new tasks for the schools and suggested the compulsory education of all children. The modern idea of elementary education appears to be an outgrowth of the principles involved in the Reformation.[3]

Reformation educators. It is almost impossible to differentiate between humanistic and religious educators of the sixteenth century. Most Reformation educators were humanists also. For the most part the religious aspect of the work of these educators is seen in the purpose and organization of education, while the humanistic aspect is seen in educational content. Generally, religious leaders seized upon education for bringing about religious reform. The major Protestant educational theorists are Luther and Melanchthon, but a host of figures, Reformation and Counter Reformation, appear in the history of education in the sixteenth century. Three lesser figures (although giants in religious reform) in Protestant educational theory include John Calvin (1509–1564), who organized in Geneva a school which was a consolidation of several Latin schools. The school was thoroughly humanistic and was organized into seven grades (or classes); attached to it was a higher academy. Again, the primary aim was religious, with religious training forming the bulk of the curriculum. Although some historians have attributed to Calvin the origin of the common school,[4] this

[3] Luther asked for compulsory school attendance as early as 1526. See Preserved Smith and Charles M. Jacobs, *Luther's Correspondence and Other Contemporary Letters,* Philadelphia, 1918. The untranslatable German *Schulpflichtigkeit,* means that children are "due at school."

[4] W. Walker, *John Calvin,* New York, 1906; also, Herbert D. Foster, "Calvinists and Education," in Paul Monroe, ed., *A Cyclopedia of Education,* vol. I, pp. 491–499.

is doubtful; rather, Calvin's significance in education lies in the subtle coloring that his theory of "total depravity" gave sixteenth and seventeenth century educational theories, and the reaction against this influence in the philosophic enlightenment of the eighteenth century.[5] Ulrich Zwingli (1484–1534), the Swiss religious reformer, summarized his views on education in his *Christian Education of Youth* (1523), essentially humanistic in tone and method; in his interest in the founding and supervision of schools, Zwingli's purpose was to teach a greater knowledge of God. John Knox (1505–1572), the leader of the Scotch Reformation, was the chief influence in the establishment of the parish school system of Scotland, although the rejection of his *First Book of Discipline* (1560; actually a comprehensive system of education) deferred a scheme of national education in Scotland for three centuries.[6]

1. **Martin Luther** (1483–1546) was the greatest protagonist of the Reformation, who epitomized the educational movement that had begun in Germany to (1) remove education from the control of the Church; (2) extend the opportunities of education; (3) redefine the nature of education, both secular and religious. Most of Luther's educational views are not in writings on education as such but rather in sermons and other primarily religious writings. Luther was essentially a religious reformer, not an educational theorist.[7] Two important educational statements include: "Letter to the Mayors and Aldermen of All Cities of Germany in Behalf of Christian Schools" in which he reminded the public officials of their duty to build schools and to assume the education of the young, and bitterly denounced the monastic schools; and *A Sermon on the Duty of Sending Children to School* (1530), an explanation of (1) the spiritual benefits derived from sending the children to school, (2) the temporal

[5] Calvin believed the child to be inherently bad and called for the suppression of all his natural instincts and inclinations. See Herbert D. Foster, *loc. cit.*

[6] J. Edgar, *History of Early Scottish Education,* Edinburgh, 1893; W. J. Gibson, *Education in Scotland,* London, 1912.

[7] F. V. N. Painter, *Luther on Education,* St. Louis, 1928, also, G. M. Bruce, *Luther as an Educator,* Minneapolis, 1928.

benefits and service to the state. Although no systematic statement of education is found in Luther's writings, the following recommendations may be discerned: (1) a broad (if humanistic) plan of education which included Latin and Greek, but did not neglect history, science, and music; (2) the fundamental importance of universal education for all children framed within state laws for compulsory attendance, state supported and state controlled. The concrete work of carrying out his educational ideas was left to his followers.[8]

2. **Philip Melanchthon** (1479–1560), called the *Praeceptor Germaniae,* he was long associated with Luther, and assumed the labors of implementing his educational reforms. Melanchthon is generally regarded as the chief Protestant educational reformer in the establishment of schools in Lutheran lands, and in the reorganization of the German universities.[9] At his death there was not a city in all Germany that had not modified its schools according to his direct advice or suggestions.[10] His influence lay in five directions: (1) as a university teacher (Wittenberg), he trained a large number of scholars; (2) in visitation articles (e.g., *Visitation Articles of Saxony,* 1528), he made direct recommendations for the erection of schools; (3) as an organizer of schools (e.g., Eisleben, Nuremberg), he established a tradition which was followed everywhere; (4) reorganization of universities along humanistic lines (e.g., Marburg, Jena); (5) as author of textbooks and editor of classical and theological works. As with Luther, Melanchthon's aim in education was to prepare men for ecclesiastical and civil offices. The Saxony church-school ordinance provided in every town for schools which would consist of three groups of pupils. The first group learned Latin; the second group extensively and minutely studied Latin grammar; and the third group took up advanced lin-

[8] Luther adopted the view that every child must be taught the Lutheran confession only, out of which emerged the concept *Cuius regio, eius religio,* that every man must profess the religion of his prince.

[9] J. W. Richard, *Philip Melanchthon, The Protestant Preceptor of Germany,* New York, 1898.

[10] F. Paulsen, *German Universities and University Study,* New York, 1906, p. 33.

guistic studies. The vernacular was rejected; all instruction was in Latin, and religious instruction was emphasized.[11]

Religious schools of the Reformation. In the German states, the Protestants generally stressed not only the religious conception of education, but also the idea of its universality. Education was to be civil as well as religious, existing as much for the sake of the Church as for the state. In order to promote this ideal, the reformers desired to cooperate with the civil authorities in matters of education, and to have the schools managed, and to some extent supported, by the state.

1. **The universities.** In the German states, the progress of the universities was almost identical with the progress of Protestant theology. Wittenberg (founded in 1502) became the very center of the new learning and was the residence of Luther and Melanchthon. Gradually, the universities threw off the allegiance to the Pope, and transferred it to the German princes who began to exercise more control. Marburg (1527) was the first of the Protestant universities, and those at Königsberg, Jena, Helmstadt, Dorpat, followed within a century. By the opening of the seventeenth century, the work of these universities had deteriorated into the lifeless formalism of rigid humanism.[12] A similar course was followed in England.

2. **The Protestant elementary and secondary schools.** The public schools of the German states were the first of the modern type that embodied the principles of state support and universal, compulsory attendance. In Würtemburg, as early as 1559 (approved by the state in 1565), provision was made in every village for elementary vernacular schools in which reading, writing, religion, and church music were to be taught. A modification of Melanchthon's Saxony plan, it was later adopted by other German cities. The movement toward the secularization of the Latin secondary schools, begun in the fifteenth century, was completed by the Reformation movement in the sixteenth. But even under state con-

[11] Other Lutheran educational reformers included John Bugenhagen (1485-1558); John Brenz (1499-1570); Valentin Trotzendorf (1490-1556).

[12] G. Bush, *Origin of the First German Universities,* Boston, 1884.

trol, the major educational aim was religious. For the most part, no attention was paid to the vernacular, and the curriculum was largely Latin, with a little Greek and mathematics added. The first distinctly Protestant gymnasium was that at Magdeburg, founded in 1524. In time, these schools were organized into systems, largely modeled on the plan that Melanchthon had drawn up for Eisleben in 1525. Outside Germany, no great success was achieved in the organization of systems of schools in Protestant lands. Until late in the nineteenth century, England left all educational effort to the family or the church.[13] In Scotland, no church-state system was achieved until 1696.[14] In Holland, a system of elementary schools was established under the auspices of the reformed churches, but the Spanish wars of the sixteenth century delayed until 1618 (Synod of Dort) a church-state system of elementary schools.[15]

Catholic Reformation and the Society of Jesus. The struggle for control between the Roman Catholic Church and Protestantism resulted in religious wars, with the failure of the conciliatory Council of Trent (1543–1563). Bloody warfare in Holland (1567–1609), persecutions in France and Italy, religious strife in Germany, all intensified the struggle.[16] As an educational countermove, new religious societies were founded whose main endeavor, unlike the medieval monastic establishments, was the direct involvement in practical affairs, principally education.[17] The Society of Jesus, organized in 1540, became the chief instrument of counter reformation. Founded by Ignatius of Loyola (1491–1556), the society strove through missionary labors to win back

[13] Foster Watson, *English Grammar Schools to 1660,* New York, 1908.

[14] W. L. Mathieson, *Church and Reform in Scotland,* Edinburgh, 1916.

[15] For some background material on Dutch education in this period, see W. H. Kilpatrick, *The Dutch Schools of New Netherland and Colonial New York,* Washington, D.C., Government Printing Office, 1912.

[16] P. Janelle, *Catholic Reformation,* Milwaukee, 1949.

[17] For a list of Catholic societies, see P. J. Marique, *History of Christian Education,* New York, 1924-32, vol. II, p. 128.

Protestant territory, and by means of its schools to hold converts and to educate peoples to submission.[18]

1. **Constitution of the Society of Jesus.** This consisted of ten parts, the fourth one of which was the *Ratio Studiorum,* or system of studies, the instrument that guided Jesuit schools and teaching. A third edition of the *Ratio* appeared in 1599 (earlier editions in 1589, 1591), and in his form it remained unchanged until 1832.[19] It dealt with administration of the schools, methodology, and curriculum.

a) **Administration.** The order was headed by a general, and each administrative province presided over by a provincial. On the educational side were rectors of various colleges, under whom functioned prefects of studies, and the teachers, who were supervised by both rector and prefect.

b) **Curriculum.** Generally speaking, Jesuits were not interested in elementary education and made no provision for it. Their schools were secondary and university, and curriculum concerned itself with the relative importance of the humanities, philosophy, and theology in the order of studies. Mathematics and science were given a subordinate position; both Latin and Greek were taught, with some use of the vernacular. Subject matter was of the characteristic humanistic order, and in this respect they did not differ from the schools of the time, their superiority being achieved by the observation of the high standard of the *Ratio.* Two types of colleges were conducted by the Jesuits: (1) the lower, which covered five or six years, divided into three grammar classes followed by a fourth called "rhetoric" and humanities; (2) higher college (university), which allowed for three years of study of philosophy, mathematics, and natural science, all subordinated to scholastic theology.

2. **Preparation of teachers.** The teaching force was largely made up of those who had passed through the rigid course of the lower and higher college, while permanent teachers were trained through a long university and teaching career.

[18] T. Hughes, *Loyola and the Educational System of the Jesuits,* New York, 1892; J. W. Donohue, *Jesuit Education,* New York, 1963.

[19] For the *Ratio,* see A. P. Farrell, *The Jesuit Code of Liberal Education,* Milwaukee, 1938.

3. **Methodology.** Jesuit education was characterized by memorization, frequent reviews of subject matter (daily, weekly, yearly), rejection of corporal punishment,[20] and the promotion of rivalry and competition among the students.

4. **Extent of influence.** At the time of its suppression in 1773, the Society of Jesus conducted 865 schools; its members included 22,000 individuals, the majority of whom were devoted to education.[21] The primary importance of Jesuit education lay in Loyola's recognition of the necessity of superior educational training as an effective religious weapon against Protestantism; a second, but not less important, influence of the Jesuits lay in the stimulus they provided other orders in making education an integral part of their work, e.g., the Dominicans and the Franciscans. The work of the Jesuits, coupled with that of new orders such as the Oratorians, Jansenists, Piarists, and the Christian Brothers of the seventeenth century, demonstrated the power of educational organization.

Selected References

Part III: The Renaissance and Reformation

Allen, Percy S. *The Age of Erasmus.* Oxford, 1934.

Cannon, M. A. *The Education of Women During the Renaissance.* Catholic University of America Press, 1916.

Donohue, John W. *Jesuit Education. . . .* Fordham University Press, 1963.

Eby Frederick, ed. *Early Protestant Educators.* New York, 1931.

Ferguson, Wallace. *The Renaissance in Historical Thought.* Boston, 1948.

Fife, Robert H. *The Revolt of Martin Luther.* New York, 1957.

[20] Unusual for the time when corporal punishment was common. Jesuits used a *corrector,* usually from outside the order, to discipline more difficult students.

[21] For the Jesuits in America, see Thomas A. Hughes, *History of Society of Jesus in North America,* 2 vols., New York, 1907-17; G. J. Garraghan, *The Jesuits of the Middle United States,* New York, 1938.

Fitzpatrick, Edward A. *St. Ignatius and the Ratio Studiorum.* New York, 1933.

Haydn, Hiram. *The Counter Renaissance.* New York, 1950.

Hamlyn, V. W. C. *The Universities of Europe at the Period of the Reformation.* Oxford, 1876.

Hay, Dennis. *The Italian Renaissance in its Historical Background.* Cambridge University Press, 1961.

Hyma, Albert. *Erasmus and the Humanists.* New York, 1930.

———. *Renaissance to Reformation.* Grand Rapids, 1951.

Laurie, Samuel S. *Studies in the History of Educational Opinion from the Renaissance.* Cambridge University Press, 1904.

Leach, A. F. *English Schools at the Reformation.* London, 1896.

McMahon, Clara P. *Education in Fifteenth Century England.* Baltimore, 1947.

Painter, F. V. N. *Great Pedagogical Essays.* New York, 1905.

Paulsen, Friedrich. *German Education, Past and Present.* New York, 1912.

Phillips, Margaret. *Erasmus and the Northern Reformation.* London, 1949.

Robbins, C. L. *Teachers in Germany in the Sixteenth Century.* New York, 1912.

Schwickerath, Robert. *Jesuit Education: Its History and Principles.* St. Louis, 1904.

Schwiebert, E. G. *Luther and his Times.* St. Louis, 1950.

Tobriner, Marian L., ed. *Vives' Introduction to Wisdom: A Renaissance Textbook.* New York, 1968.

Watson, Foster. *Vives and the Renaissance Education of Women.* New York, 1912.

Watson, Foster, ed. *Vives on Education. A translation of the De Tradendis Disciplinis.* Cambridge, 1913. (Reissued with a Foreword by Francesco Cordasco, Rowman and Littlefield, 1971)

Weiss, R. *Humanism in England During the Fifteenth Century.* Oxford, 1957.

Wood, Norman. *The Reformation and English Education.* London, 1931.

Woodward, William H. *Vittorino da Feltre and other Humanist Educators.* New York, 1905.

———. *Studies in Education During the Age of the Renaissance, 1400–1600.* New York, 1924.

Part IV

THE MODERN ERA (1600-1900)

Chronological Table of Educational Development during the Seventeenth and Eighteenth Centuries

Political Events and Personages	Literary Men, Religious Leaders, etc.	Scientists, Philosophers, etc.	Educational Writings and Educators	Educational Events
1600. 1618–1648. Thirty Years' War. 1620. Plymouth settled. 1648. Peace of Westphalia. 1649. Charles I beheaded. 1660. Restoration. Louis XIV 1643–1715 1679. Habeas Corpus Act. 1688 English Revolution.	Bunyan 1628–1688 George Fox 1624–1691 Spener (Pietist) 1637–1702 1673. Test Act, Eng. 1685. Edict of Nantes revoked. 1695. Toleration Act, Eng. Corneille 1606–1684 La Fontaine 1621–1685 Racine 1639–1699	Galileo 1564–1642 Hugo Grotius 1583–1645 Bacon 1561–1626 Harvey 1578–1657 Hobbes 1588–1679 Des Cartes 1596–1650 Boyle 1627–1691	Ratich . 1571–1635 Comenius 1592–1671 Comenius's *Great Didactic* . 1630 Comenius's *Orbis Pictus* . . 1657 Milton's *Tractate* . 1644 Fenelon's *Ed. of Girls* . . 1687 Lasalle's *Institutes*, 1684 Locke's *Thoughts* . 1693	1619. First Natural Science Association (Rostock). 1619. First comp. ed. (Weimar) 1633. First el. school in America (N. Y.). 1635. Boston Latin Grammar School. 1636. Harvard founded. 1642. School reforms of Gotha. 1643. Port Royal "Little Schools." 1647. Comp. School law in Mass. 1693. William and Mary founded. 1694. First modern university. (Halle founded.) 1697. Teachers' seminary at Halle. 1699. Soc. for Prom. of Chris. Knowl. founded.
1700. 1713. Peace of Utrecht. Queen Anne 1702–1714 Frederick William of Prussia 1713–1740 Frederick the Great 1740–1786 1756–1763. Seven Years' War. 1757. British East India Empire founded. 1772. Partition of Poland. 1759–1773 to 1814. Jesuit Order suppressed. 1775–1783. American Revolution. 1789. First President inaugurated. 1789. States General. Louis XVI 1774–1792 1799. Bonaparte overthrows Directory. 1800.	Fenelon 1651–1715 Montesquieu 1689–1755 Voltaire 1694–1778 Pope 1688–1744 Richardson 1689–1761 De Foe 1661–1731 Addison 1672–1719 Fielding 1707–1757 Gray 1716–1771 Jonathan Edwards 1703–1758 John Wesley 1703–1791 Diderot 1713–1784 Helvétius 1715–1771 Condillac 1715–1780 Burns 1759–1796 Schiller 1759–1805	Newton 1642–1727 Leibnitz 1646–1716 Halley 1656–1742 Buffon 1707–1788 Linnæus 1707–1778 Franklin 1706–1790 Hume 1711–1776 Watt 1736–1819 Lavoisier 1743–1794 Priestley 1733–1804 Adam Smith 1723–1790 Lamarck 1744–1829 Werner 1750–1817 Kant 1724–1804 Herschel 1738–1832 Schleiermacher 1768–1834 Fichte 1762–1814 Laplace 1749–1827 Humboldt 1767–1835	Francke, 1663–1727 Rollin . 1661–1741 Julius Hecker 1707–1768 Rousseau 1712–1778 Rousseau's *Émile* . . 1762 Johann Basedow 1723–1790 Salzmann 1744–1811 Campe . 1746–1818 Pestalozzi 1746–1827 Pestalozzi's *Leonard and Gertrude* . 1781 Knox, *Liberal Education* 1781 Edgeworth, *Practical Education* 1798 Jean Paul Richter 1763–1825 Frederick Augustus Wolf 1759–1824 Bell's *Experiment in Education*, 1798 Lancaster's *Monitorial System* . 1798 Andrew Bell 1753–1832 Joseph Lancaster 1778–1838 Noah Webster 1758–1843	1700. Yale College founded. 1704. First American newspaper. 1709. First daily newspaper. 1724. Compulsory education of both sexes in Saxony. 1746. Princeton founded. 1747. First *real schule* (in Berlin). 1748. First *Lehrerseminar* founded. 1751. Academy of Philadelphia founded. 1754. Kings' (now Columbia) College founded. 1764. Expulsion of Jesuits from France. 1763. Special training required of all German teachers. 1763. Founding of present system of Prussian schools. 1774–1793. Basedow's *Philanthropinum*. 1783. Sunday-schools founded. 1784. University of State of New York. 1785. Land endowments for public schools in United States. 1785. Webster's *Speller*. 1794. All Prussian teachers declared State officials. 1793. Decree of Rev. Convention on education. 1794. National Normal School in France. 1795. Primary education established in France. 1795. Lindley Murray's English grammar. 1798. Monitorial System established.

Chapter VII

REALISM IN EDUCATION: THE SEVENTEENTH CENTURY

Historical background. Significant events include the destruction of Spanish supremacy as seen in the defeat of the Spanish Armada (1588) by the English, and the successful revolt of the Netherlands (1572–1609); the religious wars became localized in three main theaters of war. In Germany, it was the clash of the Lutherans and Catholics in the Thirty Years' War (1618–1648), which concluded in the Peace of Westphalia; in England, it was the prolonged conflict between the Puritans and the Stuarts; in France, it was the struggle between the Catholic monarchy and the Huguenots (1562–1629). The English Revolution of 1688 established parliamentary control and gave the Puritans the freedom of religious worship. The wars of the French King Louis XIV (War of the Spanish Netherlands, 1667–1668; War with the Dutch, 1672–1678; War of the Palatinate, 1688–1697; War of the Spanish Succession, 1701–1713) culminated in the Peace of Utrecht (1713), in a sense ending a period of religious and political rivalry. Against this background, utilitarian and realistic tendencies in education developed.

What is realism? Monroe's definition is, perhaps, best: "This term is applied to that type of education in which natural phenomena and social institutions, rather than languages and literature, are made the chief objects of study."[1] Actually, realism was a further development of the Renaissance. In the fifteenth century, the dominant interest was revealed in literary and aesthetic forms; in the sixteenth century, the dominant interest was moral and hence religious and social; in the seventeenth century, the same intellectual interests became impersonal and were directed toward philosophical and scientific problems. It is in the seventeenth century that modern philosophical and scientific thought begins. Sense-realism, the educational part of the movement, may be appropriately called the early scientific movement. However, sense-realism cannot be adequately understood without notice of its earlier forms, humanistic (or literary) realism and social-realism.

Humanistic realism. Essentially it was a reproduction in the sixteenth and seventeenth centuries of earlier Renaissance education, and was a protest against the narrow ciceronianism which in the late Renaissance was regarded as humanism. As against the totally literary and stylistic study of the ciceronians, the humanistic realist sought to enhance his own life, natural and social, through a knowledge of the life of the ancients. If the literature of the Greeks and the Romans remained important, it was primarily a key to the realities of thought. Physical, moral, social development were the basic concerns in education. This definition would allow the inclusion of some of the leaders of the late Renaissance,[2] but the two best representatives of humanistic realism (separated by almost a century) are Rabelais (1483–1553) and Milton (1608–1674).

1. **François Rabelais** (1483–1553). His educational importance derives from the influence he exerted on Mon-

[1] Paul Monroe, *Brief History of Education,* New York, 1907, p. 215. See also, J. W. Adamson, *Pioneers of Modern Education, 1600-1700,* New York, 1921.

[2] Erasmus might be an example of one who differentiated the study of *words* and the study of *things* in his *System of Studies,* but the definition would be too restricting applied to him. See W. H. Woodward, *Erasmus Concerning Education,* Cambridge, 1904.

taigne, Rousseau, and Locke. His most famous writings are *Pantagruel* (1533) and *Gargantua* (1535), in which the manners and education of the sixteenth century are ruthlessly satirized. Violently opposed to the scholastic formalism of his time, yet unable to get away from classical literature as the chief source of his material, Rabelais is exemplary of the twofold tendency of humanism and realism. Spontaneity and interest are substituted for formalism and authority, and the concerns of everyday life are made as important as those of the cloister. Hidden under the broad, often ribald, humor of Rabelais is a trenchant satire on the humanistic education of his day.[3]

2. **John Milton** (1608–1674). Urged by his friend, Samuel Hartlib, Milton published a brief *Tractate on Education* in 1644.[4] The *Tractate* provided for the education of boys from the age of twelve to twenty-one. He made no provision for education up to twelve, or beyond twenty-one. In rejecting the dominant education of his day, he objected to the study of mere form and recommended that the ancient authors be used to teach science and morality. Education is defined as "that which fits man to perform justly, skillfully, and magnanimously all the offices, both private and public, of peace and war." The curriculum allowed in four stages was truly encyclopedic, and led critics to observe that he legislated for "a college of Miltons." Training included Latin grammar, arithmetic, geometry, and moral training, followed by training in agriculture, architecture, physiology, natural philosophy, geography, and medicine. All of these subjects were studied through classical authors (e.g., agriculture through Cato, Columella, Varro); the Greek and Latin languages, thus, were used incidentally to the mastery of the content of the authors. This was a significant departure from the narrow humanism of the late Renaissance. Provision was made for ethics, economics, politics, history, theology,

[3] Parts of *Gargantua* and *Pantagruel* were translated into English as early as 1653 by Sir Thomas Urquhart. See Jean Plattard, *Life of Rabelais,* New York, 1931.

[4] Editions of the *Tractate* are by Oscar Browning (1897), and E. A. Morris (1895). See O. M. Ainsworth, *Milton on Education,* Yale University Press, 1928. For Hartlib, see G. H. Turnbull, *Hartlib, Dury, and Comenius,* University Press of Liverpool, 1947.

church history, logic, rhetoric, composition, and oratory; and beyond Latin and Greek were included for study Hebrew, Chaldee, Syriac, and Italian, the last acquired in what Milton called "odd hours." This education was to be acquired in an academy as the ideal educational institution, a combination secondary and university school, and its students were obviously members of the privileged classes.[5]

Humanistic realism in the schools. Its only influence was exerted by individual teachers and individual programs. It was not characterized by any great difference from the dominant humanism, either in content or method. Its greatest importance was that it led almost directly to sense-realism, which was to be both methodologically and curricularly significantly different from the formal humanism.

Social-realism. Its representatives looked upon humanistic culture at its best as inadequate preparation for the life of the gentleman. Education was viewed as a direct preparation for the life of the man of affairs, an education in which travel allowed the acquisition of practical knowledge and the learning which comes from actual contact with places and peoples made familiar through the study of books. Actually, there were many social-realists in earlier centuries but the best representation is seen in Montaigne.[6]

1. **Michel de Montaigne** (1533–1592). Ideas on education are found scattered through his *Essays,* but his clearest views on the subject are in *Of Pedantry, Of the Education of Children,* and *Of the Affection of Fathers to Their Children.* He carefully differentiates education and knowledge, since knowledge from books has little value in itself. The aim of education is virtue, which for Montaigne becomes an honest and materialistic morality. If Montaigne did not condemn studies, he asked that they be subordinated to the happy life of action. Knowledge was to be assimilated, action was to

[5] A. F. Leach, "Milton as Schoolboy and Schoolmaster," *Proceedings of the British Academy,* vol. III, 1909. The theory was impossible of "application to the common herd in a common school by a common man."

[6] For an opposite view, more representative of the period, see the *Schoolmaster* (1570) of Roger Ascham (1515-1568) in which travel is condemned and experience regarded as *costly.*

be imitated, and, above all, ideas were to be realized in conduct. In many ways, education becomes judgment, and Montaigne's insistence on things before words, action rather than books, and living before learning, has led to his characterization as a utilitarian pragmatist.[7]

2. **Social-realism in the schools.** This was not widely represented in the schools, and was antithetic to the formalistic, grammatical education of the time. In substance it was widely representative of the education of the upper classes, based in the typical humanism of the period.[8]

Sense-realism was an amalgam of humanistic and social-realism, formulated in the seventeenth century. Sense-realism contains the basic features of modern education, whether defined in psychological, sociological, or scientific terms. The term itself underscores belief that knowledge comes primarily through the senses; and education was to be founded on a training in sense perception (rather than on memory) and based on a different subject matter. Coextensive with sense-realism was the new movement in science, and sense-realism takes as one of its stimuli the new discoveries in science.[9] Interest and identification with the new science led to two main characteristics of representatives of sense-realism: (1) formulation of a rudimentary science of philosophy of education based on investigation, rather than on empiricism; (2) formulation of a new curriculum based on the natural sciences and contemporary life, rather than on literary and grammatical materials. Child psychology remained simple, but recommendation that the child first acquire the idea rather than the form represented a basic advance. Use of the vernacular was necessary in the earliest years of education, and this was an important innovation. The change in method heralded the introduction of induc-

[7] G. Compayré, *Montaigne and the Education of Judgment,* New York, 1908; G. Hodgson, *Studies in French Education from Rabelais to Rousseau,* Cambridge, 1908.

[8] For an excellent commentary on aristocratic education in the Renaissance, see J. H. Hexter, *Reappraisals in History,* Northwestern University Press, 1961.

[9] For the new science, see Herbert Butterfield, *The Origins of Modern Science, 1300–1800,* London, 1949.

tion[10] as more practical for the new aim. Sense-realism, in a way, is to be identified with movement toward the universal organization and dissemination of knowledge which was termed "pansophism."

Representative sense-realists. The movement found expression in the writings and works of many men before and during the seventeenth century. The philosophic basis for the movement was laid by Francis Bacon and René Descartes; early representatives include Vives, Ramus, and Mulcaster, primarily identified with the sixteenth century; Comenius is its chief representative, extraordinary for his time; and the English philosopher Locke epitomizes the empiricism to which realism inevitably led.

1. **Francis Bacon** (1561–1626) is the founder of modern interest in inductive logic. His chief works include *Essays* (1597); *The Advancement of Learning* (1605), *Cogitata et visa* (1612), *Novum Organum* (1620). Educational ideas are found in the unfinished *New Atlantis* and certain of the *Essays.* Bacon had little direct knowledge of or interest in education, but his work influenced education profoundly. In his directing study to nature, and away from theology and metaphysics, he led education away from the humanistic formalism toward a new realism. *The Advancement of Learning* (unfinished) was to have been a general survey of the intellectual achievements of the past; the *Novum Organum* was to provide a new method, induction, for the investigation of natural phenomena. Education, viewed as a means to knowledge, gave it new social value. The *New Atlantis* is a Renaissance utopia which describes an ideal educational institution called Solomon's House, in which the investigation of natural phenomena is a guide to the management of society, and the possession of science (knowledge) is common to society.[11]

[10] Essentially, the abandonment of *a priori* speculation; induction is the act of reasoning from the particular to the general. Inductive logic became the method of the new science. See Richard S. Westfall, *Science and Religion in Seventeenth Century England,* Yale, 1958.

[11] Other educational utopias are Campanella (1568-1639), *The City of the Sun;* and Andrea (1586-1654), the *Christian City.* See Gildo Masso, *The Place of Education in Utopias,* New York, 1927. For the struggle between the ancient and modern science, see Richard F. Jones, *Ancients and Moderns,* St. Louis, Washington University, 1961.

2. **René Descartes** (1596–1650). Although not an educational theorist, Descartes contributed in his *Discourse on Method* (1637) and other writings a framework of rationalism in which educational problems could be viewed. The Cartesian method consists of mathematical deductions generalized, and emphasizes self-observation. The following ideas establish the educational significance of the new method: (1) in establishing the distinction between mind and body, he made the disciplining of the mind the end of all study; (2) innate faculties of the mind determined the measure of all educational means; (3) he advocated the principle of evidence and free examination; the appeal to reason as the criterion, and to inquiry as the means, of true knowledge led to the principle of individual liberty. For Descartes, education was not a privilege, but a natural right. In a positive way, the practice in the Oratorian and Port Royal schools showed a direct influence of Descartes' ideas.[12]

3. **Early sense-realists.** Inevitably, some educational theorists who have all or most of the characteristics of sense-realism do not belong to the seventeenth century; some, like the Spaniard Vives, anticipate the movement by almost a century; the Frenchman Ramus and the Englishman Mulcaster are an immediate prelude to sense-realism. All have a common commitment to the use of knowledge and to the rejection of formal humanism.

a) **Juan Luis Vives** (1492–1540). A prolific writer on educational subjects,[13] tutor of Princess Mary and friend of Catherine of Aragon, Vives's main educational works include *On a Plan of Studies for Youth* (1523); *On the Instruction of a Christian Woman* (1523); *Concerning the Teaching of the Arts (De Tradendis Disciplinis),* 1531, which Foster Watson called "the most thoroughgoing educational book of the Renaissance."[14] In addition, he was the author of several

[12] E. K. B. Fischer, *Descartes and His School,* London, 1897; Jacques Maritain, *The Dream of Descartes,* New York, 1944.

[13] Lynn Thorndike, "Juan Luis Vives: His Attitude toward Learning and to Life," *Essays in Intellectual History,* New York, 1929, pp. 329-342.

[14] *Luis Vives,* Oxford, 1922, p. 100.

widely used textbooks,[15] and of a book on psychology *Concerning the Mind (De Anima)*, which was actually a precursor of empirical psychology in its concern with the workings of the mind, not with the problem of the mind's essence or substance. Although Vives is sympathetic to humanism, he is in the forefront of educational reform. Primarily, he recommended (1) the use of the vernacular; (2) a modern curriculum, e.g., one that included history and geography; (3) the education of women; (4) public support of education. If the educational aim of Vives was, in the last analysis, the making of a "good Christian," he remained pre-eminently the schoolmaster concerned with practical problems.

b) **Peter Ramus** (1515–1572). Ramus was the author of over sixty works on education and philosophy; in all of these he attacked Aristotelianism (the foundation of scholastic philosophy), attempted the reform of the work of the schools and particularly the universities, and designed a new methodology. The chief aim of Ramus was to free the liberal arts from barrenness and needless difficulties. He anticipated the sense-realists of the seventeenth century in his insistence that education be based on nature, that it be based on a system of organization of knowledge, and that it be characterized by practice in which the practical goal of use was emphasized. Ramism was debated throughout Europe for more than a century and left a great impression on philosophical and educational thought.[16]

c) **Richard Mulcaster** (1548–1611) was one of the first to recommend the use of the vernacular in education, and in 1582 published *The First Part of the Elementarie* (the second part never appeared), which deals with the correct use of written and spoken English. In 1581, he published *Positions*, which advanced the doctrine that the aim of education "is to help nature to her perfection." His doctrine of education led to the formulations of three basic principles: (1) all children

[15] For excerpts from these textbooks see Foster Watson, *Tudor School Boy Life: The Dialogues of Juan Luis Vives*, London, 1908. See also Foster Watson, "Vives: the Father of Modern Psychology," *Psychological Review*, vol. XXII, 1915, pp. 333-353.

[16] Frank P. Graves, *Peter Ramus and the Educational Reformation of the Sixteenth Century*, New York, 1912.

can profit from some form of elementary education in the vernacular and too many seek education in classical languages which is not fit for all; (2) education must be for boys and girls at all levels; (3) education must be public and not by tutors. With Ascham he opposed foreign travel, but he turned his attention almost prophetically to the subject of teacher training and recommended the establishment of training colleges at the universities parallel to those of the professional schools in law, medicine, and theology. Above all, Mulcaster argued against the formal, repressive schoolwork of the times and held that education should not aim either to force or repress the child.[17]

4. **English sense-realism.** Some representative figures in seventeenth-century England who advocated universal literacy, the teaching of practical subjects, and scientific research, and who recognized education as the supreme means for improving humanity and the duty of the state to provide schools, illustrate the rise of sense-realism: **Samuel Hartlib** (1600–1670), who wrote *A Description of the Famous Kingdom of Macaria,* a utopian romance, argued for a state-controlled system of education, publicly supported; **Hezekiah Woodward** (1590-1675), whose *A Gate to Science* recommended teaching children by realistic (intelligible books, etc.) methods; **John Dury** (1596–1680), whose *Reformed Schools* subordinated the learning of languages to the practical arts and sciences; **Sir William Petty** (1623–1687), who in his *Advice of W. P. to Mr. Samuel Hartlib* recommended a universal education for all children, and a trade education for most; **Charles Hoole** (1610–1667), who translated Comenius' *Orbis Pictus* and who advocated in his *A New Discovery of the Old Art of Teaching School* the use of the vernacular in an educational program that remained practical with the postponement of Latin to a later age. **John Brinsley** (dates unknown) might be included in this group even though his *Ludus Literarius* (1612) is more conventional and a good pic-

[17] James Oliphant, *The Educational Writings of Richard Mulcaster,* Glasgow, 1903. The *Positions* was edited by Robert H. Quick (1888) who brought Mulcaster to the attention of nineteenth-century historians.

ture of the grammar schools of the time; if nothing else, Brinsley insisted on the teaching of English.[18]

Wolfgang Ratke (1571–1635)[19] was the most influential of the Continental realists, second only to Comenius, whom he influenced. In an address to the Diet of the German Empire at Frankfort in 1612, Ratke proposed the reformation of education by (1) a new method to teach Latin, Greek, and Hebrew and to achieve better results in shorter time; (2) the use of the vernacular to give all children a thorough knowledge of all the arts and sciences; (3) through the continued use of the vernacular and the new methods, to bring about the use of one language in all of Germany, and thus to lay the basis for uniformity in religion and in government. Ratke's method was eminently realistic. He recommended that everything be learned in the natural order which the mind of the child follows; that only one thing at a time be learned; that each thing be often repeated; that the vernacular be used first for all instruction; that everything be taught wihout compulsion; that everything be learned by experience. Although Ratke appears to have been interested chiefly in Latin, Greek, and Hebrew, the method he proposed (and although his own attempts failed)[20] remained, as a form of systematic instruction, very influential.

John Amos Comenius (1592–1670) was the most important representative of the realistic movement, whether from the viewpoint of his theoretical writings on education, or from that of practical experience. Comenius "is thus among the authors who do not need to be corrected or . . . contradicted in order to bring them up to date, but merely to be translated and elaborated."[21]

[18] All of these are discussed in J. W. Adamson, *Pioneers of Modern Education, Cambridge,* 1905; and in Foster Watson, *The English Grammar Schools up to 1660,* Cambridge, 1908.

[19] Also written *Ratichius* or *Ratich.*

[20] Ratke is constantly spoken of as "too crabbed and mean" to accomplish any great reform. See Henry Barnard, *German Teachers and Educators,* Hartford, 1878.

[21] Jean Piaget, *John Amos Comenius: Selections,* Paris, Unesco, 1957, p. 30.

1. **Purpose of education.** Comenius wrote, "The ultimate end of man is eternal happiness with God" as the primary principle of education. If there was nothing new in this goal, Comenius gave it new significance by noting that the religious end was to be achieved by moral control over one's self, and this in turn achieved by knowledge of one's self and all things. Knowledge was the one element that directly related to the schools; and this advance, however, was so radical that it profoundly affected every phase of education in its organization, method, and textbooks.

2. **Content of education.** Comenius' purpose was the complete reorganization of human knowledge along Baconian lines with the consequent expansion of that knowledge and of human happiness. This was typical of the pansophic movement of the seventeenth century in which *Pansophia* meant an educational encyclopedism. Previous encyclopedias had been mere collections of facts; Comenius proposed an arrangement of facts around universal principles so that in all the arts and sciences, study could proceed slowly from what is best known to what is less familiar, until all knowledge is encompassed. In the textbooks of Comenius, each chapter leads to the next, and thus embodies his universal principle of method.

3. **Method of education.** Comenius brought the inductive method of Bacon to the school. "As far as possible," he says, "[children must] be taught to become wise by studying the heavens, the earth, . . . but not by studying books; . . . they must learn to know and investigate things themselves."[22] Learning was to be approached through the senses; things must be taught before words; subject matter was to be organized according to its difficulty, proceeding from the easy to the difficult; instruction was to be harmonized with age, interests, and capacity of the pupils, who were to be allowed to learn by doing; schools must be cheerful, equipped with illustrative materials, and staffed with sympathetic teachers. Most of these principles of method grew out of Comenius' practical experience as a teacher.

22 *Didactica Magna,* XVIII, 28. The standard English translation is by M. W. Keatinge, London, 1896.

4. **The textbooks of Comenius.** These were not theoretical, but born of the actual practical problems of the classroom, and number over one hundred.[23]

a) Janua Linguarum, or Gates of Languages Unlocked (1631) includes about 8,000 Latin words with equivalents in the vernacular, arranged into some 1,000 sentences grouped around 100 diverse topics dealing with nature, art, and society. This was the first Latin grammar especially written for children.

b) Vestibulum (Entrance Hall) (1633). Intended as an introduction to the Latin language, it was far simpler than the previous formal grammars, and selected about 1,000 of the most commonly used Latin words for the construction of some 400 simple sentences.

c) The Atrium. An enlargement of the *Janua* with a complete Latin grammar affixed.

d) Palatium and *Thesaurus.* Collections of excerpts from classical authors intended as readers.

e) Orbis Pictus (1657). Intended as a supplement to the *Vestibulum* and *Janua,* this is the first illustrated textbook for children. Each chapter was headed by a picture in which the various objects were numbered with reference to specific lines in the text.

f) The Great Didactic. Written as early as 1632 but not published in Latin translation until 1657,[24] this is not a textbook, but a theoretical summary of his educational ideas. For Comenius, the primary aims of life are knowledge, morality, and piety; and these are to be obtained through education. The *Great Didactic* concerns itself with universal education, the need for the reform of the schools, the principles of teaching and learning, the method of the sciences, the proposed organization of the schools.

5. **The schools of Comenius.** Comenius provided for a definite school organization in which his curriculum and

[23] For lists of the texts, see Matthew Spinka, *John Amos Comenius,* University of Chicago, 1943; W. S. Monroe, *Comenius and the Beginnings of Educational Reform,* New York, 1900.

[24] As part of *Opera Didactica Omnia,* a collection of his works, published in 4 vols., Amsterdam, 1657. See S. S. Laurie, *John Amos Comenius,* Cambridge, 1904, pp. 98-100.

method were to be implemented. Four grades of schools, each some six years long, covered birth to maturity: (a) infant school; (b) vernacular school; (c) Latin school or gymnasium; (d) university and travel. Despite the extraordinary work of Comenius, his educational influence was slight, save in the scientific manner of teaching languages, and this derived almost totally from the use of his textbooks. His theoretical writings remained unknown until the nineteenth century when their rediscovery and publication influenced many thinkers of that period.[25]

John Locke (1632–1704): Realism and Empiricism. Among those who most directly felt the influence of Comenius was Locke. His chief works are *An Essay Concerning Human Understanding* (1690); *Two Treatises on Government* (1690); *Some Thoughts Concerning Education* (1693).[26]

1. **Locke's philosophical position** is empiricist and materialistic, arguing that experience is the sole original source of knowledge. There are no innate ideas in the mind, which unformed at birth is given definiteness through experience. Experience is the source of all knowledge, which comes to man through sensation and reason. The *tabula rasa* theory held that man's mind is passive and, like a wax tablet, can receive only the impressions made upon it.[27] His philosophical position allows for a theory of human development and, in substance, rejects theological argument of innate total depravity.

2. **Educational ideas.** Locke was concerned only with the education of the aristocratic class, suggesting that if the gentry were properly educated "they will quickly bring all the rest into order." Four essentials of education are virtue, wisdom, breeding, and learning: virtue—good character; wisdom—sound judgment; breeding—manners; learning—knowledge, placed last because it is subservient to greater

[25] Jean Piaget, *op. cit.*

[26] *Of the Conduct of the Understanding* was published posthumously in 1706. See J. W. Adamson, *The Educational Writings of John Locke*, New York, 1912.

[27] For the philosophy of Locke, see B. A. G. Fuller, *History of Philosophy*, 2nd ed., New York, 1957.

qualities. Private education is preferred to public education; and around a program of physical education, Locke constructs a utilitarian curriculum that hardens the body and develops habits of moral discipline and self-control. Humanistic training is rejected, with vernacular recommended as the means of instruction in geography, geometry, French, Latin, and a knowledge of things.

3. **The doctrine of formal mental discipline.** Locke has been identified with this doctrine, which maintains that the memory is strengthened by practice, although he seems not to have taken a clear position on this matter; if anything, Locke rejects the idea that any faculties are capable of growth and development.[28]

4. **The influence of Locke** was widespread and profound. In philosophy, his empiricism influenced Berkeley, Hume, and Kant; in education, his views influenced Rousseau, Basedow, Pestalozzi, and Herbart. If Locke's great importance lies in his investigation of the problem of epistemology (i.e., of knowledge, of how we know), his importance in the history of education lies in his analysis of human nature as it is before experience and without innate ideas.[29]

Sense-realism in the schools. Most of the sense-realists had little connection with the universities, and in these slight influence of the movement was felt. The first schools to embody realism were those of the Pietistic movement of Hermann Francke (1663–1727), and from the middle of the seventeenth century, the textbooks of Comenius came into common use in the German *gymnasien,* primarily as aids to the study of Latin. The German *Ritterakademien* (schools for nobles), which came into prominence at the close of the Thirty Years' War, were largely based on the social-realism of Montaigne, rather than on the scientific realism of Bacon or Comenius. The *Real-Schulen of Germany* (largely as a

[28] There are grounds for designating Locke as a humanist, realist, utilitarian, empiricist, and disciplinarian. See further Walter B. Kolesnik, *Mental Discipline in Modern Education,* University of Wisconsin Press, 1958.

[29] R. I. Aaron, *John Locke,* 2nd ed., New York, 1955; Maurice Cranston, *John Locke,* London, 1957.

result of Francke's influence) date from the middle of the eighteenth century. In England, "real studies" made their way into the curriculum of the academies that were developed by the nonconforming churches. After the restoration of the Stuarts in 1660, the dissenting clergymen were expelled from their parishes and excluded from the schools and the universities. Most of this clergy turned to the foundation of private academies, which figured prominently in English educational history after the Toleration Act of 1689.[30] The University of Halle (1694) is the first modern university in which the new science was first taught in the vernacular, and it became the center of the new learning and the educational freedoms of *Lehrfreiheit* and *Lernfreiheit* (freedom of teaching and learning) which distinguished the German universities in the succeeding centuries.

Religious education in the seventeenth century. Two important attempts to adapt sense-realism to the pressing problems of seventeenth-century society and to use education as the handmaiden of religion were the schools of the Christian Brothers, and those founded by the Pietists.

1. **August Hermann Francke (1663–1727) and the Pietistic schools.** The movement was founded by Philip Jacob Spener (1635–1705) in the middle of the seventeenth century, following the spiritual and economic havoc of the Thirty Years' War. It was primarily a benevolent, evangelical reaction against formalism and rationalism, and was critical of existing schools because they failed to give emphasis to the development of Christian virtues and practical piety. Beginning in 1692, Francke established at Halle a group of educational and charitable institutions. In the schools he aimed to combine a practical preparation for life, Christian training, and an integration of knowledge and piety. Some years later provision was made for a teachers' college (*Seminarium Praeceptorum*). Although religion was paramount in the Pietist schools, their great importance at-

30 This had an American counterpart in the academies in the colonies which were largely founded by religious dissenters. See H. McLachlan, *English Education under the Test Acts: The History of the Non-Conformist Academies,* University of Manchester Press, 1931.

taches to the opening of hundreds of schools intended for the middle and lower classes, and to the model they furnished of the practicability of a universal, sponsored program of education.[31]

2. **John Baptist de la Salle (1651–1719) and the Brothers of the Christian Schools.** The Institute of the Brothers of the Christian Schools was founded by John Baptist de la Salle in 1684 and was committed to elementary education much as the Jesuits were dedicated to secondary education. The first school was established at Rheims in 1679, before the foundation of the order; La Salle opened a seminary for teachers as early as 1685; the order's *Conduct of the Schools* (first published in 1720) was drawn up about 1695.[32] The curriculum of the schools was limited to religion, good manners, reading, and arithmetic; and some of the order's technical schools taught industrial and commercial subjects. Pupils were graded into classes, and class method of instruction was introduced. The importance of the work of the Christian Brothers is perhaps best recognized in their dedicated efforts (like the Pietists) to poor and orphaned children, many of whom they literally rescued from the streets.[33]

31 See further F. Eby, *Early Protestant Educators,* New York, 1931.

32 *The Conduct of the Schools* was translated and edited by F. de la Fontainerie, New York, 1935. See further W. J. Battersby, *John Baptist de la Salle,* New York, 1957.

33 Other teaching orders organized within the Catholic Church include the *Oratory of Jesus,* which became a teaching order in France in 1611 and established a system of secondary schools; the *Jansenists* or *Gentlemen of Port Royal,* who in 1643 started a school at Port Royal in France for the education of young children which was distinguished for the improvements effected in the teaching of languages and logic, the use of French in instruction, and the influence of Descartes in the organization of its curriculum and methods. Before the close of the seventeenth century, some attempt was made by Catholic educators and writers for the training and education of girls. The most important of these recommendations was *On the Education of Girls* (1687) by the French prelate, François de Salignac de la Mothe Fenelon (1651-1715), whose main thesis was that "women are weak, but must be strengthened for duties that lie at the foundation of all human life." See further H. C. Barnard, *The French Tradition in Education,* New York, 1922.

Chapter VIII

NATURALISM IN EDUCATION: THE EIGHTEENTH CENTURY

Historical background. The eighteenth century Enlightenment was a reaction against the authoritarianism of the Reformation, against absolute monarchy, against social privilege and stratification, and against the domination of intellectual life by ancient and medieval concepts of knowledge. The doctrine of political liberalism had been clearly stated by John Locke, for whom the social contract was an agreement where citizens delegated authority to government in return for the government's protection of the natural rights of life, liberty, and property; in France, the work of Locke was examined and reaffirmed by Montesquieu in his *Spirit of Laws* (1748). In essence, the middle-class constitutionalism of Locke became the agency of revolution, both in Europe and America. During the long reign of Louis XV (1715–1774), France lost her supremacy in Europe, not to be regained until Napoleon, and in 1789 was engulfed in revolution. The French First Republic (1792–1804) culminated in the empire of Napoleon. Under Frederick I (1713–1740), Prussia emerged strengthened and expanded; under Frederick the Great (1740–1786), Prussia became a first-rate political power. In England, the expulsion of the

Stuarts in the Glorious Rebellion of 1688 assured parliamentarian government, and educational movements in eighteenth-century England were largely the outgrowth of a middle-class philanthropy. Throughout the Enlightenment the organization and control of education reflect changes that are political, economic, and religious. As national governments became stronger, attempts were made to construct national systems of education; almost coincident with liberalism and humanitarianism was the rise of a theory of education as a necessary agency of democracy; with the growth of middle-class power, education was reshaped to meet their interests; and with the advent of new religious ideas (Methodism in England), education was revitalized. For the student of the history of education, the key concepts of the eighteenth century include: (1) rationalism, as illustrated in Voltaire and the French Encyclopedists, which held that the world is completely subject to natural law and ruled out everything supernatural and all revealed religion as contrary to the natural law; (2) in economics, the doctrine of laissez-faire, or noninterference, as applied by Adam Smith (*The Wealth of Nations,* 1776) and the French physiocrats; (3) the effort to base education on child psychology, as dramatically seen in Rousseau, which culminates in the attempt of Pestalozzi "to psychologize education."

French educational theory and nationalization. For the most part, education in France from the middle of the sixteenth century to about the middle of the eighteenth was almost entirely conducted by the Jesuits and other religious orders. With the suppression of the Jesuits in 1763[1] and the closing of their schools, French theorists turned their attention to education and began to present plans for a complete system of national schools to replace the teaching orders of the Church.[2]

1. **Claud Adrien Helvetius** (1715–1771). In *On the Soul* (*De l'Esprit*), 1758, Helvetius had argued that the differences

[1] T. Hughes, *Loyola and the Educational System of the Jesuits,* London, 1892.

[2] For background see Shelby T. McCloy, *The Humanitarian Movement in 18th Century France,* University of Kentucky Press, 1957.

of character and personality in men depend on the inequalities of intellectual attainment due to education. The *Treatise on Man* (published 1772) reasserts this position and further maintains that all education should be subject to civil authority.

2. **Louis René de Caradeuc de la Chalotais** (1701–1785) recommended the reformation of secondary education in his *Essay on National Education* (1763). Concerned primarily with an education that would prepare the student for citizenship, he deplored the inadequacy of existing institutions, laid down principles for fixing the number of secondary schools, discussed method, and devised an elaborate curriculum which allowed physical education, modern language study, and a secular (as opposed to clerical) faculty.

3. **Barthelemy Rolland D'Erceville** (1734–1794). *Compte-rendu* (1768), presented to the Parliament of Paris, was in part intended to meet the problem of the closing of the Jesuit schools. Rolland advocated a program of universal education, the establishment of a teachers' college, the use of the national language, the use of special teachers for science and mathematics (as opposed to the philosophers commonly used), and the adaptation of instruction to the needs of various classes. His highly centralized system of educational control was later adopted by Napoleon in his organization of the Imperial University in 1808. His *Plan of Education* (1783) reaffirmed these recommendations.

4. **Aune Robert Jacques Turgot** (1727–1781) proposed in *Memoirs* (1775) the creation of a Council of National Education that should control all education. In the primary grades, Turgot recommended the teaching of the social duties of citizens, manners and customs, the rudiments of writing and reading, with some elementary geometry, and the principles of mechanics.

5. **Denis Diderot** (1713–1784). The great monument of his career was the *Encyclopedia* (28 vols., 1750–1772),[3] which assumed the principle of religious toleration and freedom of speculation, and argued that the principal concern

[3] J. Morley, *Diderot and the Encyclopedists,* London, 1905; N. L. Torrey, ed., *Diderot Studies,* New York, 1949.

of government was the welfare of the common people. His chief educational works include the *Systematic Refutation of the Book of Helvetius on Man* (1773) and *Plan of a University* (1776), the latter written at the request of Catherine II of Russia. In these works he advocated (1) that instruction is necessary for all, should be compulsory, and under State direction; (2) the reconstruction of the curriculum of the secondary schools; (3) that utility should be the measure of values in all schooling, and that the sciences are to be preferred.

6. **Marie Jean Antoine Nicolas Caritat, Marquise de Condorcet** (1743–1794)—mathematician, philosopher, and educational theorist. In 1792, he presented to the French National Assembly a report on the state of education and a project for a new system; the report was drawn from a series of memoranda that he had published earlier. Condorcet's main ideas on education include the following: (1) education is necessary for liberty and equality, and forms the basis of morality and human progress; (2) instruction should be universal; (3) although the state should subsidize education, all instruction must be free of political and religious control; (4) education must be allowed women; (5) education must include the sciences. Organizationally, Condorcet provided for elementary schools, secondary schools, colleges, and a National Society for Sciences and the Arts.[4]

7. To the work of these theorists may be added that of **Etienne Bonnot de Condillac** (1715–1780), whose *Cours d'Etudes* (1767–1773) showed the influence of Locke and maintained that the mind is the product of sensation.[5] But it remained for Rousseau in the second half of the eighteenth century to attempt the reconciliation of reason and the emotions, science and morality, and to construct for man a society in which he could live the balanced life.

Jean-Jacques Rousseau (1712–1778) was a moralist, who attacked the notion that progress results from advances in

[4] For some notices of Condorcet's educational theory, see J. S. Shapiro, *Condorcet and the Rise of Liberalism*, New York, 1934.

[5] Zora Schaupp, *The Naturalism of Condillac*, University of Nebraska Press, 1926.

science and technology; was the originator of romantic sensibility as opposed to the dominant rationalism; and was a revolutionary political thinker.[6]

1. **Political writings.** In the *Discourse on the Moral Effects of the Arts and Sciences* (1749), Rousseau advanced the doctrine of the "natural state." Written in answer to the question, "Has the restoration of the sciences contributed to purifying or corrupting manners?" Rousseau's answer was negative: time had created all the institutions of corrupt society; evil was in society, not in man; society was to be reconstructed by the "return to nature." *On the Origin of Inequality Among Men* (1754) concluded that in a state of nature men were more equal than they are under civilization, and that education greatly increases the natural inequality between men. Rousseau next defined the right state of nature for man, and attempted the construction of a society for man's newly discovered true nature. This was the theme of the *Social Contract* (1762), which maintained that man was brought into society by his own consent, i.e., by way of a social contract. Such a society can devote itself to the development of an ideal life in which the "natural state" is not infringed, freedom is not lost, and the arts and sciences of polite (rationalistic) society are not developed.[7] All of these writings allow a better understanding of the *Nouvelle Hélöise* (1761) and of *Émile* (1762), which consider education in the "natural state" and life in response to the promptings of the heart and the inner voice of conscience.[8]

2. ***Émile*** (1762). A long tale (500 pages in five books) part novel, part exposition, in which Rousseau describes the education of the young appropriate to the ideal society. The

[6] F. C. Green, *Rousseau,* Cambridge, 1955; and Ernst Cassirer, *The Question of Jean-Jacques Rousseau,* New York, 1954. For the relation of Rousseau to the other French educational theorists, see F. de la Fontainerie, *French Liberalism and Education in the 18th Century,* New York, 1932.

[7] The political writings are translated and edited by C. E. Vaughan, *The Political Writings of Jean-Jacques Rousseau,* 2 vols., Cambridge, 1915.

[8] The *New Hélőise* considers family education whose major ideas are repeated in *Émile.* The *Émile* is available in many editions; See W. Boyd, *Rousseau's Émile,* London, 1957. See also W. Boyd, *The Minor Educational Writings of Jean-Jacques Rousseau,* Glasgow, 1910.

child, taken from his parents and isolated from society, is put in the hands of a tutor who instructs him "in a natural state." Education according to nature is the theme with four characters: Émile, the boy who is being educated; Sophy, to whom the fifth book is devoted; the tutor; and Rousseau who constantly explains, expostulates, and admonishes.

a) **Meaning of nature in *Émile*.** The fundamental principle is in the opening sentence of the book: "Everything is good as it comes from the hand of the author of nature; but everything degenerates in the hands of man." Although Rousseau does not completely define "nature," hc appears to assign three meanings to it—(1) social meaning: education must be based on a knowledge of the true nature of man; "natural man" is not the savage man, but man governed and directed by the laws of his own nature; and such laws are discoverable, as are other laws, through investigation; (2) instinctive judgment: this is more trustworthy than reflection or experience that comes from association with others; formation of habits must be prevented; only the primary habit of personal disposition must be followed: (3) inanimate identity: a fearless, intimate association with animals, plants, and all physical phenomena and forces must be encouraged in the child, who must become a "lover of nature." Rousseau noted that "Cities are the graves of the human species."[9]

b) **The negative education of *Émile*.** In his opposition to the prevailing sentiment that human nature was bad, and that religious training and education were to eradicate original nature, Rousseau recommended what he called "negative education"; the entire education of the child was to come from free development of his own nature, his own powers, his own natural inclinations. But this did not mean that there was to be no education; the training was to be very different from that which prevailed at the time. Rousseau's statement in paradoxical form has made some of his thinking ambiguous, and difficult to understand, e.g., "A negative education does not mean a time of idleness; far

[9] On the romanticism of Rousseau see Irving Babbitt, *Rousseau and Romanticism,* Boston, 1930; and Jacques Barzun, *Romanticism and the Modern Ego,* Boston, 1943.

from it. It does not give virtue, it protects from vice; it does not inculcate truth, it protects from error."

c) **Education from one to five in *Émile*.** This includes condemnation of restraints on freedom of the child, on the injurious effects of swaddling clothes, on the need to avoid the thwarting of natural inclinations and desires, and the rejection of all punishment that the child cannot understand because he has no conception of the nature of wrong. It recommends that little attention be paid to intellectual or moral education, with more concern for the development of words rather than ideas. Above all, the child is to have a regimen of exercise, freedom, sports, and games in the country.

d) **Education from five to twelve in *Émile*.** Two central principles control this critical period: (1) negative education; (2) moral training must develop through natural consequences. Childhood exists for its own sake. The child is not to be taught to read, and education is to be largely a training of the senses as can be obtained by intimate contact with nature. In this period the child will measure, weigh, count, compare, draw conclusions, and discover principles.

e) **Education from twelve to fifteen in *Émile*.** In this period the strength of the individual is greater than his needs, and it is in this period that knowledge is to be acquired. Defoe's *Robinson Crusoe* is recommended, and a knowledge that is eminently practical. Among other things, Émile will learn a trade, and at the end of this period he will be "industrious, temperate, patient, firm, and full of courage. . . ."

f) **Education from fifteen to twenty in *Émile*.** In this period the child is to be educated for life with others and social relationships are to be developed; in this period moral and religious education is to be introduced. The true method of moral education is to delay the growth of the passions until judgment and self-control have had time to develop; and this is the period to study mankind.[10]

[10] Sophy appears in the last book of *Émile* to be trained to serve and charm Émile; Rousseau makes no contribution to the education of women.

3. **Recapitulation of Rousseau's educational theory.** *Émile* shows certain basic theories that form the foundation of Rousseau's theory of education. These include: (1) education is a natural, not an artificial process; its development is from within and is life itself; (2) the child is the positive factor in education, and education is to find its purpose, its process, and its means totally within the child life and experience.[11]

4. **Influence of Rousseau.** Most of the nineteenth-century educational theory was based on Rousseau. His nature concept allowed the development of educational psychology (study of native instincts, tendencies, etc.), and the formulation of an educational theory that viewed education as a natural process; his insistence on the study of the phenomena of nature prepared the way for the scientific movement in education; and his advocacy of an education that prepared the individual to live in society led to sociological theories in education. Rousseau's naturalism was the most radical of all of the theories that came out of the Enlightenment; if it proved impracticable in education, still the advocacy of an educational methodology that would follow the natural stages of development through which children grow to maturity remained the most influential educational concept of the eighteenth century.[12]

Basedow and German educational reform. In Germany, above all, considerable progress was made in establishing national education in the eighteenth century. The work of Francke in the preceding century, and the rapid development of the Pietistic schools led to the decree of 1717 in which Frederick William I made attendance in the elementary schools of Prussia compulsory; in a sense, this culminated in the General School Regulations (1763) of Frederick the Great, which made attendance in school compulsory for all children between the ages of five and fourteen.[13]

[11] W. Boyd, *The Educational Theory of Rousseau,* New York, 1911.

[12] Romain Rolland, *et al., French Thought in the 18th Century, New* York, 1953.

[13] Friedrich Paulsen, *German Education, Past and Present,* New York, 1912.

Much of the stimulus for educational reform in eighteenth-century Germany resulted from the work of Johann Bernard Basedow.

1. **Johann Bernard Basedow** (1724–1790). Chiefly influenced by Rousseau and La Chalotais, Basedow attempted to implement Rousseau's theory that children learn through natural experiences into a basic methodology for teachers, which would allow the development of a national system of education, not unlike that proposed by La Chalotais.

2. **Basedow's educational writings.** Among his most important works was *Appeal to the Friends of Mankind . . .* (1768), in which he outlined his plans for reform in educational organization, curriculum, and methods. This was an appeal for funds that would allow him to write a textbook for parents. In 1770, his *Book of Methods for Fathers and Mothers of Families and for Nations* appeared, and in 1771, his *Elementary Book;* both of these were combined in 1774 as a text and method called the *Elementarwerk,* published in four volumes and elaborately illustrated with copper engravings.

3. **The Philanthropinum** was established in 1774 by Basedow as a small experimental school to demonstrate his principles. The name expresses the idea that the school was the child of philanthropy, the love of men for mankind, and instructed the young to humanitarian ends. The stated aim was to prepare boys of the upper classes for useful and happy lives; the school was to be opened to children of all religious views, and was to be the prototype of a nationally sponsored system of schools.[14]

4. **Basedow's methods.** Actually most of Basedow's educational principles are not new, but suggest the influence of many education-thinkers. His principles include: (a) everything should be taught by objects, pictures, and models; (b) all languages, including Latin and Greek, should be taught by the direct conversational method; (c) education is more important than instruction; (d) all learning must be

[14] Basedow urged the creation of a State Superior Council for the Supervision of Public Instruction. This may have influenced the establishment of the *Oberschul-Collegium* in 1787, when Prussia assumed control of the schools.

useful; (e) no harsh discipline should be used. In keeping with the temper of realistic studies, Basedow's curriculum was encyclopedic but not humanistic in the classical sense. It included natural history, carpentering, geography, history; and the pupils went on excursions visiting shops, farms, and industries. The teaching of religion was undenominational; special textbooks were recommended for children;[15] and great stress was laid on physical education.

5. **Influence of Basedow.** His model school was copied everywhere, and some of his suggested reforms adopted. Primarily, Basedow's importance lies in (a) the vitalization of interest in educational reform, and its promotion by the upper classes; (b) the appeal of the concrete program he recommended; (c) the new emphasis and importance attached to realistic studies, and the demonstration of their practicability; (d) the movement toward secular and national control of the schools. In Prussia, where Basedow's influence was most felt, the work of Baron von Zedlitz, who served as Prussian minister of education from 1771–1789, illustrates the movement toward national control. It was Von Zedlitz who brought about the creation of the Supreme Council of Public Instruction (*Oberschul-collegium*) to supervise all education in Prussia (1787), and established the first chair in pedagogy at the University of Halle (1779). Colleagues and followers of Basedow include C. H. Wolke (1741–1825); J. H. Campe (1746–1818), who was the author of *Robinson the Younger,* an imitation of Defoe's classic; E. C. Trapp (1745–1818), who became professor of pedagogy at the University of Halle and director of the practice school founded there in 1779, perhaps the first example of a university practice school for the training of teachers; and Christian G. Salzmann (1744–1811), the only member of Basedow's staff who succeeded in founding a permanent Philanthropinum. Important in his own right, Salzmann recommended that immediate interests and the life of the present should occupy the child's attention; a prolific writer,

[15] An important contribution by the Philanthropinists was the creation of a children's literature in German, which appears to be directly due to the influence of Rousseau and his recommendation of *Robinson Crusoe* in the *Émile.*

he was the author of the very popular *Stories for Children* (1778) which reaffirmed the great interest in the creation of a genuine literature for children. Salzmann's associates included C. F. Guts Muths, the founder of systematic school gymnastics, and Karl Ritter, who was the founder of the "natural method" in geography.[16]

English educational practice in the eighteenth century. Although some educational reform was suggested in the period of the Puritan Commonwealth (1649–1660), the restoration of the monarchy (1660) delayed any effective measures, and successful attempts at the national level were delayed for almost two centuries. At the beginning of the eighteenth century, an exensive system of charity schools developed in London and the surrounding towns, largely providing free rudimentary education to poor boys and girls. Most of these efforts were the work of the Society for the Promotion of Christian Knowledge (S.P.C.K.), founded in 1698 by Thomas Bray and others. The Society has always been connected with the Church of England. The curriculum was limited to reading, writing, and catechism, and the avowed aim was the elimination of vice and degradation among the lower classes. Later provision was made for manual work and for the preparation of children to earn a living, with girls taught to sew and knit, and boys apprenticed to trades.[17] To carry on the work in the English colonies, the Society for the Propagation of the Gospel in Foreign Parts (S.P.G.), was founded, which continued very active in America down through the end of the eighteenth century.[18] Further efforts

[16] Although not part of the Basedow group, the work of the Swiss educators, Martin Planta (1727-1772) and John George Sulzer (1720-1779), is worthy of note. Both anticipated Rousseau and attempted the *realistic* innovation of the curriculum. Planta developed a Philanthropinum more than a decade before Basedow. See Auguste Pinloche, *La Reforme de l'Education en Allemagne au dix-huitieme Siècle,* Paris, 1889. Much of this material is in the same author's study of *Pestalozzi* (1901), which is in English translation.

[17] See the *Annual Reports* of the society; also, W. C. B. Allen and E. McClure, *Two Hundred Years: The History of the Society for Promoting Christian Knowledge,* London, 1898.

[18] C. F. Pascoe, *Two Hundred Years of the S.P.G., 1701-1900,* London, 1901. For both societies, see Jewell Lochhead, *The Education of Young Children in England,* Columbia University Press, 1932.

in elementary education were made by the Sunday School movement, largely the work of the Gloucester publisher, Robert Raikes, and directly promoted by the Methodists and other religious groups.[19] These schools, which came into prominence in the last decades of the eighteenth century, taught rudimentary education and religion to working children during their free time on Sundays. In a sense, their origin is to be understood as a reaction to the industrial revolution and the employment of children in the factories. In addition to these activities, two other movements that developed in the nineteenth century should be noted. The infant school, which received children "at one year or as soon as they could walk" and retained them until the age of six when they were transferred to the elementary school, was introduced into England by Robert Owen (1771–1858); with the founding of the London Infant School Society in 1824 and through the efforts of its first superintendent, Samuel Wilderspin (1792–1866), the infant schools became an important force in English education. Some critics have argued that the schools simply allowed both mothers and fathers to work and freed them from the care of their children, but it is true that the infant schools allowed the ideas of Froebel a fertile ground for growth.[20] Equally important were the monitorial schools, which were largely the result of the efforts of Joseph Lancaster (1778–1838) and Andrew Bell (1753–1832). In these schools a headmaster taught the brighter or more mature pupils, who then (as pupil-teachers or monitors) taught small groups of pupils. In this fashion, one headmaster could teach many hundreds of children. Organized along military lines and limited to the most elementary rudiments, the monitorial schools recommended themselves because of their low cost, and two societies were set up to promote them, the British and Foreign Society (1810),[21] to establish Lancasterian schools; and the National

[19] For Robert Raikes (1735-1811), see Charles Birchenough, *History of Elementary Education in England and Wales,* London, 1938.

[20] For Robert Owen, see Lloyd Jones, *Robert Owen,* London, 1905; also, D. Salmon and W. Hindshaw, *Infant Schools: Their History and Theory,* London, 1904.

[21] Henry B. Binns, *A Century of Education, 1808-1908: A History of the British and Foreign School Society,* London, 1908.

Society, to establish those of Rev. Andrew Bell. The chief difference between the groups was that Lancaster's schools were non-sectarian, and those of Bell were Anglican. The outlines of the monitorial method can be found in Bell's *An Experiment in Education Made at the Male Asylum of Madras* (1797) and in Lancaster's *Improvements in Education as It Respects the Industrious Classes* (1803). The monitorial schools were important, not only in their very wide use and influence, but in the combined effort they afforded with the S.P.C.K. and Sunday School movements toward the achievement of public education in England.[22]

Johann Heinrich Pestalozzi (1746–1827) was a Swiss educator and reformer, a pioneer in "psychologizing education" (his own phrase), whose theories laid the foundation of modern elementary education. Inspired by the theory of Rousseau, Pestalozzi tried to apply this theory in practice. Two chief schools conducted by Pestalozzi were the institute at Burgdorf (1800–1804) and the institute at Yverdun (1805–1825), both of which were boarding schools for boys ranging from six or seven to eighteen years of age.

1. **Organization of Pestalozzi's schools.** Boys under eight were combined in a primary class; above this was the school proper, consisting of two groups: the lower class of boys eight to eleven, and the upper class eleven to eighteen.

2. **Pestalozzi's educational writings.** Most important of these is the didactic novel *Leonard and Gertrude* (1781–1785), which stresses two important points of Pestalozzian theory: the extension of sympathy to the poor; and the essence of mother-love personified in the heroine, Gertrude. The reformation of the ills of society was to be sought in its schools, and *Leonard and Gertrude* emphasizes an education

[22] A voluminous literature on the controversy of the origin of the monitorial schools (Lancaster or Bell?) is noted in David Salmon, *Joseph Lancaster,* London, 1904. The monitorial schools had a wide success in America; see, e.g., John F. Reigart, *The Lancastrian System of Instruction in the Schools of New York City,* Columbia University, Teachers College, 1916. See also D. Salmon, ed., *The Practical Parts of Lancaster's Improvements and Bell's Experiment,* Cambridge University Press, 1932.

based on nature, good teaching, and love. Many of the theories of *Leonard and Gertrude* are practically explained in *How Gertrude Teaches Her Children* (1801), the main idea being that first impressions of objects or sense perceptions are the basis for knowledge. Allowing this, Pestalozzi further claimed that the knowledge gained from sense perceptions could be clarified and developed by means of three concepts: number, form, and language. Through the use of objects that gave the child the sense perceptions essential to learning, the child was able to discern real and meaningful substance to his observations. Other works include the early philosophical treatise, *My Investigations into the Course of Nature in the Development of the Human Race* (1797) and *Mother's Guide* (1803).[23]

3. **Main features of the Pestalozzian system.** From Pestalozzi's writings and practices certain principles may be discerned. These include: (a) The ideal educational institution is the home, as it is the center of love and activity for the common welfare; (b) Since society requires an educational framework that the home cannot completely supply, schools must be provided, and these should be modeled on the good home; love must guide the teacher and a compassionate, yet firm, discipline maintained; (c) The aim of education is the harmonious development of man's powers and the development of social responsibility; (d) Pestalozzi's early endeavors were directed to the improvement of the social conditions of the lower classes, largely through industrial education; (e) The "psychologizing" of education demands the grading of pupils, the presentation of subject matter in harmony with the stages of growth, and the encouragement of the child's self-activities; (f) Instruction is to be carried on by "observation" and by graduated activities, always beginning with the simplest elements; (g) The curriculum must be reformed along practical and scientific lines; (h) Provision must be made for teacher education, and teachers will best learn their

[23] J. A. Green, *Pestalozzi's Educational Writings,* New York, 1912; also, the same author's *Life and Work of Pestalozzi,* London, 1913. *How Gertrude Teaches Her Children* was translated and edited by Lucy E. Holland and F. C. Turner, 5th ed., Syracuse, 1915.

needed skills in experimental schools that are committed to a program of continuing improvement.[24]

4. **The influence of Pestalozzi.** In Prussia, the influence was very strong since it allowed the continuance of the efforts made in establishing a national school system. The philosopher Fichte (1762–1814) stimulated interest in Pestalozzian methods by his endorsement, and the defeat of Prussia by Napoleon at Jena (1806) turned Prussia's attention to a complete social revolution that would regenerate the country. Both Herbart and Froebel were directly influenced by Pestalozzi. Prussian teachers were trained at the school in Yverdon at government expense, and the German educator-historian Diesterweg (1790–1866) referred to the "Prussian-Pestalozzian school system" that had brought fame to the German popular schools.[25] Two agencies led to a popularization of Pestalozzian methods in England: (a) the publication of books on object teaching, and (b) the organization of an infant-school society to use Pestalozzian methods. The work of **Charles Mayo** (1792–1846) and the Home and Colonial Infant School Society (1836) in founding model Pestalozzian schools greatly influenced educational practice in nineteenth-century England. In America, Pestalozzian methods were particularly influential because of the early work of **Joseph Neef** (1770–1854), one of Pestalozzi's teachers who taught in Philadelphia; the general attention paid to Pestalozzian methods by American periodicals and official reports; and the influence of the movement on the American normal schools, particularly the Normal School at Oswego and the pioneering work of **Edward A. Sheldon** (1823–1897).[26] Related to the Pestalozzian movement is the work of the Swiss educator, **Emanuel Fellenberg** (1771–1844), who developed a plan of agricultural schools for Switzerland and who conducted a school at Hofwyl along Pestalozzian lines between 1806 and 1844. This school included not only industrial education for the poor but also the training of teachers for rural schools.

[24] Lewis F. Anderson, *Pestalozzi,* New York, 1931; Roger de Guimps, *Pestalozzi: His Life and Work,* New York, 1914.

[25] Henry Barnard, *Pestalozzi and His Educational System,* Syracuse, n.d.

[26] See Part V.

Chronological Table of Educational Development during the Nineteenth Century

Political Events and Personages	Literary Men, Religious Leaders, etc.	Scientists and Philosophers	Educational Writings and Educators	Educational Events
1800. 1804. Bonaparte emperor. 1807. Class distinctions and serfdom abolished in Germany. 1814. Bonaparte at Elba. 1815. Congress of Vienna. Frederick William 1797–1840 1810–1830. Freedom of South American States. 1817. Wartburg demonstration for freedom. 1830. July Revolution in France. 1830. Reform bill in England. 1833. Slavery abolished in British colonies. 1846. Corn laws repealed. 1848. French Revolution. 1851. New French Empire. 1854. Crimean War. 1870. Franco-Prussian War. 1871. German Empire founded. 1871. The Union of Italy.	Goethe 1749–1832 Wordsworth 1770–1850 Byron 1788–1824 Scott 1771–1832 Coleridge 1772–1834 Irving 1783–1859 Cooper 1789–1851 Emerson 1803–1882 Thackeray 1811–1863 Dickens 1812–1870	Hegel 1770–1831 Cuvier 1769–1832 Comte 1798–1857 Faraday 1791–1867 Hamilton 1788–1856 Liebig 1803–1873 J. S. Mill 1806–1873 Herbert Spencer 1820–1903 Buckle, *History of Civilization* 1857 Darwin, *Origin of Species* 1859 Agassiz 1807–1873 Darwin 1811–1882 Wallace 1820	Pestalozzi, *How Gertrude Teaches* . 1801 Jacotot 1770–1840 Herbart, 1776–1841 Froebel 1782–1852 Thomas Arnold 1795–1842 Rosmini 1797–1855 Herbart's *General Pedagogics*, 1806 Horace Mann 1796–1859 Rosenkranz 1805–1879 George Combe 1788–1858 Froebel, *Education of Man* . . . 1826 Spencer, *Essay on Education*, 1861 Alexander Bain 1818–1887 Henry Barnard 1811–1900 Stoy . 1815–1885 Otto Frick 1832–1892 Tuiskon Zeller 1817–1883 R. H. Quick 1831–1891	1803. Sunday-school Union f. 1805. Public School Society of New York. 1806. University of France f. 1806. Neef introduces Pestalozzi in United States. 1808. First treatise on education published in United States. 1809. University of Berlin founded. 1808–1811. Von Humboldt head of German schools. 1804–1844. Fellenberg's School at Hofwyl. 1811. National Society for Promotion of Ed. of the Poor. 1813. First State superintendent of ed. in United States (N.Y.). 1814. British and Foreign School Society. 1818. Lancaster comes to U.S. 1821. First legislative aid for education of women (N.Y.). 1821. First High School (Boston). 1827. All schools free in Massachusetts. 1835. Cousin's *Report* published in United States. 1837. Mount Holyoke seminary for women. 1837–1849. Mann Secretary of Mass. Bureau of Ed. 1837. First kindergarten. 1837. First city superintendent of schools. 1838. First State normal school in United States (Mass.). 1843. School Board in New York City. 1850. Kindergartens forbidden in Germany. 1860. First kindergarten in U.S. 1861. First Ph.D. in U.S. 1862. Morrell land grant for agricultural and technical education. 1867. Elective system at Harvard. 1867. United States Commissioner of Education. 1867. All State schools free in New York. 1869. English Endowed School Act. 1870. Elem. Ed. Act in Eng. 1873. Kindergarten part of public school (St. Louis). 1890. Berlin School Conference. 1896–1897. University of France reorganized.

Chapter IX

NATIONALISM AND SCIENCE IN EDUCATION: THE NINETEENTH CENTURY

Historical background. In the nineteenth century, four social trends are discernible that have largely influenced educational development; the interaction of these four trends produced (or were the result of) most of the social conflict of the nineteenth and twentieth centuries.

1. **Nationalism.** Political and cultural nationalism concomitantly produced many of the revolutions and wars of the nineteenth century in the attempt to transform cultural unity into political unity. Education was used as a means to develop the spirit of nationalism.

2. **Liberalism and democracy.** Largely a continuation of the humanitarian impulses of the eighteenth-century Enlightenment, one aspect of which recommended the state's positive reorganization of social institutions (including education) to better serve the common welfare.

3. **Industrialism.** Perhaps the most fundamental change in nineteenth-century Europe was the new technology that wrought great changes in social conditions, the rise of the

factory system, urbanization, and the conflict between labor and the new entrepreneurs.

4. **Capitalism.** The industrial capitalism of the nineteenth century was a development from the early mercantilism (strict government control) and laissez-faire capitalism (free competition, open markets, private ownership of property) in which, with the development of the factory system, a new and great power was concentrated in managerial hands.

Education, quite normally, reflected the influences of these trends in the graphic changes that they made on society.

Important political history. The Congress of Vienna (1815) following Napoleon's overthrow; the system of Metternich (1815–1830); the liberal revolutions of 1830–1833 (France, Belgium, parts of Germany, Italy, Switzerland, Poland); the national revolutions of 1848–1850 (Sicily, Second French Republic, Germany and Austria-Hungary, Turkey); the Crimean War (1854–1856); unifications of Italy and of Germany (1870–1871); imperial rivalries and international relations (1871–1914).[1]

National school systems in nineteenth-century Europe. The changing economic scene and the causes that produced it in the late eighteenth century and throughout the nineteenth century brought about an intensification of the emphasis on national ideals, and the establishment under lay auspices of national school systems. European nations set out to achieve a system of elementary education that would be free, compulsory, universal, and to a large degree secular.

Prussia. Until the late eighteenth century education was largely dominated by the Lutheran State Church. Separation of the administration of the church from that of the schools was achieved in 1787 by the creation of the *Oberschulcollegium,* a central board of experts, and by bringing the schools under greater state control. The Prussian law (Code, 1794) defined education as a function of the state, not of parents or of the church. In 1817, the Bureau of Education

[1] For nineteenth-century European political and cultural history, see David Thomson, *Europe Since Napoleon,* New York, 1961.

was made a national Department of Education, and in 1825, provincial school boards were set up throughout Prussia to replace the local church-school boards. The provinces were divided into districts, and in each district a school board was organized whose responsibility was the establishment of schools that met standards set up by the national educational authority. By 1840, an efficient machinery had been set up to enforce the compulsory education law, and the *Volksschulen* (folk-schools) were supported mainly by local property taxes. For the most part, the elementary *Volksschulen* were free, even though as late as 1888 pupils who could afford it paid small fees.[2]

Nineteenth-century German schools. Throughout the nineteenth century, the middle class in the German states was far less powerful and influential than that in England and France; in the class society of Prussia, the character of the schools was determined by the national and political purposes that the schools were created to serve. The basic elementary schools (*Volksschulen:* folk-schools) were the schools of the laboring classes, and attendance was required between the ages of six and fourteen. The curriculum (particularly after 1871) emphasized religious instruction, German language and literature, arithmetic, drawing, history, geography, elementary science, gymnastics for boys, needlework for girls. The religion taught was that of the predominant church group in the district, and as a class-structured school, the *Volksschule* student could not use this school to better his social position; in a sense, the school assured his retention in the class of his parents. The *Mittelschule* (after 1872) met the educational needs of the children of the lower middle classes; it was a six-year pay school that served as a path to lower positions in the civil service and commerce. Children entered this school at age ten, and the only difference between its curriculum and that of the upper grades of the *Volksschule* was the addition of a foreign language in the last three years of its program.

1. **Prussian secondary education.** At the beginning of the nineteenth century Prussia had two types of secondary

[2] T. Alexander, *The Prussian Elementary Schools,* New York, 1918.

schools: (a) the *gymnasien,* or classical schools; (b) the *realschulen,* which emphasized modern studies. By decree of the *Oberschulcollegium,* only the *gymnasien* were permitted to issue certificates of admission to the universities; students from the other schools had to pass the examinations of the universities for entrance to higher studies. With the abolition of the university entrance examinations in 1834, only the *gymnasien* students were assured entrance to the universities. However, by 1859, the reorganization of the *realschulen* into the *realgymnasium* (a nine-year academic modern course), and the *realschule* (a shorter academic course) began a movement which, by the end of the century, opened up university privileges to the students of these schools. Further developments after the unification of Germany led to the organization of three six-year secondary schools: *realschule, progymnasium,* and *realprogymnasium,* in which national interests and modern studies enjoyed greater importance, but the universities still continued to draw most of their students from the *gymnasien,* which outnumbered the other schools. In Prussia, and in the united Germany, all secondary education was under the supervision of state authorities.[3]

2. **Vocational education.** In keeping with the development of the pre-vocational *Mittelschule,* a vast program of trade and vocational education (for the most part established in the cities) was developed for the graduates of the *volksschulen,* and as an adjunct to these schools, technical institutes that met the needs of expanding commerce and industry.

3. **German universities in the nineteenth century.** The University of Berlin (1810) served as a prototype to the other universities, and developed as a great center of research and subject specialization, and pre-eminently as a graduate institution. The ideals of academic freedom (*Lehrfreiheit* and *Lernfreiheit*) became the great achievement of the German universities, but academic freedom was largely the prerogative of the institutions, not of the individual professors, who for the most part were orthodox in their political, economic, and social views. Above all, research was

[3] For German secondary education, see James E. Russell, *German Higher Schools,* New York, 1899.

the distinguishing characteristic, and in the second half of the nineteenth century, the German universities enjoyed a great influence and prestige.[4]

France. Out of the philosophical turmoil of the French Revolution came many proposals for French educational reform and legislation; the culmination was the passage of the Daunou Law (1795), which provided for the establishment of primary schools in the large cities, administered by the local authorities, limited to the very rudiments of curriculum, and free only to the neediest students. The law also allowed for a limited number of secondary schools (Central Schools), which were not unlike the German *realschulen* in their emphasis on modern studies; but for the most part these schools were not popular, with children attending private and church schools.

1. **Napoleonic reform of education** (1799–1815). Napoleon advocated national education for state ends, with political indoctrination of the curriculum. He reorganized the schools by establishing the Imperial University as a national ministry of education with full control of all education; by subdividing France into academies, each with a rector and educational council; and by supervisory authority vested in national school inspectors. Some provision was made for the training of secondary school teachers in a national normal school (1808). Actually more interested in secondary education, Napoleon established state (lycées) and municipal (collèges) secondary schools, but did little for elementary education.

2. **The primary school law of 1833.** The restoration of the monarchy (1815–1848), following the overthrow of Napoleon (1815), saw the enactment of the school law of 1833, which established lower and higher primary schools, and in each department (largest political subdivision), a primary normal school. The curriculum of the lower primary in-

[4] Friedrich Paulsen, *German Education, Past and Present,* New York, 1908; Charles Thwing, *The American and German University,* New York, 1928. Thwing maintained that 10,000 Americans received the Ph.D. at German universities in the nineteenth century.

cluded reading, writing, French language, morals, and religion; and in the higher primary were added geometry, elements of science, history, and geography. Fees were required in these schools of students able to pay, and additional support was obtained from local taxation.[5] Infant schools became part of the system in 1837 and important concessions were made to the religious schools. No provision was made for effective compulsory attendance. Under the Second Republic (1848–1852) and the Second Empire (1852–1870), many repressive measures were enacted by conservative groups, and the law of 1850 restored much of the former power of the church in education, even with its strengthening of the educational authority of the Minister of Public Instruction and its improvement of educational administration.

3. **French national education, 1870–1900.** The basic form of French national education was achieved under the Third Republic, founded after the defeat of Napoleon III (1870) by the Germans. Laws were enacted severely restricting the religious societies, and a bitter struggle was begun against clerical control of education and for the establishment of a system of free public schools. Significant developments included: (a) in 1881–1882, primary education was made free and compulsory for all children between the ages of six and thirteen; (b) in 1882, the teaching of religion in the schools was abolished; (c) in 1886, the unification of French education into one single national system was achieved, with total state administrative and supervisory control; (d) the law of 1886 allowed the development of vocational schools (post-primary or higher primary) to meet the commercial and industrial needs of their areas. Private schools (mostly Catholic) were permitted, for the most part free from state requirements in curriculum and methods.[6]

[5] The school reforms of 1833 were largely the result of Victor Cousin's *Report . . . on Public Instruction in Germany,* Paris, 1831. Cousin had great influence in French education from 1830-1851, and in 1840 was appointed Minister of Public Instruction.

[6] Frederic E. Farrington, *The Public Primary System of France,* Columbia University, Teachers College, 1906; P. Gay and O. Montreux, *French Elementary Schools,* Columbia University, Teachers College, 1926.

Secondary school education was based on a seven-year curriculum, and as late as 1930 all secondary schools charged fees. Under the Third Republic six successive reforms of the secondary curriculum were undertaken, all of which turned on the question of the classics *versus* modern subjects. Although the Ribot Commission (1898) concluded that the classical curriculum should be maintained, this was to parallel a modern course. In 1902, reforms were instituted to provide for four secondary school curricula of seven years (ages eleven to eighteen), which were (a) Latin-Greek; (b) Latin-Modern Languages; (c) Latin-Scientific; (d) Modern Languages-Scientific. In all curricula, great attention was paid to French.[7]

England. At the beginning of the nineteenth century, two types of schools were found in England, both provided by voluntary effort of churches and private philanthropy: (a) elementary schools for the poor; (b) grammar schools (secondary schools) for the upper classes, of which the "Great Public Schools"[8] are representative. What the elementary schools were unable to do for the poor, an apprenticeship system attempted. For the most part, attendance in the elementary schools was irregular, short, and of limited value. Much of the philanthropic effort in education arose to correct the social ends to which children were exposed as the result of industrialization and urbanization. Between 1833 and 1870, some effort was made to systematize education. In 1833, and again in 1839, grants were made to the National Society and to the British and Foreign School Society, and these grants were gradually increased. But until 1870, elementary education for the masses in England was the work of private, voluntary (largely religious) agencies to which the government gave little support and over which it exercised little supervision.[9]

7 Isaac L. Kandel, *The Reform of Secondary Education in France,* Columbia University, Teachers College, 1924.

8 See pp. 47-48 for founding of "Public Schools." These were class schools and largely the entrance schools to Oxford and Cambridge Universities. See Edward C. Mack, *Public Schools and British Opinion,* 2 vols., Columbia University Press, 1941.

9 John W. Adamson, *English Education 1789-1902,* Cambridge University Press, 1930.

1. **Elementary Education Act of 1870.** This provided for the election of school boards, which imposed local taxation for elementary schools. Government grants to "voluntary schools" were continued, with the provision that no child be instructed in religion against his will, and the further stipulation that no denominational religion be taught in board schools. In substance, the Act of 1870 provided England with two school systems, one public and one religious. Subsequent developments included compulsory elementary education to the age of ten (1876), and in 1891 elementary education was made free in state-aided schools; in 1899 compulsory attendance was extended to age twelve, and in the same year a national Board of Education was created. The Balfour Act (1902) continued the dual system of education, and brought all schools under the control of the elected councils of the political administrative English divisions. These councils known as L.E.A.'s (local education authorities) controlled education. Despite some further reforms (The Fisher Act of 1918), English education essentially retained its form until the recasting of the national system in 1944.[10]

2. **The elementary curriculum.** Unlike the Prussian and French governments, which prescribed the curriculum of their schools, the English left the curriculum to local authorities. Before the Newcastle Commission (1858–1861), the curriculum of most of the schools was limited to religion and reading, with a few schools adding writing, arithmetic, geography, history, grammar, drawing, and general elementary science. After the Act of 1870, religion ceased to be the core of the curriculum, but the expansion of the schools and their studies largely remained local matters.[11]

3. **Developments in secondary education.** Before the Balfour Act of 1902, English secondary education was limited to the aristocratic "public schools," and to grammar schools,

[10] R. Barker, ed., *The Education Act of 1944*, London, 1944; S. J. Curtis, *History of Education in Great Britain*, London, 1948.

[11] M. Sadler, *Our Public Elementary Schools*, London, 1926. See also the contemporary criticisms of Matthew Arnold, *Reports on Elementary Schools*, London, 1852-1882.

which had arisen in the late nineteenth century to meet the needs of the middle class for modern and practical studies.[12] All of these schools were private. In 1902, the local educational authorities were allowed to establish secondary schools which qualified for state support if they provided free places for public elementary school students. English secondary education did not become free until the Education Act of 1944 provided that all schools maintained by the L.E.A.'s be free. Thus, free secondary school education in England is a very recent matter.[13]

Nineteenth century educational theory. Most prominent in nineteenth century educational thought is the attempt to base an educational philosophy on some system of psychology. If the writers of the Renaissance (and later Comenius and Locke) discovered the individual, and Rousseau pushed this individualism to a dangerous extreme, Pestalozzi tried to balance individualism and to advocate the education of children as children before they could become men. It remained for Johann Friedrich Herbart (1776–1841) and Friedrich A. W. Froebel (1782–1852) to attempt the formulation of a scientific educational psychology to allow learning and growth.

Johann Friedrich Herbart (1776–1841) was a German philosopher and educator, who advanced associationism as the basis of an educational psychology. His main writings include *Science of Education* (1806) and *Outlines of Educational Doctrine* (1835).

1. **Herbart's educational aim.** His primary aim was the development of the religious, moral, and cultural man. Social environment was of great importance, and particularly the cultivation of "many-sidedness" of interest, which is not the means but the end of education. Interest springs out of the physical and human worlds, the latter being the more important. Herbart's "cycle of thought" begins with knowledge

[12] R. L. Archer, *Secondary Education in the 19th Century,* London, 1921.

[13] S. J. Curtis, *Education in Great Britain since 1900,* London, 1952; G. A. N. Lowndes, *The British Educational System,* New York, 1955

(clear ideas), is followed by action, and the formation of moral character.[14]

2. **Herbart's psychology.** Ideas group themselves as "apperceptive masses" according to similarities between them, and this process of "apperception" is the learning process. The task of the teacher is to direct that process. Interest (though distinct from ideas) has its origin in ideas, and interest acts to retain ideas in consciousness and to recall them to consciousness. The power of interest is increased by the presentation of the idea to consciousness, and by the association of ideas (apperception). Herbart's method is based on his theory of the mind and apperception. The method evolved into the "Five Formal Steps of the Recitation," which (modified by later Herbartians) were: (1) Preparation, or preparing the student's mind for the assimilation of the new idea; (2) Presentation of the new idea; (3) Association, or assimilation of the new idea by the old; (4) Generalization, or the general idea that comes from the combination of old and new ideas; (5) Application, or the use of the new knowledge in solving problems. Although Herbart did not regard the steps as fixed and invariably followed, the steps were formalized and became the basis of the "model lesson plan" of the normal schools, and were taught as mechanical devices.[15]

3. **Herbart's influence.** Herbartian principles that had wide influence include his doctrines of apperception and interest, and his rejection of the faculty psychology and the doctrine of formal discipline. In Germany, the universities of Jena and Leipzig were centers of Herbartianism. Tuiskon Ziller (1817–1883) developed a theory of unification of all instruction beginning in the elementary grades, and reformulated Herbart's five formal steps. Wilhelm Rein (1847–1929) applied Herbartian principles to the curriculum. After 1890, Herbartianism spread to the United States, largely because of teachers who had studied at Jena. American Herbartians

[14] Christian Ufer, *Introduction to the Pedagogy of Herbart,* Boston, 1901.

[15] John Adams, *The Herbartian Psychology,* Boston, 1906; Gardner Murphy, *An Historical Introduction to Modern Psychology,* New York, 1932.

include Charles DeGarmo, who wrote *Essentials of Method* (1889); Charles McMurray and Frank McMurry, who published *General Method* (1892) and the *Method of Recitation* (1897). The National Herbartian Society (1892) was founded to promote Herbart's ideas in America (name changed to National Society for the Study of Education in 1902), and by 1900, teacher-training institutions in America had largely adopted Herbartianism. The great appeal of Herbartianism lay in its method of instruction and in the practical application of its "Five Formal Steps of Instruction" to the teaching of the subjects of the curriculum.[16]

Friedrich Froebel (1782–1852). In many ways directly influenced by Pestalozzi and Rousseau, Froebel in his *Education of Man* (1826) recommended a principle of unity that derived from a doctrine of mystical idealism and from which his educational theories evolve. All things derive from the "Divine Unity." Man is viewed as a developing unity according to a law of nature unfolding within him. As basic components in the education of the child, Froebel embodied in this mystical philosophy doctrines of (1) free self-activity; (2) creativeness; (3) social participation; (4) motor expression. By divine law, free self-activity directs the growth of the child and allows him through creativeness and social participation to merge his individuality with the spirit of humanity. Motor expression (activism) was for Froebel to learn a thing by doing, not by verbal communication alone, and made the educative process productive.[17]

1. **Froebel and the kindergarten.** Established first in 1837 by Froebel, the kindergarten was the result of his study of infant schools, and represented an attempt to find the best materials and activities that would cultivate the young child's powers of observation and understanding. As materials for children's play, Froebel selected the sphere,

[16] Charles DeGarmo, *Herbart and the Herbartians*, New York, 1895; A. F. Lange, *Herbart's Outlines of Educational Doctrine*, New York, 1901. Educational journals issued in the United States between 1890-1910 contain a great deal of material on Herbart.

[17] S. S. Fletcher and J. Welton, *Froebel's Chief Writings on Education*, New York, 1912; H. C. Bowen, *Froebel and Education by Self-Activity*, New York, 1899.

the cube, and the cylinder. As the kindergarten developed, much of Froebel's symbolism was abandoned. The kindergarten (not unlike the nursery school)[18] came to provide supervision of children between two and five years of age in the crowded slums of the large cities. In America, the first kindergarten was opened at Watertown, Wisconsin, in 1855 by Mrs. Carl Schurz, and rapidly developed but with serious modification of the mysticism of Froebel.[19]

Educational theory and nineteenth-century science. After the middle of the nineteenth century, the biological and physical sciences vastly influenced thought, and the educational writings of some theorists were in direct response to the new science. Perhaps the most important scientific publication of the century was Charles Darwin's *Origin of Species* (1859), which advanced the theory of "natural selection" in biological evolution. Herbert Spencer (1820–1903) worked out a theory of evolution on a philosophic basis, and in his *Essays on Education* (1861) advocated a curriculum based on science as that of the greatest value. Thomas Henry Huxley (1825–1895) similarly advocated a place for science in the curriculum and advanced these views in many publications and addresses.

Selected References

Part IV: The Modern Era (1600–1900)

Adams, J. *The Evolution of Educational Theory*. London, 1912.
Adamson, J. W. *English Education, 1789–1902*. Cambridge, 1930. (Rep., 1964)
Adamson, J. W. *Pioneers of Modern Education, 1600–1700*. New York, 1921.

[18] Cf. the work of Maria Montessori (1870-1952) in Italy and her *Montessori Method*, 1912.

[19] Nina C. Vandwalker, *The Kindergarten in American Education*, New York, 1908; Susan Blow, *Educational Issues in the Kindergarten*, New York, 1908; W. H. Kilpatrick, *Froebel's Kindergarten Principles Critically Examined*, New York, 1916.

Archer, R. L. *Secondary Education in the 19th Century.* London, 1921.
Aries, Philippe. *Centuries of Childhood: A Social History of Family Life.* New York, 1962.
Atkinson, Carroll, and Eugene T. Maleska. *The Story of Education.* Philadelphia, 1962.
Cole, P. R. *Herbart and Froebel: An Attempt at Synthesis.* Columbia University, Teachers College, 1907.
Curtis, S. J., and M. Boultwood. *A Short History of Educational Ideas.* London, 1966.
Dobbs, A. E. *Education and Social Movements, 1700–1850.* New York, 1919.
Eby, F. *Early Protestant Educators.* New York, 1931.
Fitzpatrick, Edward A. *LaSalle, Patron of All Teachers.* Milwaukee, 1951.
Gay, Peter, ed. *John Locke on Education.* New York, 1964.
Hayward, F. H. *Three Historical Educators: Pestalozzi, Froebel, Herbart.* London, 1905.
Jarmon, Thomas. *Landmarks in the History of Education.* London, 1950.
Kandel, Isaac L. *History of Secondary Education.* Boston, 1930.
———. *Comparative Education.* Boston, 1933.
King, Edmund J. *World Perspectives in Education.* Indianapolis, 1962.
Krikorian, Y. H., ed. *Naturalism and the Human Spirit.* Columbia University Press, 1944.
Laurie, S. S. *Studies in the History of Educational Opinion from the Renaissance.* London, 1904.
Lawrence, Evelyn, ed. *Friedrich Froebel and English Education.* New York, 1953.
Mayer, Frederick. *Education—Past and Present.* New York, 1962.
Misawa, Tadasu. *Modern Educators and Their Ideals.* New York, 1909.
Moehlman, A. H., and J. S. Roucek, eds. *Comparative Education.* New York, 1952.
Monroe, W. S., and M. Engelhardt. *The Scientific Study of Educational Problems.* New York, 1937.
Ogilvie, Vivian. *The English Public School.* London, 1957.
Paulsen, Friedrich. *German Education, Past and Present.* New York, 1912.

Peterson, Alexander D. C. *A Hundred Years of Education.* New York, 1962.

Pollard, Hugh M. *Pioneers of Popular Education.* Harvard University Press, 1957.

Quick, R. H. *Essays on Educational Reformers.* New York, 1890. (Rep., Littlefield, 1970)

Reisner, Edward. *Nationalism and Education Since 1789.* New York, 1923.

———. *Historical Foundations of Modern Education.* New York, 1927.

Rice, E. A., J. L. Hutchinson, and M. Lee. *A Brief History of Physical Education.* New York, 1958.

Rusk, Robert R. *The Doctrines of the Great Educators*, rev. ed. London, 1969.

Sadler, John E. *Comenius and the Concept of Universal Education.* New York, 1966.

Smith, F. *History of English Elementary Education since 1760.* London, 1931.

Smith, W. O. L. *Education in Great Britain.* Oxford University Press, 1958.

Ulich, Robert. *The Education of Nations: A Comparison in Historical Perspective.* Harvard University Press, 1962.

Watson, Foster. *English Grammar Schools to 1660.* London, 1908.

Weinberg, Ian. *The English Public Schools.* New York, 1967.

Wodehouse, H. *A Survey of the History of Education.* London, 1924.

Part V

AMERICAN EDUCATION

The periods of American education are usually divided into the Colonial Period (1607–1787) and the National Period (1787–present). The adoption of the Constitution in 1787, with the establishment of a federal republic with limited powers (and no power over education) is a good point at which to divide American education. The large periods may be further subdivided to allow for fuller notice of particular educational developments that fall into relatively smaller time-areas. The Colonial Period divides into (1) the transplantation of European institutions and ideals, 1607–1700; (2) the age of enlightenment in colonial America, 1700–1787. The National Period divides into (1) 1787–1830, the academy movement, the formulation of a national theory of education, and the plans for state educational systems; (2) 1830–1890, the rise of state systems, the land-grant colleges, new methods and theories; (3) 1890–present, democracy and science in education, progressive education, challenges to education in a democratic society.[1]

[1] H. G. Good, *A History of American Education*, New York, 1973.

Chapter X

THE COLONIAL PERIOD (1607-1787)

Historical background. Permanent British settlements in North America began at Jamestown, Virginia, in 1607. Other settlements include Plymouth (1620); Massachusetts Bay (1630); Maryland (1632); Connecticut (1635); Providence (1636); Carolinas (1663); New Jersey and New York (1664); Pennsylvania (1681). The Puritan Commonwealth in England extended from 1649 to 1660, when the Stuart kings were restored. The migration of Germans and Scots into the middle and southern colonies extended from 1702–1713, and the colony of Georgia was chartered in 1734. Important dates for the American Revolution (1776–1783) include the Declaration of Independence (1776); the Articles of Confederation (1781); the Peace of Paris, recognizing independence (1783); the Constitutional Convention (1787).[2] Much of the social change of the period can be understood by reference to the religious practices of the early settlements. New England was Calvinist (Puritan), and a theocracy; the middle colonies were largely settled by religious dissenters (Quakers, Anabaptists); the southern colonies were

[2] C. M. Andrews, *The Colonial Period of American History*, 4 vols., New York, 1934-1938.

Anglican. State churches were the rule. Calvinism (Puritanism) was the legal church of New England. The Anglican was the legal church of New York, New Jersey, and the South. The Dutch Reformed Church lost its legal right with the English conquest of the Hudson-Delaware region (1664–1674).[3]

The transplantation of European institutions and ideals, and Colonial Enlightenment, 1607–1787. The dominant motive for the establishment of schools was for religious instruction. In New England, the church-state commonwealths established schools to preserve the Puritan faith; in New Netherlands, Dutch Calvinists established parish schools; in Pennsylvania, Delaware, and New Jersey, Quakers and Swedish Lutherans set up schools for their congregations; in Maryland, the Catholics founded schools; and in Virginia and the southern colonies, the Anglican church superintended instruction.

Elementary education and secondary schools

1. **Southern colonies.** Here there were many diverse practices, with education (excepting apprenticeship training) at a minimum. In Anglican Maryland, some provision was made to establish "Public Schools (1728) in which some poor children were taught without fee. In Virginia, the schools received no assistance, and between 1624 and 1660, laws were enacted requiring religious (Anglican) instruction of children. In Virginia, the "old field school" developed. These were schools largely taught by Anglican ministers for the children of the rich. In South Carolina, the "Charleston Free School" was chartered in 1710, but was free to only a few students. In South Carolina and Georgia, the work of the S.P.G.[4] was at times the only educational activity, and many of the rich planters sent their sons to England for education.[5]

2. **The middle colonies.** In Pennsylvania, some schools

[3] Harvey Wish, *Society and Thought in Early America,* 2 vols., New York, 1950.

[4] See pp. 87-89, above.

[5] S. Bell, *The Church and State in Virginia,* Lancaster (Pa.), 1930.

were organized by the S.P.G., the Presbyterian Synod of Philadelphia, and the Moravians. Education was not a public concern, although apprenticeship education widely existed. The Quakers provided some schools (e.g., William Penn Charter School, 1689), but continued to affirm that education was a private concern. In New Jersey, the situation remained essentially the same.[6] In Dutch New Netherlands, the schools were adjuncts of the state-church, and most of the Dutch towns (Albany to lower Delaware) seem to have had elementary schools in 1664. These schools, while allowed to continue, changed after the English occupation, with public funds appropriated to them and with the teachers supervised by church officials.[7] In New York City, the English allowed the S.P.G. to maintain schools. In 1702 and 1732, the legislature provided for secondary education in the establishment of a "Grammar Free School," but this was not free except to a few and very limited number of students.

3. **New England.** With the exception of Rhode Island, the New England colonies adopted some form of school legislation, and collected local taxes for school support. The motive was entirely religious and attempted the continuance of the Puritan theocracy. The General Court of Massachusetts enacted laws that required the proper employment and instruction (1642), and that required every town of fifty families to employ a teacher of reading and writing whose fees were to be paid by the community or by the parents of the students (1647). Connecticut adopted similar legislation in 1650, and New Hampshire in 1680; the effectiveness of these laws is difficult to assess. The "Dame School" developed as a private pay school, conducted by women in their homes, with instruction limited to the basic rudiments.[8]

[6] T. Woody, *Early Quaker Education in Pennsylvania,* New York, 1920; and his *Quaker Education in the Colony and State of New Jersey,* Philadelphia, 1923. See also J. P. Wickersham, *History of Education in Pennsylvania,* Lancaster (Pa.), 1886; J. Mulhern, *History of Secondary Education in Pennsylvania,* Lancaster (Pa.), 1933; N. R. Burr, *Education in New Jersey, 1630-1871,* Princeton University Press, 1942.

[7] W. H. Kilpatrick, *The Dutch Schools of New Netherland and Colonial New York,* Washington (D.C.), 1912.

[8] C. Merriwether, *Our Colonial Curriculum,* Washington (D.C.), 1907.

Widely used as a children's reader was *The New England Primer,* first published in 1690 and republished for almost 200 years. Heavily religious, illustrated, and in rhyme, this primer is representative of colonial aims in education.[9] Secondary education in New England begins with the founding of the Boston Latin School (1635–1636),[10] essentially like its European counterpart. The immediate aim of the Latin schools was college preparation; and the curriculum was that of the narrow humanistic school of the Old World. In the eighteenth century, town schools declined and were replaced by district schools. Connecticut provided for district schools in 1715 and 1717, and Massachusetts in 1789.

Higher education

Largely following the Puritan example in the founding of Harvard College (1636),[11] all pre-Revolutionary colleges (with the exception of the College of Philadelphia, 1755) were denominational. The early colleges include William and Mary (1693); Yale College (1701); Princeton College (1746); King's College (Columbia, 1754); Brown College (1764); Dartmouth (1769); Rutgers College (1770, founded as Queen's College). The college curriculum was limited mostly to the classics and theology, with some work in rhetoric, ethics, logic, geometry, astronomy, and history. In the eighteenth century both secular and national interest became more pronounced, with science making its way into the curriculum.[12]

[9] P. L. Ford, *The New England Primer,* New York, 1898. The general scarcity of books resulted in the use of *Hornbooks* (a sheet of paper with the alphabet, numerals, Lord's Prayer, and other reading material pasted on a paddle-shaped implement and the whole covered with sheets of transparent horn) and the *Battledore* (made of stiff paper containing similar materials). See A. W. Tuer, *History of the Hornbook,* New York, 1896.

[10] P. Holmes, *A Tercentenary History of the Boston Latin School,* 1635-1935, Harvard University Press, 1935.

[11] S. E. Morison, *Harvard College in the 17th Century,* 2 vols., Harvard University Press, 1936.

[12] Frederick Rudolph, *The American College and University: A History,* New York, 1962; Samuel E. Morison, *The Intellectual Life of New England,* Ithaca, 1956; Bernard Bailyn, *Education in the Forming of American Society,* University of North Carolina, 1960.

Apprenticeship education

The colonists brought from England the practice of apprenticeship education of dependent children. Essentially, the British laws of 1562 and 1601 had shaped apprenticing into a national system, and the system was re-established in the Massachusetts laws of 1642 and 1648, and by many other statutes in the other colonies. In many ways, apprenticeship education became associated with the class structure of colonial society, and remained the chief provision for the servant class.[13]

Textbooks and educational theory

Down to the time of the American Revolution, the dominant religious purpose is shown in the textbooks used: *The New England Primer,* the *Hornbook,* the *Psalter,* the *Testament,* the *Bible,* and the *Westminster Catechism.* In the eighteenth century, texts by English writers supplemented the list. The Latin grammar of Ezekiel Cheever (1614–1708) was used for a century in New England and was representative of the few texts available.[14] Pre-revolutionary educational theory is almost wholly limited to Benjamin Franklin's *Proposals Relating to the Education of Youth in Pennsylvania* (1749), which formed the theoretic basis for the academy.[15] Of lesser importance are *General Idea of the College of Mirania* (1753) by William Smith (1727–1803), a plan of a college course which Smith, as its first provost, later adopted at the University of Pennsylvania; and Christopher Dock's (1698–1771) *Schulordnung* (written 1750; published

13 M. W. Jernegan, *Laboring and Dependent Classes in Colonial America, 1607-1783,* Chicago, 1931.

14 Cheever taught in the grammar schools of New England for seventy years. The texts of the English schoolmaster Thomas Dillworth (d. 1780) were reprinted and extensively used in colonial America. Particularly influential were his *New Guide to the English Tongue* (1740) and *Schoolmaster's Assistant* (1743). Isaac Greenwood's *Arithmetic, Vulgar and Decimal* (1729) was also widely used. See John A. Nietz, *Old Textbooks,* University of Pittsburgh Press, 1961.

15 See reprint of University of Pennsylvania Press, 1931; Thomas Woody, ed., *The Educational Views of Benjamin Franklin,* New York, 1931; John H. Best, ed., *Benjamin Franklin on Education,* Columbia University, Teachers College, 1962.

1770), a text on teaching methods, written in German by a teacher in the Pennsylvania Mennonite community. In Franklin's *Proposals,* the influence of seventeenth- and eighteenth-century European realism is discerned; in the *Academy* that he proposed, boys were to study the achievements of science, and the study of the mother tongue was to be given priority over the classics, with emphasis placed on history, mathematics, physics, chemistry. Out of these proposals came a new kind of education for America, and the ultimate collapse of the classical Latin grammar school.[16]

[16] The American Philosophical Society (founded under the leadership of Benjamin Franklin in 1743) was instrumental in bringing about educational reform.

Chapter XI

THE NATIONAL PERIOD (1787-1900)

Historical background. Nineteenth-century American history divides into several distinct periods: (1) The New Nation (1787–1810), in which the transition from colonial status to independence and successful federation was achieved; (2) National Growth (1810–1865), in which the War of 1812 freed the United States from the danger of foreign domination, and attention was turned to internal expansion, the settlement of the West, and "manifest destiny." This period saw the emergence of the common man and Jacksonian democracy, and the industrial transformation of the Northeast, which (combined with a reform movement) set North and South against each other on the issue of slavery. The Civil War settled the question of secession and started the country on a new road. (3) Reconstruction and World Power (1865–1914), in which the South, handicapped by post-bellum problems and new chaos, rebuilt itself slowly, and in which the North witnessed a period of great industrial expansion. The last half of the nineteenth century saw the growth of manufacturing industry, the growth of large corporations, the continuing growth of great cities, the revolution in farming, the rise of the labor movement, and an era of new immigration. The growth of nationalism culminated in the Spanish-American War (1898), and the ultimate involvement in World War I (1917). At the beginning of the nineteenth century, there was (in the strict sense) no American educational system; at the century's close, the educational system was complete and its structure clearly cast.[1]

Early educational developments (1787–1820)

Constitutional provisions for education. Educational theories of the Revolution were first put into public practice in state constitutions. Broad provisions for establishment of schools and encouragement of useful learning were embodied in clauses in the constitutions of Pennsylvania (1776), North Carolina (1776), Georgia (1777), Massachusetts (1780), New Hampshire (1784), and Delaware (1792). The United States Constitution is silent on the subject of education, and its Tenth Amendment grants educational power and control to the states.[2]

Thomas Jefferson (1743–1826) was convinced that education was the guardian of democracy, and he made important proposals to the Virginia Assembly.

Bill for the more general diffusion of knowledge (1779). Jefferson's proposals included an elementary school system maintained at public expense for all free children. A rudimentary curriculum was offered for three years, after which continuance was at private expense. A system of secondary schools was proposed, which was a combination of Latin grammar school and academy, with some provision for scholarship students. Qualified students would enter the College of William and Mary, but Jefferson proposed the creation of a state university, the University of Virginia, in

[1] Charles Beard and Mary Beard, *The Rise of American Civilization,* New York, 1927; Nelson M. Blake, *A Short History of American Life,* New York, 1952.

[2] Allen Oscar Hansen, *Liberalism and American Education in the 18th Century,* New York, 1926.

which religion would not intrude. The bill was rejected by the Virginia legislature in 1779, and again in 1817.[3]

The academy movement

1. The academy was a product of the realistic movement in education, established in opposition to the formalized Latin grammar school. Some academies were denominational, but most were secular and scientific. Democratic in spirit, they encouraged the education of women and provided a wide range of educational opportunities.

2. The first of the academies was that of Benjamin Franklin (founded in 1751; reorganized in 1779 as the College of Philadelphia). Academies flourished through the entire country and declined only after 1860, as the American high school developed. Some academies were known as institutes, seminaries, military schools, manual-labor schools, all with a great variety of curricula.

3. Academies were not public schools, but some provision was made by scholarship for poor children.[4]

The American state university

1. **National university movement.** There was considerable discussion in the early federal period for formation of a national university. Benjamin Rush (1745–1813) originated the movement and President Washington in his message to Congress (1790) recommended a national university, but nothing came of the proposal.[5]

2. **First state universities.** Most of the state universities of the original thirteen colonies were established in the period from 1791 to 1825. They were largely in the South, and included the University of Georgia (1785), North Carolina (1789), and Virginia (1825). Opposed by church groups, economic conservatives, and educational conservatives, the

[3] Roy J. Honeywell, *The Educational Work of Thomas Jefferson,* Harvard University Press, 1931.

[4] A full account of the academies is in Elmer E. Brown, *The Making of Our Middle Schools,* New York, 1928.

[5] Edgar B. Wesley, *Proposed: The University of the United States,* University of Minnesota Press, 1936.

state universities were little more than liberal arts colleges until after the Civil War and the passage of the Morrill Act (1862), which provided for land-grant colleges.[6]

Elementary school practices

1. Many elementary school practices in the early years of the nation laid the groundwork for the growth of a public elementary school system after 1840.[7]

2. **The infant school.** This was largely an importation of the ideas of Robert Owen (1771–1858) and Samuel Wilderspin (1792–1866). In 1818, Boston appropriated money to aid infant schools, and the practice spread to other cities, e.g., New York (1827), where the Infant School Society was founded. The infant school provided rudimentary education to children between the ages of four and eight; and when the name was changed to "primary department" and it was united with regularly established schools, it formed the lower level of the American public school system.[8]

3. **The monitorial schools.** These originated in England as the result of the work of Joseph Lancaster (1778–1838) and Andrew Bell (1753–1832). They provided a method by which mass education could be cheaply achieved. In these schools a headmaster taught the brighter students, who then (as pupil-teachers or monitors) taught small groups of students. In this way one headmaster could teach hundreds of children. A Lancasterian school was opened in New York City in 1806, and the movement spread to other cities. In 1818, Lancaster came to the United States to promote the movement. He remained, until 1830, the greatest single force in mass public education.[9]

[6] Allan Nevins, *The State Universities and Democracy,* University of Illinois Press, 1962. See also Earle D. Ross, *Democracy's College: The Land Grant Movement in the Formative State,* Iowa State College Press, 1942; and Edward D. Eddy, Jr., *Colleges for Our Land and Time,* New York, 1956.

[7] Paul Monroe, *Founding of the American Public School System,* New York, 1940.

[8] See pp. 87-89.

[9] See pp. 87-89; in New York City it was estimated that the education of a pupil in the monitorial schools cost one dollar and twenty-two cents a year. See John Reigart, *The Lancasterian System of Instruction in the Schools of New York City,* New York, 1916.

4. **The Sunday School.** This was largely due to the work of the Englishman, Robert Raikes, and was directly promoted by the Methodists and other religious groups. These schools taught rudimentary principles to working children during their free time on Sundays. A Sunday School Society was organized in Philadelphia in 1791, and Sunday Schools were opened in most of the larger cities for the benefit of poor children. In its early stages, the Sunday School helped promote the idea of public education.

Curriculum changes

1. Liberal ideas from Europe, the frontier, and dissatisfaction with colonial schools slowly produced changes in curriculum.

2. Many changes occurred in the fields of English grammar, history, geography, mathematics, and commerce; and science made its way into the curriculum in the subjects of chemistry, botany, and astronomy. Important textbooks included that of Lindley Murray on *English Grammar* (1795); the American *Universal Geography* (1789) of Jedidiah Morse; Nicholas Pike's *A New and Complete System of Arithmetic* (1788); and the texts of Peter Parley (Samuel G. Goodrich, 1793–1860), who published eighty-four textbooks and reading books for children.[10]

3. **Noah Webster** (1758–1843), "schoolmaster to America," published his *Grammatical Institute of the English Language* in 1783, of which some seventy-five million copies were sold. His *American Dictionary of the English Language* appeared in 1828.[11]

The Northwest Ordinances (1785, 1787)

1. Although no references were made in the Constitution to the federal support of education, significant steps were taken in the Ordinances of 1785 and 1787.

[10] Clifton Johnson, *Old Time Schools and Schoolbooks,* New York, 1904; Alice W. Spieseke, *The First Textbooks in American History,* New York, 1938.

[11] H. R. Warfel, *Noah Webster: Schoolmaster to America,* New York, 1936; Ervin S. Shoemaker, *Noah Webster: Pioneer of Learning,* New York, 1936.

2. The Ordinance of 1785, which made possible the sale of public lands, provided that the sixteenth lot in each township was to be set aside for educational purposes.

3. The Ordinance of 1787 followed with a plan of administration and encouraged education. "Religion, morality and knowledge being necessary to good government and the happiness of mankind, schools and the means of education shall forever be encouraged."

4. These ordinances promoted the cause of public education and laid the basis for future federal educational support.

The nineteenth-century public school

Origin of the public schools. Although some disagreement exists, the American public school system appears to have arisen out of native experience and European influence.[12]

1. Pre-nineteenth-century forces contributing to the development of public schools were: (a) establishment of the district schools of Colonial New England and the Massachusetts laws of 1642 and 1647; (b) American revolutionary ideas and the influence of progressive eighteenth-century European thought.

2. Early state school laws included Massachusetts (1789), which legalized the school district, and New York (1812); but rates were charged to all who could pay.

3. State school laws enacted after 1825 mark the beginning of the public school system.

Early state laws and practices. In the early decades of the nineteenth century, a major difficulty was in the definition of local district control of education as against the development of a state system.

1. **Beginnings of state boards of education.** The state board of education and state superintendent of schools had

[12] Sidney L. Jackson, *America's Struggle for Free Schools,* Washington (D. C.), 1941; Lawrence A. Cremin, *The American Common School,* Columbia University, Teachers College, 1951.

their origins in the state committees set up for the disposition of funds from the sale of public lands, designated for education under the Northwest Ordinance of 1785.

2. In 1784–1787, the New York legislature established the University of the State of New York, which was actually a state board of education.

3. New York established a state school fund in 1805, and in 1812 provided for a "superintendent of common schools." The office was abolished in 1821, but re-established in 1854.

4. Support of public schools prior to 1825 attempted to avoid property tax. Lotteries were extensively used, and the rate bill (a tax on parents of school children) was widely introduced.

5. In many cities, special chartered school districts were set up, independent of the state system, to offset the backwardness of rural communities and the difficulty of obtaining a general state school law. Schools were so organized in Philadelphia (1812) and in Baltimore (1825).

6. The right of school taxation was finally realized in the Pennsylvania School Law of 1834, and that of Massachusetts in 1837. The Massachusetts Law created a state board of education and provided for a state superintendent of schools.

7. **Permanent public school funds** were derived from the sale of lands under the federal land-grant acts in the western states. In the older states, comparable funds were set up as endowments, the interest being used for public school support. Surplus Revenue Act (1827), Federal Internal Improvements Land Act (1841), and Swamp Land Grant Act (1850) made additional federal grants, which many of the states put into school funds.[13]

The public school movement. Many forces were enlisted in the struggle to establish public schools and to answer opposition of those who were against tax support of the schools, of those who argued that secular schools were non-Christian

[13] F. H. Swift, *A History of Public Permanent Common School Funds in the United States, 1795-1905,* New York, 1911.

and ungodly, and of those who argued that education would remove desirable social barriers.

1. Educational magazines and journals supported public education. These included Albert Pickett's *Academician* (1818); Horace Mann's *Common School Journal* (1838); Henry Barnard's *Connecticut Common School Journal* (1838); Calvin H. Wiley's *North Carolina Journal of Education* (1843); William Russell's *American Journal of Education* (1826–1830).[14]

2. **Reports on European education** were enlisted to support the creation of the American public school system. These reports, largely on education in Prussia, were very influential and included those made by Calvin E. Stowe (1837), Alexander D. Bache (1839), Henry Barnard (1835), and Horace Mann (1843). The report on the Prussian schools by the French philosopher Victor Cousin (1832) was translated into English (1834) and was widely circulated.[15]

3. **The organization of free school societies** between 1800 and 1825 was motivated by the plight of poor children in cities for whom no educational facilities existed. Free school societies collected funds and opened schools. The New York Free School Society (1805), founded by DeWitt Clinton, organized schools, and in 1826 became the Public School Society of New York.[16]

4. **The American Lyceum** and other academic institutions aided the public school movement. The American Lyceum, organized by Josiah Holbrook in 1826, was committed to the advancement of popular education and to the improvement of its members in useful knowledge. By 1831, it was a national organization and in nineteenth-century America became the most effective instrument of adult education.[17] The Western Academic Institute and Board of Education

[14] Sheldon E. Davis, *Educational Periodicals during the 19th Century,* Washington (D.C.), 1919.

[15] Edgar W. Knight, ed., *Reports on European Education,* New York, 1930.

[16] William O. Bourne, *History of the Public School Society of the City of New York,* Baltimore, 1870.

[17] Cecil B. Hayes, *The American Lyceum: Its History and Contribution to Education,* Washington (D.C.), 1932.

was established by Albert Pickett at Cincinnati, Ohio, in 1829. Reorganized as The Western Literary Institute and College of Professional Teachers (1832), it exerted influence in every area of the Middle West.

Leaders of the public school movement

1. **Horace Mann** (1796–1859) was the first secretary of the Massachusetts state board of education, serving from 1837 to 1848. During these years, he assured the success of the Massachusetts school program by answering the objections of those forces that he classified as "religious orthodoxy, the politicians, the moneyed class, and the old-time schoolmasters." Annual reports as secretary include an account of six months' study of European schools (*Seventh Annual Report,* 1843). He aided the teacher education movement by promoting the establishment of normal schools.[18]

2. **Henry Barnard** (1811–1900) served as secretary of the board of commissioners of public schools in Connecticut (1838–1842) and did similar work in Rhode Island (1843–1848). Between 1851 and 1855, he served as Connecticut superintendent of schools, and as principal of the normal school at New Britain. Brief periods of service at the University of Wisconsin (1858–1860) and at St. John's College in Maryland (1866) were followed by his service as first United States Commissioner of Education (1867–1870). Barnard's greatest service to education was in the editing and publishing of his *American Journal of Education* (1855–1881), a mammoth encyclopedia of educational information.[19]

3. **William T. Harris** (1835–1909) did much to advance the cause of public school administration in his work as superintendent of public schools in St. Louis (1868–1880)

18 B. A. Hinsdale, *Horace Mann and the Common School Revival in the United States,* New York, 1898; E. I. F. Williams, *Horace Mann, Educational Statesman, New York,* 1937; Louise Hall Tharp, *Until Victory: Horace Mann and Mary Peabody,* Boston, 1953.

19 Richard E. Thursfield, *Henry Barnard's American Journal of Education,* Johns Hopkins University Press, 1945; Anna L. Blair, *Henry Barnard: School Administrator,* New York, 1938.

and as United States Commissioner of Education (1889–1906).[20]

4. Other leaders in the public school movement include Calvin H. Wiley of North Carolina, Caleb Mills of Indiana, John D. Pierce of Michigan, William F. Perry of Alabama, and John Swett of California.

The graded elementary school

1. Beginnings of a graded elementary school go back to 1818, when the primary school in Boston was organized into six classes, from which children were admitted to the grammar (classical secondary) school.

2. By 1823, the grammar school was divided vertically into reading and writing schools, with the reading school further divided into four classes. This general pattern prevailed with grading as new schools were opened. The development allowed a room for each grade and a grade for each year between six and fourteen years.

3. Between 1810 and 1860, there was a great variety of elementary school organization.

4. The first fully-graded elementary school in the United States was Quincy Grammar School in Boston, which opened in 1848 with John D. Philbrick as principal. This school set the pattern for the graded elementary schools of the cities.

5. The nine-year elementary school was typical of New England, and the eight-year school for the rest of the country.

6. In rural communities, most children continued to attend ungraded, poorly equipped and staffed one-room schools.

7. Many factors impeded the growth of the graded elementary school, chief of which were inadequate tax support, child labor, and the absence of compulsory attendance laws. The first compulsory attendance law was passed in Massachusetts in 1852.

[20] Carl L. Byerly, *Contributions of William T. Harris to Public School Administration*, New York, 1946.

8. By the end of the nineteenth century, a rigid uniformity in the structuring of the elementary school, with an emphasis upon subjects rather than upon children, led to a general revolt against the formal graded elementary school that had evolved through the century.[21]

The American public high school. This developed as a result of a growing industrialized and urbanized America.[22]

1. The first American public high school was founded as the English Classical School in Boston (1821), and renamed English High School (1824). Intended to meet the needs of boys who would not go on to college, this school served as the type provided by the Massachusetts Law of 1827, which required the opening of a high school in all cities with a population of five-hundred families or more.

2. Development of the high school in America was slow due to: (a) its urban and middle-class nature; (b) competition from the academies; (c) slowness of development of elementary schools in urban areas; (d) lack of need for the children of the great mass of urban workers.

3. In 1860, there were some 321 high schools in the United States, with 167 of these located in Massachusetts, Ohio, and New York. Representative establishment dates include Providence, Rhode Island (1843); Pittsburgh, Pennsylvania (1849); St. Louis (1853); Chicago (1856); San Francisco (1858); Burlington, Iowa (1863).

4. **Tax support for the public high school.** Although many of the city high schools were supported by tuition, the movement had been toward their tax support. Many objections finally led to the Kalamazoo (Michigan) case of 1872–1874 in which Judge Thomas Cooley of the State Supreme Court ruled that the public high schools were to be free and supported by "taxation levied on the people at large." Similar decision was rendered in Illinois in 1878,

[21] Lawrence A. Cremin, *The Transformation of the School: Progressivism in American Education, 1876-1957*, New York, 1961.

[22] I. L. Kandel, *History of Secondary Education*, Boston, 1930; Elmer E. Brown, *The Making of Our Middle Schools,* New York, 1928; Emit D. Grizzell, *Origin and Development of the High School in New England before 1865*, New York, 1923.

and a great incentive was given to the public high schools, which by 1900 numbered over 20,000.[23]

5. **Standardizing associations for the secondary schools.** The expanding note of the high school and controversy over its curriculum led to the formation of standardizing associations which helped to standardize the length of the school year, the class period, preparation of teachers, graduation units, classroom size, libraries, science facilities, etc. Associations include the New England Association of Colleges and Secondary Schools (1879); the Middle Atlantic States Association of Secondary Schools and Colleges (1892); the North Central Association (1894); the Association of Colleges and Preparatory Schools of the Southern States (1895); the Northwest Association of Secondary and Higher Schools (1918).[24]

6. **The Committee of Ten.** This was set up by the National Education Association in 1892 to define the function of the high school. Its report (1893) upheld the doctrine of formal transfer, and recommended more thorough study of the classics, history, literature, and grammar. In a sense, it postponed the problem of defining the function of a high school that served the needs of all its students, not only those intended for college.[25]

Public education in the South, 1860–1900. Generally poor before the Civil War, education in the South presents particular problems because of the impact and ruin of the Civil War.[26]

[23] For a discussion of the case, see I. L. Kandel, *op. cit.*, pp. 443-444.

[24] For the history of these associations, see Edwin C. Broome, *A Historical and Critical Discussion of College Admission Requirements*, New York, 1903; William K. Selden, *Accreditation: A Struggle Over Standards in Higher Education*, New York, 1960.

[25] Excerpts from the report are in Edgar W. Knight and Clifton L. Hall, *Readings in American Educational History*, New York, 1951, pp. 555-556.

[26] Edgar W. Knight, *Public Education in the South*, Boston, 1922; and the same author's *Influence of Reconstruction on Education in the South*, Boston, 1913.

1. What there was of public education in the South collapsed after the Civil War and was further aggravated by the problems of Reconstruction (1865–1867; 1868–1877).

2. Some progress was made in the education of the Negro by the **Freedmen's Bureau** (1865–1872).

3. **George Peabody Educational Fund.** Money from the fund established by George Peabody (1795–1869) has been used to ameliorate and aid educational conditions in the South.[27]

4. Despite the work of education conferences (The Ogden Movement), education continued to lag in the South, with many problems carrying over into the twentieth century.

Religious and private schools in nineteenth-century America

Adoption of the First Amendment to the Federal Constitution removed any possibility of an alliance between church and state in national government.

1. Gradually, church control over education in Virginia, Maryland, and Massachusetts declined.

2. The development of free public elementary schools under state control caused continuing controversy over such questions as state aid for religious educational programs, and a common religious educational program in the public schools.[28]

[27] Jabez Curry, *Brief Sketch of George Peabody and a History of the Peabody Education Fund through 30 years,* Cambridge (Mass.), 1898. In 1907, Anna T. Jeanes set aside one million dollars for the improvement of Negro rural education; in 1909, the Phelps Stokes Fund was created to help Negro education; and in 1917, the Julius Rosenwald Fund was directed to help all aspects of Southern education.

[28] Alvin W. Johnson, *The Legal Status of Church-State Relationships in the United States,* University of Minnesota Press, 1934; Ernest F. Johnson, *American Education and Religion,* New York, 1952; William W. Brickman and Stanley Lehrer, eds., *Religion, Government, and Education,* New York, 1961.

The Catholic parochial school

1. Schools were operated under Catholic auspices in the seventeenth and eighteenth centuries, but large scale development took place in the nineteenth century.

2. Important ecclesiastical councils that promulgated establishment of Catholic schools include the First Provincial Council of Baltimore (1829); the First Plenary Council of Baltimore (1852); the Third Plenary Council of Baltimore (1884).

4. The parish high school developed as an extension of the parish elementary school.

5. The leading figure in nineteenth-century Catholic education was Bishop John L. Spaulding, who emphasized "Americanism" in Catholic thought, and recommended a denominational public school system.[29]

The Lutheran parochial school

1. Strongly committed to religious education, German Lutherans had an extensive system of parochial schools by the early nineteenth century.

2. During the nineteenth century, Lutherans were organized into various synods throughout the United States. All of these maintained schools.

3. In 1900, the Missouri Synod was operating 1787 schools.[30]

Other denominational schools

1. Quakers (Society of Friends) supported education for all races and classes, and operated many schools that were for the most part absorbed into the public elementary school.[31]

[29] Roy J. Deferrari, *Essays on Catholic Education in the United States*, Washington (D.C.), 1942; J. A. Burns and Bernard J. Kohlbrenner, *A History of Catholic Education in the United States*, New York, 1937.

[30] Walter H. Beck, *Lutheran Elementary Schools in the United States*, St. Louis, 1939.

[31] Howard H. Brinton, *Quaker Education in Theory and Practice*, Wallingford (Pa.), 1940.

2. Jewish education was varied, but generally rejected the maintenance of separate schools. In the nineteenth century, Jews developed a number of Congregational Day Schools (German Jews), Sunday Schools (Reform Jews), Yeshivah (Russian Jews)—reflecting a variety of culture among the Jewish immigrants.[32]

Private schools and agencies

1. Many of the experimental programs in education were first conducted in private schools or agencies. These include education of the blind (1832); education of the deaf-mute (1817; the work of Thomas H. Gallaudet).

2. The strong tradition of the academy continued in some private institutions after the academy declined in the latter part of the nineteenth century. Mostly reserved for the wealthy, some of the best-known academies include Phillips Academy (1778), Deerfield Academy (1797), Bradford Junior College (1803), Groton (1884), Howe Military School (1884), and the Thacher School (1889).[33]

Higher education in nineteenth-century America

Major issues in nineteenth-century American higher education include (1) private *versus* state control of colleges; (2) definition of the college curriculum; (3) the college *versus* the university.[34]

1. Following the Revolution many attempts were made to change the colonial colleges into state institutions. In the

[32] Alexander M. Dushkin, *Jewish Education in New York City,* New York, 1918.

[33] Oscar F. Adams, *Some Famous American Schools,* Boston, 1903.

[34] George Schmidt, *The Liberal Arts College,* Rutgers University Press, 1957; Richard Hofstadter and C. DeWitt Hardy, *The Development and Scope of Higher Education in the United States,* Columbia University Press, 1952; John S. Brubacher and Willis Rudy, *Higher Education in Transition,* New York, 1968; Frederick Rudolph, *The American College and University, A History,* New York, 1962; William W. Brickman and Stanley Lehrer, eds., *A Century of Higher Education,* New York, 1962.

Dartmouth College Case (1819), the United States Supreme Court held that states could not abrogate vested rights and privileges of college charters. The decision opened the way for the development of church and private colleges.

2. Struggle between a rigid classical curriculum and one that allowed subject election more responsive to the new science dominated much of the college thinking of the century. The classical conservative view was stated in the *Yale Report* of 1825. Leaders in the fight for the elective program included President Francis Wayland of Brown University, President Andrew D. White of Cornell, and President Charles W. Eliot of Harvard. By the end of the century, the elective system had largely won, with the problem essentially defined as the degree of election.

3. Expansion of higher education caused conflict between advocates of the liberal arts college (English college tradition) and the concept of the research university (European, German) wherein all knowledge was taught and investigated.

State and national higher education

1. State colleges and universities were of three origins: (a) those founded in the original thirteen colonies; (b) those created out of the original land grants of the Northwest Ordinances and the Louisiana Purchase; (c) those created out of the Morrill Act of 1862.

2. **The Morrill Act of 1862** granted each of the states 30,000 acres of public land for each senator and representative; those states without public lands were given scrip. Funds were to be used for "the endowment, support, and maintenance" of at least one college in each state for the teaching of agriculture and mechanic arts. The Hatch Act (1887) and the Adams Act (1906) provided for agricultural experimental stations in the land-grant colleges. A second Morrill Act (1890) carefully defined the use of federal funds for instruction in agriculture and mechanic arts.[35]

[35] Edward D. Eddy, *Colleges for Our Land and Time: The Land Grant Idea in American Education,* New York, 1956; James L. Morrill, *The On Going State University,* New York, 1960.

3. Although a national university was never established, Congress set up the United States Military Academy at West Point (1802) and the Naval Academy at Annapolis (1845).

4. In a class by themselves were municipal colleges and universities. These included College of Charleston, South Carolina (1837, founded in 1785); University of Louisville (1837); College of the City of New York (1849); University of Cincinnati (1870).[36]

Denominational colleges

1. These were largely agencies of religious and cultural advancement in frontier America.

2. Over 500 denominational colleges were founded in nineteenth-century America, many of them short-lived.[37]

Professional education

1. Early professional schools were theological academies. Over 150 theological schools were founded in the nineteenth century.[38]

2. **Technical education.** In addition to the United States Military Academy (1802), important foundations include Rennsselaer Polytechnic Institute at Troy, New York (1824), Lawrence Scientific School at Harvard (1847), Sheffield Scientific School at Yale (1852). Technical schools were also found in land-grant colleges and in state schools of mines, which included the Colorado School of Mines (1871), South Dakota State School of Mines (1885), and the Michigan College of Mining and Technology (1886).[39]

3. **Medical education.** The first medical department was established in Philadelphia (1765), with later medical depart-

[36] Roscoe H. Eckelberry, *History of the Municipal University in the United States,* Washington (D.C.), 1932.

[37] Donald G. Tewksbury, *The Founding of American Colleges and Universities Before the Civil War,* Columbia University, Teachers College, 1932.

[38] Robert L. Kelly, *Theological Education in America,* New York, 1924.

[39] Charles R. Mann, *A Study of Engineering Education,* New York, 1918.

ments established at King's (Columbia) College (1767), Harvard (1782), Dartmouth (1797), Yale (1811). Before 1860, medical instruction was given largely by practicing physicians with some college affiliation. The American Medical Association was founded in 1847. Reforms in medical education came with the reorganization of the Harvard Medical School (1871) and the opening of the Johns Hopkins University Medical School (1893). Many of the inadequate, proprietary medical schools closed after the publication of the Flexner Report in 1910.[40]

4. **Legal education.** The first law school granting a degree was at William and Mary (1779). The Harvard Law School was founded in 1817. "Case method" was originated by Christopher C. Langdell (1826–1906) at Harvard in 1870.[41]

5. **Graduate education**

a) For most of the nineteenth century, American colleges remained liberal arts colleges, with little or no provision for graduate study. The M.A., where it was granted, was bestowed for the payment of a fee and without additional study.

b) Graduate study was first significantly organized at Yale (1858), with conferment of the first Ph. D. in 1861.

c) The example of German research universities and the study of American students in Germany brought about a movement for change.

d) The first truly graduate university was organized at Johns Hopkins University (1876) under the leadership of Daniel Coit Gilman.[42]

Higher education for women

1. Leaders in the movement include Mary Lyon, Emma Willard, Ellen H. Richards, and Catherine Beecher.

[40] William F. Norwood, *Medical Education in the United States Before the Civil War,* Philadelphia, 1944; Abraham Flexner, *Medical Education in the United States and Canada,* New York, 1910.

[41] William Hurst, *The Growth of American Law,* Boston, 1950.

[42] W. Carson Ryan, *Studies in Early Graduate Education,* New York, 1939; Richard J. Storr, *The Beginnings of Graduate Education in America,* University of Chicago, 1953.

2. Mary Lyon opened Mount Holyoke (1837); Emma Willard founded a seminary at Troy (1821) and continued an advocate for women's education.

3. Co-education dates from the founding of Oberlin College, Ohio (1834), and gained strong support in midwestern state universities.

4. Women's colleges include Smith (1871), Vassar (1861), Wellesley (1877), Bryn Mawr (1880), Radcliffe (1874) as a Harvard annex, Barnard (1894).[43]

Teacher education

1. The success of state normal schools abroad attracted the attention of leaders in American education.

2. Samuel R. Hall's *Lectures on Schoolkeeping* (1829) was one of the earliest texts in teacher education and widely used in the normal schools of the East before 1860.

3. State and city normal schools progressed rapidly from 1835 to 1860, with the first state normal school opened at Lexington, Massachusetts, in 1839. A normal school was established at Albany, New York, in 1844; in Connecticut in 1850; and by 1865, in many principal cities.

4. Oswego Normal School (Oswego, New York) was founded in 1853, with Edward A. Sheldon as its first principal.

5. Teacher training at colleges and universities developed slowly. Significant developments were the establishment of George Peabody College for Teachers (1875; reorganized 1911), and Teachers College, Columbia University (1887; part of Columbia, 1898).

6. The National Teachers' Association was founded in 1857; the name was changed to National Education Association in 1870.

7. By 1870, better normal schools had a three-year curriculum, with the tendency toward expansion to a four-year

[43] Thomas Woody, *A History of Women's Education in the United States,* 2 vols., New York, 1929; Mabel Newcomer, *A Century of Higher Education for American Women,* New York, 1959.

program. In the university departments of education, few specialized courses were offered before 1900.[44]

[44] Merle L. Borrowman, ed., *Teacher Education in America: A Documentary History*, New York, 1965; *Professional Teacher Education*, Washington, D.C.: American Association of Colleges for Teacher Education, 1968; F. Cordasco, *Teacher Education in the United States: A Guide for Foreign Students*, New York (Institute for International Education), 1971; Kevin Ryan, *Teacher Education* (74th Yearbook of the National Society for the Study of Education), Chicago, 1975.

Chapter XII

AMERICAN EDUCATION IN THE TWENTIETH CENTURY

Historical background. Many of the changes in the nineteenth century were consolidated in the twentieth; much of the educational change was translated into innovations dictated by vast social and economic reverberations graphically highlighted by the two world wars. The presidencies of Theodore Roosevelt (1901–1909) and William H. Taft (1909–1913) witnessed overseas expansion and American involvement in world politics. Woodrow Wilson brought to his presidency (1913–1921) a zealous ardor to correct the inequalities of the American social and economic order and guided the nation through World War I (1917–1918) and postwar adjustments. Postwar prosperity was succeeded by a depression in 1929. Election of Franklin D. Roosevelt in 1932 brought the nation to the staggering economic task imposed by eleven million unemployed and threatened social collapse. The New Deal program of Roosevelt represented emergency measures to deal with the economic crisis. In the decade 1931 to 1941, political conditions throughout the world were having increased impact on the United States, with ultimate involvement in World War II (1939–1945). The presidencies of Harry S. Truman (1945–1953) and Dwight D. Eisenhower (1953–1961) saw American idealism turned to collective security as an answer to aggression and world tension. Adoption by forty-six nations of the United Nations Charter (1945) suggested means of attaining world security. United States foreign policy was dominated by the effort to develop a peaceful coexistence of the communist and the free world. The presidencies of John F. Kennedy (1960-1963) and Lyndon B. Johnson (1963-1968)) witnessed the initiations and implementation of broad programs of domestic social reformation, but the inauguration of Richard M. Nixon as president in 1969 found the country bitterly divided over the issues of the Vietnam War, race relations, and urban deterioration. The controversy over the Watergate revelations, President Nixon's resignation in 1974, and the early presidency of Gerald R. Ford (1974) found the country in a deepening economic recession, with some evidences of economic upturn in mid-1975.[1]

Educational growth (1900–1960)

From 1890 to 1960, American educational history is a history of growth.

1. By 1918, all states had compulsory education laws, which made universal education a reality.
2. From 1890 to 1930, the school year was increased from 135 to 172 days.
3. By 1960, the school year in most states was 180 days.
4. Figures of growth are averages; some states and regions were far below the averages.[2]

A complete American school system had been established by 1900, but with the role of the private school undefined.

[1] Arthur S. Link, *American Epoch: A History of the United States since the 1890's*, New York, 1967; Harold U. Faulkner, *American Political and Social History*, 7th ed., New York, 1957; Oliver W. Larkin, *Art and Life in America*, New York, 1960; Barton J. Bernstein, ed., *Towards a New Past: Dissenting Essays in American History*, New York, 1968; Theodore H. White, *Breach of Faith: The Fall of Richard Nixon*, New York, 1975.

[2] Harry Moore, *Modern Education in America*, Boston, 1962; Edward J. Power, *Education for American Democracy*, New York, 1958; Norman Woelfel, *Educational Goals for America*, Washington (D.C.), 1962.

1. State control of education resulted in problems of definition of the role of private schools.

2. In *Pierce et al* v. *Society of Sisters* (268 U.S. 510, 1925) the United States Supreme Court decided that a state law compelling parents, who had sent their children to Catholic and other private schools, to send them only to public schools was unconstitutional.[3]

Educational opportunity

1. Extension of educational opportunity in twentieth-century America saw the general development of the nursery school, the junior high school, the community college, and the study of educational opportunity for minority groups.

2. Attack on the doctrine of "separate but equal facilities" in education for the American Negro led to its overthrow by the United States Supreme Court in *Brown* v. *Kansas* (347 U.S. 483, 1954), which notified states that public schools were to be integrated with "all deliberate speed."[4]

3. Many communities in the North and South integrated their schools, but some difficulties developed in the integration of the public schools of Little Rock, Arkansas (1958–1959), New Orleans (1961–1962), and in the enrollment of the first Negro student at the University of Mississippi (1962).

4. The peaceful enrollment of a Negro student at Clemson College, South Carolina (1963), where no integration of

[3] Other significant cases and materials on the role of the private school, religion, and that of government include: (a) *Cochran* v. *Louisiana Board of Education* (281 U.S. 370, 1930), in which it was held that a state may furnish free textbooks to parochial school pupils on the theory of child benefits; (b) *Everson* v. *Board of Education* (330 U.S. 1, 1947), which held that states may furnish bus transportation to parochial school pupils; (c) *Zorach* v. *Clauson* (343 U.S. 306, 1952), which allowed released time classes on school time outside public school buildings; (d) National Education Act (1958) allowed private schools loans from the federal government for improvement of their programs in science, mathematics, and foreign languages. See William W. Brickman and Stanley Lehrer, eds., *Religion, Government and Education,* New York, 1961. See also John J. McGrath, *Church and State in America,* Milwaukee, 1962.

[4] Don Shoemaker, ed., *With All Deliberate Speed,* New York, 1957; William W. Brickman and Stanley Lehrer, eds., *The Countdown on Segregated Education,* New York, 1960.

schools had been implemented, suggested a growing compliance with the law of the land.

The science of education

Herbart's influence in the United States was extended along scientific lines by the study of Americans at European universities in the late nineteenth century.[5]

1. The German psychologist Wilhelm Wundt's (1832–1920) publication of his *Principles of Psychology* (1874) opened the way for the growth of experimental psychology.
2. In America, William James (1842–1910) influenced educators on the role of psychology and teaching. His *Principles of Psychology* (1890) was widely read and stimulated much of the work of James McKeen Cattell (1860–1944) and of G. Stanley Hall (1844–1924).

Edward L. Thorndike (1874–1949) formulated the system of connectionistic, stimulus-response, psychology in his *Educational Psychology* (1913).

1. Connectionism and its explanation of learning followed the "laws" of effects, exercise, and readiness.
2. Although mechanistic, Thorndike's explanation of learning influenced most of the teachers of the early twentieth century.[6]

The mental testing movement

1. Mental testing was first successfully demonstrated by the French psychologists Alfred Binet (1875–1911) and Theodore Simon (1873–   ).
2. In America the testing movement was inaugurated by Lewis B. Terman (1877–1956), who revised and published Binet's test in 1916.
3. The movement introduced the IQ (Intelligence Quo-

[5] See pp. 101-103.

[6] Ernest R. Hilgard and Gordon H. Bower, *Theories of Learning* 3rd ed., New York, 1966.

tient) into American education, and led to the standardization of tests and to their wide use.[7]

Educational theory

Progressive education, which advocated the elimination of the nineteenth-century class formalism and the substitution of a new learning-living methodology, begins with the work of Francis W. Parker (1837–1902) in Quincy, Massachusetts. The work of John Dewey (1859–1952) was to formulate a new educational philosophy that challenged both the ends and means of traditional education.[8]

1. Dewey's principles were experimentally evolved at the Laboratory School at the University of Chicago (1896–1903) and during his long tenure at Columbia University.

2. His chief works include *School and Society* (1899), *How We Think* (1909), *Democracy and Education* (1916), *Human Nature and Conduct* (1922), *Experience and Education* (1938).

3. Basic Dewey ideas include: (a) a closer relationship between the schools and life; (b) "Teach students, not subjects"; (c) "Education is not a preparation for life; it is life"; (d) rejection of formalism that characterized the graded elementary school and its curriculum.

4. The Progressive Education Association (1918–1944) largely advocated Dewey's ideas, although Dewey was critical of some of its measures.

5. Important figures in the progressive movement include William H. Kilpatrick (1871-1965) and Harold O. Rugg (1866-1960).[9]

[7] J. Raymond Gerberich, Harry A. Greene, and A. N. Jorgensen, *Measurement and Evaluation in the Modern School,* New York, 1962.

[8] For a guide to the enormous material on Dewey, see Milton H. Thomas, *A Bibliography of John Dewey,* 2nd ed., New York, 1962; Melvin C. Baker, *Foundation of John Dewey's Educational Theory,* New York, 1955; William W. Brickman and Stanley Lehrer, eds., *John Dewey: Master Educator,* 2nd ed., New York, 1961; Martin S. Dworkin, ed., *Dewey on Education: Selections,* New York, 1959.

[9] Harold O. Rugg, *Foundations for American Education,* New York, 1947.

6. Experiments resulting from Dewey's influence include: University of Missouri Laboratory School, J. L. Meriam (1904); Speyer School of Teachers College, Columbia University, Frank M. McMurry (1904); MacDonald County Rural School, Missouri, Ellsworth Collins (*ca.* 1905); School of Organic Education, Fairhope, Alabama, Marrietta Johnson (1907); The Dalton Contract Plan, Helen Parkhurst (1919); The Winnetka Plan, Carleton Washburne (1919); The Gary (Platoon) Plan, William Wirt (1908–1915).[10]

Opposition to progressive education

1. Opposition, called essentialism, arose out of the belief that the educational practices of progressives were anti-educational.

2. The leader of the essentialists was William C. Bagley (1874–1946), who advocated a return to the fundamentals in education.

3. In their opposition to progressive methodology, essentialists eventually included many groups that advocated different educational theories, which embraced realism, idealism, rational humanism, and Christian humanism.[11]

The eight-year study

1. The study (1930-1938) involved a comparison of the performance of high school students who were instructed under the old methodology and those in the progressive schools.

2. Generally, the study confirmed the superiority of the new progressive methods.[12]

[10] For all of these experiments and the history of progressive education, see Lawrence A. Cremin, *The Transformation of the School,* New York, 1961.

[11] After 1946, powerful support for the essentialist point of view came from the subject matter departments of the colleges. Arthur Bestor has led the essentialists (traditionalists) since 1952 and took part in the establishment of the Council for Basic Education in 1956. See Arthur Bestor, *Educational Wastelands,* University of Illinois Press, 1953; and his *Restoration of Learning,* New York, 1955. See also Ernest E. Bayles, "The Present State of Educational Theory in the United States," *School and Society,* January 17, 1959, pp. 5-8.

[12] Wilfred M. Aiken, *The Story of the Eight Year Study,* New York, 1942.

Educational crisis

1. Criticism of American public schools (1948–1970's) arose from (a) self-appointed critics of the public school and its program; (b) comparison of European (particularly Russian) and American education; (c) efforts to study and improve public schools.[13]

2. Problems that have emerged from these criticisms include:

a) Shall public education and its curriculum for all children be continued at the high school level, or shall high school education become again highly selective, as it was in the early decades of the century?

b) To the fundamentals of the elementary school, shall we add the continuation of basic or general education on the junior and senior high school levels?[14]

c) Shall the emerging junior high school curriculum be freed to perform the special functions for which it was established?

d) What shall comprise the curriculum for more effective work in international and intercultural education?[15]

e) How must the grave curricular issues be faced as desegregation takes place in the schools?[16]

f) How and where shall we include in our curriculum

[13] C. W. Scott, *et al.*, eds., *Public Education Under Criticism,* Englewood Cliffs (N.J.), 1959.

[14] *Behavioral Goals of General Education in High School,* Russell Sage Foundation, New York, 1957; F. S. Chase and H. A. Anderson, *The High School in a New Era,* University of Chicago Press, 1958; James B. Conant, *The American High School Today,* New York, 1959; *Education in the Junior High School Years,* New York, 1960; *Slums and Suburbs,* New York, 1961.

[15] *Intergroup Relations Bibliography* (Connecticut State Inter-Racial Commission, 1948) lists twenty-nine independent organizations and eleven state agencies engaged in some phase of intergroup activity. See Robert B. Knapp, *Social Integration in Urban Communities,* New York, 1960.

[16] *Action Patterns in School Desegregation,* Phi Delta Kappa, 1959; the *Southern School News* (Southern Education Reporting Service) offers factual and impartial information on desegregation.

the problems and knowledge of the nuclear age, which were not in existence a little more than a decade ago?

g) What shall be done for the gifted and talented students?[17]

h) How can we make maximum effective use of newer methods, newer media, new departures in teach-in?[18]

i) How can we provide an adequate program of general and specialized education for *all* children when our school age population is growing so fast that we cannot build additional schools fast enough to house them, and our population has become so mobile that 20 per cent of the people in most communities change school each year?[19]

j) How can the schools, labor, and industry cooperate to start "work programs" for youth as early as the junior high school grades?[20]

3. **The federal government and the educational crisis**

a) The 85th Congress passed the National Defense Education Act (1958), which appropriated money through 1966 for loans to college students; graduate fellowships; guidance counseling and testing, primarily on the secondary level; and provided money to strengthen programs in science, mathematics, foreign languages.

b) The presidencies of John F. Kennedy (1961–1963) and Lyndon B. Johnson (1963–1968) witnessed the initiations and implementation of broad programs of domestic social re-

[17] A. Harry Passow, "The Talented Youth Project: A Report on Research Under Way," *Educational Research Bulletin*, vol. 36 (September 11, 1957), pp. 199-206; Maurice E. Freehill, *The Gifted Student*, New York, 1960.

[18] F. B. Stratemeyer, *et al.*, *Developing a Curriculum for Modern Living*, rev. ed., New York, 1958.

[19] J. Lloyd Trump and Dorsey Baynham, *Focus on Change: Guide to Better Schools*, Chicago, 1961; C. S. Fletcher, ed., *Education: The Challenges Ahead*, New York, 1962.

[20] I. Minor Gwynn, *Curriculum Principles and Social Trends*, 4th ed., New York, 1969.

formation; the programs affecting education (although undergoing continual change) have largely been continued during the presidencies of Richard M. Nixon (1969–1974), and Gerald R. Ford (1974 —).

The major catalyst of this new awareness and direct federal intervention was the Civil Rights agitation and ideological struggle out of which emerged the enactment of the Civil Rights Act of 1964. The principal educational legislation enacted by the Congress in the 1960s and 1970s included:

1964	Economic Opportunity Act
1964	Civil Rights Act
1965	Elementary and Secondary Education Act
1965	Higher Education Act
1966	Adult Education Act (Amendments, ESEA)
1967	Bilingual Education (Title VII of ESEA)
1967	Education Professions Development Act
1968	Vocational Education Act Amendments
1968	Juvenile Delinquency and Control Act
1972	Education Amendments of 1972
1974	Education Amendments of 1974
1976	Education Appropriations Act

Each of the acts includes many components, and many of the acts were (and are) being amended to meet new needs. The *Economic Opportunity Act* included Headstart, different facets of community action programs, the Job Corps, Vista; the *Elementary and Secondary Education Act*, in a broad range of titles, addressed itself to meeting the educational needs of socio-economically deprived children (in 1969, ESEA expended $1.314 billion); the *Education Professions Development Act* brought together under a single administrative management all programs concerned with educational personnel.[21]

Educational issues of the 1970s

American education in the 1970s has sought to consolidate

[21] See generally, *Catalog of Federal Domestic Assistance*: Compiled *by the Office of Economic Opportunity*, Washington, 1969, and *Supplements*; also, F. Cordasco, *The Equality of Educational Opportunity: A Bibliography of Selected References*, Totowa, N.J., 1973.

the gains of the 1960s and to resolve many of the problems which remain, *e.g.*:[22]

a) The controversy over equality of educational opportunity: the legal-financial issue. As important as the struggle to achieve integration was the legal-financial controversy to change the pattern of local district school finance designed to benefit poorer communities. Significant cases include *Serrano v. Priest* (1971) in which the California Supreme Court held that the traditional pattern of local school finance discriminated against those living in poorer communities; and the U.S. Supreme Court's reversal of this view in the *Rodriguez* case (1973).[23]

b) Conflicts over genetic and environmental determinants of intelligence. In the late 1960s, inspired by the reemergence of the genetic view of intelligence, controversy developed over the "nature"-"nurture" interactive effects in the educational process.[24]

c) Conflicts over the education of culturally different groups. Controversy continues in relating American schools and their programs to the conflicts which exist between middle-class assumptions of the schools and the divergent values and cultures of minority groups.[25]

d) Emerging power relationships in school control. The continuing issue of "Who should control the schools?" besets American education. The center of the question is the role to be played by the national government, religious and private schools, and by parents and the community. With the Civil Rights movement of the 1960s and 1970s, traditional arrangements of power and control have been challenged.[26]

[22] Julius Menacker and Erwin Pollock, eds., *Emerging Educational Issues: Conflicts and Contrasts*, Boston, 1974.

[23] Thomas A. Shannon, "Rodriguez: A Dream Shattered or a Call for Reform," *Phi Delta Kappan* (May 1973), pp. 587–588, 640.

[24] David K. Cohen, "Does I.Q. Matter," *Commentary* (April 1972), pp. 51–59. See also the controversial genetic views of Arthur R. Jensen, "How Much Can We Boost I.Q. and Scholastic Achievement?" *Harvard Educational Review* (Winter 1969), pp. 78–88.

[25] James S. Coleman, "Social and Cultural Integration and Educational Policy," in Herbert J. Walberg and Andrew T. Kopans, eds., *Rethinking Urban Education* (1972), pp. 125–132.

[26] See generally, *Schools for the 1970's and Beyond: A Call to Action,* Washington, D.C.: National Education Association, 1970.

e) Alternatives to traditional schooling. Critics of the public schools have proposed a wide range of alternatives: open schools, schools without walls, educational parks, street academies, magnet schools, schools-within-a-school, integration modes. The free school movement included (March 1973 estimate) some 15,000 students and 3000 staff members. The *idea* of alternatives to public schooling was more important than its concrete applications and greater development was expected in the 1970s.[27]

f) The schools and the counterculture. In the late 1960s (and continuing across the 1970s) the schools were confronted by the emergence of a youth counterculture which opposed a wide range of established values.[28]

g) The challenge of accountability. A major development in the 1970s has been for better accounting of professional educational practice, and growing dissatisfaction with the quantity and quality of common school education.[29]

Selected References

Part V: American Education

A. GENERAL WORKS

Bereday, George Z., and Luigi Volpicelli, eds. *Public Education in America.* New York, 1958.

Boone, Richard G. *Education in the United States: Its History from the Earliest Settlements.* New York, 1889.

Butts, R. Freeman, and Lawrence A. Cremin. *A History of Education in American Culture.* New York, 1953.

Cordasco, Francesco, and William W. Brickman. *A Bibliography of American Educational History: An Annotated and Classified Guide.* New York, 1975. (Some 3000 entries including sections on collections of source materials, historiography, etc.)

[27] Vernon H. Smith, "Options in Public Education: The Quiet Revolution," *Phi Delta Kappan*, vol. 54, No. 7 (1973), pp. 434–435.

[28] James S. Coleman, "How Do the Young Become Adults?" *Phi Delta Kappan* (December 1972), pp. 226–230.

[29] Gene V. Glass, "The Many Faces of Educational Accountability," *Phi Delta Kappan* (June 1972), pp. 636–639.

Cremin, Lawrence A. *History of American Education.* New York, 1970 —. [Projected as a 3 volume comprehensive history: Volume I, *American Education: The Colonial Experience, 1607–1783* (1970)].

Cubberley, Ellwood P. *Public Education in the United States,* rev. ed. Boston, 1934.

Curti, Merle. *The Social Ideas of American Educators.* New York, 1935. Reissued with additional material, New Jersey, Littlefield, Adams & Co., 1959.

Dexter, Edwin G. *A History of Education in the United States.* New York, 1904.

Drake, William E. *The American School in Transition.* New York, 1955.

Edwards, Newton, and Herman G. Richey. *The School in the American Social Order,* 2nd ed. Boston, 1963.

Good, H. G., and James D. Teller. *A History of American Education,* 3rd ed. New York, 1973.

Gutek, Gerald L. *An Historical Introduction to American Education.* New York, 1970.

Kandel, I. L. *American Education in the Twentieth Century.* Cambridge, 1957.

Knight, Edgar W. *Education in the United States,* 3rd rev. ed. Boston, 1951.

———. *Fifty Years of American Education.* New York, 1952.

Meyer, Adolphe E. *An Educational History of the American People,* 2nd ed. New York, 1967.

Monroe, Paul. *Founding of the American Public School System.* New York, 1940.

Noble, Stuart G. *History of American Education,* rev. ed. New York, 1954.

Park, Joe. *The Rise of American Education: An Annotated Bibliography.* Northwestern University Press, 1965.

Potter, Robert E. *The Stream of American Education.* New York, 1967.

Pulliam, John D. *History of Education in America.* Columbus, Ohio, 1968.

Rippa, S. Alexander. *Education in a Free Society: An American History,* rev. ed. New York, 1971.

Slosson, Edwin E. *The American Spirit in Education.* New York, 1900.

Thayer, V. T. *The Role of the School in American Society.* New York, 1960.

———. *Formative Ideas in American Education.* New York, 1967.

Thwing, Charles F. *A History of Education in the United States Since the Civil War.* Boston, 1910.

Wiggin, Gladys A. *Education and Nationalism: An Historical Interpretation of American Education.* New York, 1962.

Winship, Albert E. *Great American Educators.* New York, 1900.

B. READINGS AND COLLECTION OF SOURCES

Arrowood, Charles F. *Thomas Jefferson and Education in a Republic.* New York, 1930.

Brubacher, John S., ed. *Henry Barnard on Education.* New York, 1931.

Best, John Hardin, and Robert T. Sidwell. *The American Legacy of Learning: Readings in the History of Education.* Philadelphia, 1967.

Bremner, Robert H., ed. *Children and Youth in America: A Documentary History.* 3 vols. in 5. Cambridge, Mass., 1970–1974.

Calhoun, Daniel, ed. *The Educating of Americans: A Documentary History.* Boston, 1969.

Cohen, Sol, ed. *Education in the United States: A Documentary History.* 5 vols. New York, 1974.

Cremin, Lawrence A., ed. *Classics in Education.* New York, 1957 —.

Cubberley, Ellwood P. *Readings in Public Education in the United States.* Boston, 1934.

Goodsell, Willystine, ed. *Pioneers of Women's Education.* New York, 1931.

Gross, Carl H., and Charles C. Chandler. *The History of American Education Through Readings.* New York, 1964.

Knight, Edgar W. *A Documentary History of Education in the South Before 1860*, 5 vols. Chapel Hill, 1949–1953.

———, and Clifton L. Hall. *Readings in American Educational History.* New York, 1951.

Monroe, Paul, ed. *Readings in the Founding of the American Public School System.* New York, 1940.

Rippa, S. Alexander. *Educational Ideas in America: A Documentary History.* New York, 1969.

Seybolt, Robert F. *Source Studies in American Colonial Education: The Private School.* Urbana, 1925.

Woody, Thomas, ed. *Educational Views of Benjamin Franklin.* New York, 1931.

C. SOME RECENT SPECIALIZED STUDIES

Barzun, Jacques. *The American University.* New York, 1968.

Binder, Frederick M. *The Age of the Common School, 1830–1865.* New York, 1974.

Brauner, Charles J. *American Educational Theory.* New York, 1964.

Brickman, William W., and Stanley Lehrer, eds. *Religion, Government, and Education.* New York, 1961.

Brown, E. Ellsworth. *The Making of Our Middle Schools.* New York, 1907. (Rep., Littlefield, 1970)

Brubacher, John S., and W. S. Rudy. *Higher Education in Transition: An American History, 1636–1968.* New York, 1968.

Cohen, Sheldon S. *A History of Colonial Education, 1607–1776.* New York, 1974.

Cordasco, Francesco. *Daniel C. Gilman and the Protean Ph.D.: The Shaping of American Graduate Education.* Leiden, 1960. (Rep., Rowman and Littlefield, 1973)

———, and Eugene Bucchioni. *Puerto Rican Children in Mainland Schools.* New York, 1968. Rev. ed., 1972.

Cremin, Lawrence A. *The Transformation of the School: Progressivism in American Education, 1876–1957.* New York, 1961.

Economics and Politics of Public Education, 12 nos. Syracuse University Press, 1962–1963.

Graham, Patricia A. *Community and Class in American Education, 1865–1918.* New York, 1974.

Greer, Colin. *The Great School Legend: A Revisionist Interpretation of American Public Education.* New York, 1972.

Gumbert, Edgar B., and Joel H. Spring. *The Superschool and the Superstate: American Education in the Twentieth Century, 1918–1970.* New York, 1974.

Hillson, Maurie, Francesco Cordasco, and Francis P. Purcell. *Education in the Urban Community: The Schools and the Crisis of the Cities.* New York, 1969.

Karier, Clarence J., ed. *Shaping the American Educational State, 1900 to the Present.* New York, 1975.

Keppel, Francis. *The Necessary Revolution in American Education.* New York, 1966.

Krug, Edward A. *The Shaping of the American High School*, 2 vols. Madison, Wisconsin, 1969. (Vol. I: 1880–1920; Vol. II: 1920–1941)

McCluskey, Neil G., S. J. *Public Schools and Moral Education: The Influence of Horace Mann, William Torrey Harris, and John Dewey*. New York, 1958.

McLaughlin, Milbery W. *Evaluation and Reform: The Elementary and Secondary Education Act of 1965, Title I.* Cambridge, Mass., 1975.

Madsen, David L. *Early National Education, 1776–1830*. New York, 1974.

Nietz, John A. *Old Textbooks*. Pittsburgh, 1961.

Perkinson, Henry J. *The Imperfect Panacea: American Faith in Education, 1865–1965*. New York, 1968.

Pratte, Richard. *The Public School Movement: A Critical Study*. New York, 1973.

Rudolph, Frederick. *The American College and University: A History*. New York, 1962.

Sanford, Nevitt, ed. *The American College*. New York, 1962.

Thomas, Russell. *The Search for a Common Learning: General Education, 1800–1960*. New York, 1962.

Tyack, David B. *The One Best System: A History of American Urban Education*. Cambridge, Mass., 1974.

Wesley, Edgar B. *NEA: The First Hundred Years*. New York, 1957.

Part VI

SOME RECENT EUROPEAN DEVELOPMENTS

Chapter XIII

SOME RECENT EUROPEAN DEVELOPMENTS

German education since World War I

Developments in the Weimar Republic (1919–1933)

1. A common four-year foundation school (*Grundschule*) was made compulsory for all German children.

2. *Grundschule* was to provide basic preparation for the work of the upper four grades (*oberstufe*) of the elementary schools and for entrance to the traditional middle and secondary schools.

3. New secondary schools were established (six-year *Aufbauschule; Deutsche Oberschule*) from which students might enter universities.

4. Reforms in teacher education were intended to abolish caste in education.

5. Liberal scholarship aid for higher education was promoted.

Education under the Nazi regime (1933–1945)

1. The general aim was to bring every individual into harmony with the will of the nation.

2. It was anti-intellectual and based on the idea of the *Volk-State,* with the state as the only legal education authority.

3. The few changes in the organization of the schools included: (a) the establishment of nursery schools for children of working mothers; (b) one additional year of compulsory education for city children, which was spent among farmers and peasants for physical training and political indoctrination (*The Landjahr*); (c) the establishment of political schools for leaders (*Ordensburgen,* Adolf Hitler Schools, etc.).

4. Secondary and elementary curricula drew their inspiration from local environment and Nazi ideology.

5. On all educational levels, teachers and school administrators were predominantly Nazi in allegiance and spirit.

Postwar reorganization of German education (1945–1949)

1. Germany was decentralized following its defeat in 1945.

2. Each of the areas (*Lander*) had its own ministry of education.

3. The Allied Control Council set up an Education Committee, although no uniform system of education for all of occupied Germany was achieved.

Education in the German Federal Republic (West Germany) 1949–

1. The German Federal Republic is a federation of independent states, which send to the central government at Bonn their elected representatives.

2. Education is under the supervisory authority of the states, in which great variety exists.

3. Generally, the states have established a foundation school (*Grundschule*) of four or six grades, leading to *Mittelschulen,* and a variety of secondary schools, which lead to "the maturity examination" and the universities.

British education since World War I

The Fisher Act (1918) led to many organizational changes in English education.

1. The school leaving age was advanced from twelve to fourteen.

2. The school leaving age was further extended (Act of 1921) to sixteen, at the option of the local educational authority.

3. Those not "beneficially employed" were required (Act of 1936) to stay in school until age fifteen.

4. A national ministry of education was created (Act of 1944).

The Education Act of 1944 laid a legal basis for progressive education.

1. The compulsory school age was defined as that between five and fifteen.

2. The number of L.E.A.'s was reduced and the function of county authority was enlarged.

3. Religious instruction was made compulsory, but parents may ask exemption.

4. Schools were classied into: (a) county schools; (b) controlled schools; (c) aided schools.

5. Controlled and aided schools are largely denominational, and the degree of control depends on the amount of money furnished by L.E.A.

6. The stages of education are: (a) primary, for pupils under twelve; (b) secondary, for pupils over twelve, who are of compulsory school age; (c) further education.

English schools in operation

The primary school is divided into two divisions: infant school (five to seven); junior school (seven to eleven plus).

2. The pupil goes from primary school to one of three types of secondary schools: modern secondary; technical high school; grammar school.

3. Fitness examination of students for secondary schools is taken by primary school students at age eleven plus, and the decision for choice of school is in most cases final.

4. The modern secondary school is generally non-selective and is similar to the multi-curricular American high school.

5. Grammar schools prepare students for universities and open opportunities in business, civil, and military life.

6. The technical high school prepares students for engineering, building trades, etc.

The comprehensive secondary school

1. The creation of a single secondary school for all students, regardless of ability and social position, is the avowed aim of some members of the Labor Party.

2. The issue is both political and educational.

French education since 1918

Reform movement dating from World War I for a common school (*l'école unique*) led to some changes.

1. Between 1930 and 1937, fees in secondary schools were abolished, and the main goal was the establishment of a foundation curriculum common to both primary and secondary schools.

2. Nazi occupation (1940–1945) arrested all attempts at reform.

The Langevin Plan (1947)

1. This called for the creation of a common school (ages seven to eleven).

2. It advocated a seven-year secondary school adapted to the academic and vocational abilities of students.

3. At age eighteen, all students would be examined and given certificates, the *baccalaureat* being reserved for those in the academic section intended for the universities.

4. The Delbos Act (1949) and the André Marie Act (1953) were intended to implement the plan, but little success has been achieved.

French schools in operation

1. Education is compulsory between the ages of six and fourteen.

2. The first stage includes preschools, elementary schools, and complementary classes attached to elementary schools (ages six to eleven).

3. French secondary education is divided into two stages: (a) first stage (*cycle d'orientation*) for students between the ages of eleven and fourteen; (b) second stage (*cycle de determination*) for students between the ages of fifteen and eighteen.

4. Two main types of secondary schools have evolved: *lycées* (national institutions); and *collèges* (municipal institutions) which are all seven-year schools.

5. The *Collège Moderne* and the *Collège Technique* are recent developments in the adaption of secondary curriculum to contemporary needs.

6. National schools in France are organized on the principle of complete neutrality in religion. State schools are closed on Thursdays, which are set aside for religious instruction by the churches.

Education in the Soviet Union

The Revolution and overthrow of the Imperial Russian Government in 1917 resulted in a complete overhauling of the Russian educational system.

1. Illiteracy in 1917 amounted to 85 or 90 per cent, with diversity of languages and nationalities.

2. The organization of the Soviet Union as a federal state placed legal control of general education in the Commissariat of Education in each of the republics.

3. Actually, educational policies are determined by the Central Executive Committee, the Council of Peoples' Commissars, and the General Committee of the Communist Party; educational planning is done by the State Planning Commission.

4. The dominant factor in all educational development in the Soviet Union is the Communist ideology, which becomes indoctrination.

Organization of the schools

1. Nurseries (*crèches*) and kindergartens, controlled by industries or the Republics, exist for children under age seven.

2. General education is provided in the ten-year school organized as *primary* (four years), *incomplete secondary* (three years), and *complete secondary* (three years).

3. Compulsory education has until recently ended with grade seven, and although the ten-year school is the basic plan of general education, many differences exist between city and rural schools.

4. In 1949, the "State Labor Reserve" was created chiefly for non-academic students between the ages of fourteen and nineteen for training in manual occupations.

5. Since 1954, many technical trade schools have been established within the Labor Reserve system with short-term courses in trade education for graduates of complete secondary schools.

6. Boarding schools for all children through age seventeen were recommended by the Twentieth Party Congress (1956) and seem to have been established on a wide basis.

7. *Technicums* are generally specialized secondary schools which in part overlap the complete secondary schools, but are outside the regular system of mass education. They provide education (usually a four-year course) in such fields as teacher education, public health, etc.

8. Admission to the universities and institutes (applied sciences) is through the complete secondary school.

Communist dictatorship exercises complete control over all aspects of Russian life, and the schools are rigidly controlled to achieve Communist ends.

Challenges to European education in the 1970s

Rapidly accelerating political and economic changes (*e.g.*, the common market, etc.) have had a great effect on educational practice in western Europe in the 1960s and 1970s. Although the Soviet Union lies outside the Western orbit politically, the world impact of Soviet education (with education recognized as the foundation for Russian development) is growing. The technological emphases in West German education account for its industrial prosperity; a radical reorientation of British education is underway to bring the country in line with its present circumstances. New movements of scholastic reform in France are enlarging its European perspectives.[1]

UNESCO and world education

The United Nations Educational, Scientific, and Cultural Organization **(UNESCO)** is a specialized agency of the United Nations (1946).

UNESCO's objectives include: (a) the elimination of illiteracy; (b) the promotion of universal educational opportunity; (c) the promotion of scientific research for the benefit of mankind; (d) the promotion of international understanding, and the international exchange of ideas and information; (e) the promotion of respect for "human rights."

UNESCO projects in education

1. Projects have been launched in those countries where there is a high rate of illiteracy, an inadequate system of education, and poor living conditions (Fundamental Education), e.g., Haiti, Peru, Nyasaland.

2. Sponsorship of conferences on educational improvement throughout the world, e.g., "The Teaching of Modern Languages," Ceylon, 1953.

3. UNESCO has become one of the most important educational publishers in the world with the publication of handbooks, textbooks, and descriptive materials for fundamental education.

4. UNESCO's International Commission on the Development of Education has been studying educational expenditures

[1] Edmund J. King, *Other Schools and Ours*, 4th ed., London, 1973; Edmund J. King, *Education and Development in Western Europe*, New York, 1969; see generally, *The International Yearbook of Education*, Geneva: International Bureau of Education.

and the linkage between education and national productivity. (Edgar Faure, *et al.*, *Learning to Be: The World of Education Today and Tomorrow*, UNESCO, Paris, 1972 —.)

Selected Readings

Part VI: Some Recent European Developments

Adler, Mortimer J., and Milton Mayer. *The Revolution in Education.* University of Chicago Press, 1958.

Alexander, W. P. *Education in England.* London, 1954.

Armytage, W. H. G. *Four Hundred Years of English Education.* Cambridge, 1964.

Bereday, George Z. F., W. W. Brickman, Gerald H. Read, eds. *The Changing Soviet School.* New York, 1960.

Blanshard, Brand. *Education in an Age of Science.* New York, 1959.

Brickman, William W., ed. *Research in Comparative Education.* Proceedings of the Sixth Annual Conference on Comparative Education, School of Education, New York University, 1959.

———. "A Historical Introduction to Comparative Education," *Comparative Education Review*, vol. III, 1959–1960, pp. 6–13.

Campbell, A. E., ed. *Modern Trends in Education.* New York, 1938.

Childs, John L. *American Pragmatism and Education.* New York, 1955.

Conant, James B. *Education in a Divided World.* Harvard University Press, 1949.

Counts, George S. *The Challenge of Soviet Education.* New York, 1957.

———. *Education and the Foundations of American Freedom.* University of Pittsburgh Press, 1963.

Cramer, John F., and George S. Browne. *Contemporary Education: A Study of National Systems*, 2nd ed. New York, 1965.

Dawson, Christopher. *The Crisis of Western Education.* New York, 1961.

Debiesse, J. *Compulsory Education in France.* Paris (UNESCO), 1951.

Dent, H. C. *The Education Act of 1944*. London, 1944.
———. *Growth in English Education*. London, 1954.
Dobinson, C. H. *Education in a Changing World*. Oxford, 1961.
Education in the USSR. Division of International Education, Bulletin No. 14, Washington, D.C., 1957.
Gruber, Frederick C., ed. *Education in Transition*. University of Pennsylvania Press, 1960.
Halls, W. D. *Society, Schools, and Progress in France*. Oxford, 1965.
Handlin, Oscar. *John Dewey's Challenge to Education*. New York, 1959.
Huebener, Theodore. *The Schools of West Germany*. New York University Press, 1962.
Jones, Howard M. *Education and World Tragedy*. Harvard University Press, 1946.
Kandel, I. L., ed. *Yearbooks*. International Institute of Teachers College, Columbia University, 1925–1944.
Kandel, Isaac L. *Conflicting Theories of Education*. New York, 1938.
———. *Education in an Era of Transition*. London, 1948.
———. *The New Era in Education*. Boston, 1955.
King, Edmund J. *Education and Development in Western Europe*. Reading, Mass., 1969.
Kline, G. L. *Soviet Education*. New York, 1957.
Korol, A. G. *Soviet Education for Science and Technology*. New York, 1957.
Lindegren, A. M. *Education in Germany*. United States Office of Education, 1938.
———. *Germany Revisited: Education in the Federal Republic*. Washington, D.C., 1957.
Malherbe, E. G., ed. *Educational Adaptations in a Changing Society*. New York, 1937.
Mallinson, Vernon. *An Introduction to the Study of Comparative Education*, 2nd ed. London, 1960.
Mayer, Martin. *The Schools*. New York, 1961.
Meyer, Adolphe E. *The Development of Education in the Twentieth Century*, 2nd ed. New York, 1949.
Moos, Elizabeth. *The Educational System of the Soviet Union*. New York, 1952.
Myers, Edward D. *Education in the Perspective of History*. New York, 1960.

Ottaway, A. K. *Education and Society*. London, 1953.

Parthemos, George S., ed. *Higher Education in a World of Conflict*. University of Georgia Press, 1962.

Pennar, Joan, *et al. Modernization and Diversity in Soviet Education*. New York, 1971.

Pillsbury, Kent. UNESCO: *Education in Action*. Ohio State University Press, 1963.

Rudman, Herbert C. *Structure and Decision Making in Soviet Education*. Washington, 1964.

Springer, Ursula K. *Recent Curriculum Developments in France, West Germany, and Italy*. New York, 1969.

Talbott, John E. *The Politics of Educational Reform in France, 1918–1940*. Princeton, 1969.

Thut, I. N., and Don Adams. *Educational Patterns in Contemporary Societies*. New York, 1964.

UNESCO. *Compulsory Education and Its Prolongation*. Geneva, 1951.

Wenke, H. *Education in Western Germany*. Washington, D.C., 1953.

INDEX

Aaron, R. I., 74*n.*
Abelard, 31
Abicenna, 35
Academician, 122
Academy, 114
Academy movement, 117, 129
Accreditation: A Struggle Over Standards in Higher Education, 126*n.*
Action Patterns in School Desegregation, 141*n.*
Adams Act, 130
Adams, John, 102*n.*
Adams, Oscar F., 129*n.*
Adamson, J. W., 62*n.*, 70*n.*, 73*n.*, 99*n.*
Adolescentia, 46
Adolf Hitler Schools, 154
Adult Education, 122
Advancement of Learning, 66
Advice of W. P. to Mr. Samuel Hartlib, 69
Age of the Reformation, 50*n.*
Agricola, Rudolph, 46
Agricultural experimental stations, 130
Agricultural schools in Switzerland, 91
Agriculture, federal funds for instruction in, 130
Aided schools, 155
Aiken, Wilfred M., 140*n.*
Ainsworth, O. M., 63*n.*
Alcuin, 27
Alexander of Hales, 32
Alexander, T., 95*n.*
Alexandria University, 10
Alfred the Great, 27
Allen, P. S., 46*n.*
Allen, W. C. B., and E. McClure, 87*n.*
American College and University: A History, 112*n.*, 129*n.*
American Common School, 120*n.*
American Dictionary of the English Language, 119
American education, 107–146; Colonial period of, 109–114; national period of (1787–1890), 115–134; twentieth century, 135–145; selected references on, 145–149
American Education and Religion, 127*n.*
American and English public schools, difference between, 48*n.*
American Epoch: A History of the United States in 1890's, 136*n.*
American and German University, 97*n.*
American Herbartians, 102, 103
American High School Today, 141*n.*
American Journal of Education, 122, 123
American Lyceum, 122
American Lyceum: Its History and Contribution to Education, 122*n.*
American Medical Association, 132

American Philosophical Society, 114*n.*
American Political and Social History, 136*n.*
American public high schools, 125, 126; standardizing associations for, 126; tax support for, 125
American public schools, criticism and problems of, 141, 142
American school system, 136, 137
American state universities, 117, 118
American students in Germany, 132
America's Struggle for Free Schools, 120*n.*
Anabaptists, 49, 50, 109
Ancients and Moderns, 66*n.*
Anderson, H. A., and F. S. Chase, 141*n.*
Anderson, Lewis F., 91*n.*
André Marie Act, 152
Andrea, 66*n.*
Andrews, C. M., 109*n.*
Andronicus, Livius, 14
Anglican church in America, 110
Anselm, 31
Apology, 7
Appeal to the Friends of Mankind, 85
Apprenticeship education in colonial America, 111
Apprenticeship system in 19th-century England, 99
Archer, R. L., 101*n.*
Archimedes, 10
Aristotle, 6, 8, 9, 26, 31, 35, 44, 68
Arithmetic, Vulgar and Decimal, 113*n.*
Arnold, Matthew, 100*n.*
Art and Life in America, 136*n.*
Artisan class of Plato's ideal society, 7
Ascham, Roger, 45, 64*n.*, 69
Association of Colleges and Preparatory Schools of the Southern States 126
Associationism, 101
Athanasius, 24
Athenaeum, 16
Athenian education, 5, 6
Athens, university of, 4, 9
Atrium, The, 72
Authoritarianism of the Reformation, 77
Averroës, 35

Babbitt, Irving, 82*n.*
Bache, Alexander D., 122
Bacon, Francis, 66, 74
Bagley, William C., 140
Bailyn, Bernard, 112*n.*
Baker, Melvin C., 139
Balfour Act, 100
Barker, R., 100*n.*
Barnard College, 133
Barnard, Henry, 47*n.*, 50*n.*, 70*n.*, 76*n.*, 91*n.*, 122, 123
Barzizza, 42
Barzun, Jacques, 82*n.*
Basedow, Johann Bernard, 84–87; influence of Locke on, 74; influence of Rousseau on, 85
Battersby, W. J., 76*n.*
Battledore, 112*n.*
Bayles, Ernest E., 140*n.*
Baynham, Dorsey, and J. Lloyd Trump, 142*n.*
Beard, Charles, and Mary Beard, 116*n.*
Beck, Walter H., 128*n.*
Beecher, Catherine, 132
Beginnings of Graduate Education in America, 132*n.*
Behavioral Goals of General Education in High School, 141*n.*
Bell, Andrew, 88, 89, 118

Bell, S., 110*n.*
Benedictine rule, 24
Benjamin Franklin on Education, 113*n.*
Berkeley, George, influence of Locke on, 74
Berlin, University of, 96
Best, John H., 113*n.*
Bestor, Arthur, 140*n.*
Bible, 113
Bibliography of John Dewey, 139*n.*
Bill for the more general diffusion of knowledge, 116, 117
Binet, Alfred, 138
Binns, Henry B., 88*n.*
Biological sciences of the 19th century, 104
Birchenough, Charles, 88*n.*
Blair, Anna L., 123*n.*
Blake, Nelson M., 116*n.*
Blind, education of, 129
Blow, Susan, 104*n.*
Boards of education, 120, 121
Boccaccio, Giovanni, 42
Boethius, 26, 27
Boke Named the Governour, 45
Bologna, University of, 33
Bonaventura, 32
Book of Methods for Fathers and Mothers of Families and for Nations, 85
Boston Latin School, 112
Bourne, William O., 122*n.*
Bowen, H. C., 103*n.*
Boyd, W., 81*n.*, 84*n.*
Bradford Junior College, 129
Bray, Thomas, 87
Brenz, John, 54*n.*
Brethren of the Common Life, 45
Brickman, William W., and Stanley Lehrer, 127*n.*, 129*n.*, 137*n.*, 139*n.*
Brief Course in the History of Education, 36*n.*
Brief History of Education, 62*n.*
Brief Sketch of George Peabody and a History of the Peabody Education Fund through 30 years, 127*n.*
Brinsley, John, 69, 70
Brinton, Howard H., 128*n.*
British (*see also* English)
British Educational System, 101*n.*
British and Foreign School Society, 99
British and Foreign Society, 88
Broome, Edwin C., 126*n.*
Brown College, 112
Brown, Elmer E., 117*n.*, 125*n.*,
Brown University, 130
Brown v. *Kansas,* 137
Browning, Oscar, 63*n.*
Brubacher, John S., and Willis Rudy, 129*n.*
Bruce, G. M., 52*n.*
Bryn Mawr College, 133
Budé, Guillaume, 44
Bugenhagen, John, 54*n.*
Burgdorf, institute at, 89
Burgher schools of the late Middle Ages, 36
Burns, J. A., and Bernard J. Kohlbrenner, 128*n.*
Burr, N. R., 111*n.*
Bush, G., 54*n.*
Butts, R. Freeman, 40
Butterfield, Herbert, 65*n.*
Byerly, Carl L., 124*n.*

Cadet education *(Ephebic)* of Athens, 5
Calvin, John, 49, 51, 52
"Calvinists and Education," 51*n.*
Calvinists of New England, 109, 110
Cambridge University, 47, 99*n.*
Campanella, Tommaso, 66*n.*
Campe, J. H., 86
Capella, Martianus, 25, 26

Capitalism, 94
Capitularies, 26, 27
"Carolingian" scholarship revival, 25
"Case method," 132
Casiglione, Baldasarre, 45*n.*
Caspari, Fritz, 45*n.*
Cassiodorus, 26
Cassirer, Ernst, 81*n.*
Catechetical schools, 24
Catherine II of Russia, 80
Catholic parochial schools, 128 (*see also* Parochial schools)
Catholic Reform movement, 49
Catholic Reformation, 55*n.*
Catholic Reformation and the Society of Jesus, 55–57
Cato, 63
Cato the Elder, 28
Cattell, James McKeen, 138
Central Executive Committee, 153
Century of Education, 88*n.*
Century of Higher Education A, 129*n.*
Century of Higher Education for American Women, 133*n.*
Certification of teachers, 17
Chantry Schools, 35
Charity schools in England in the 18th century, 87
Charlemagne, 26, 27
Charleston Free School, 110
Charter-House (English public school), 48
Chase, F. S., and H. A. Anderson, 141*n.*
Chastity as ideal of Monasticism, 24
Cheever, Ezekiel, 113
Child psychology as base of education, 78
Children's literature, creation of, in German, 86*n.*
Chivalry, educational ideals of, 34
Christian Brothers, 57; schools of, 75, 76
Christian church, education of, 18, 19
Christian City, 66*n.*
Christian Education in Youth, 52
Christian schools, early, 23–24
Chronological table of: Greek education, 2; Roman and early Christian education, 12; medieval education, 22; educational development from 14th to 17th century, 30; educational development during the 17th and 18th centuries, 60; educational development during the 19th century, 92
Chrysoloras, 42
Church control over education, decline of, 127
Church and Reform in Scotland, 55*n.*
Church and State in America, 137*n.*
Church and State in Virginia, 110*n.*
Cicero, 14, 17, 26, 42
Ciceronianism, 42, 44, 47, 62
Ciceronians, The, 44
Cincinnati. University of, 131
Citizenship, practical education in, 9
City normal schools, 133
City of the Sun, 66*n.*
Civil War, 115, 118, 126, 127
Classical curriculum *versus* subject election, 130
Classical Latin grammar school, collapse of, 114
Clement, 24
Clemson College, 137
Clinton, DeWitt, 122
Cochran v. Louisiana Board of Education, 137*n.*
Co-education, 133

Cogitata et visa, 66
Cole, P. R., 26*n.*
Colet, John, 45, 48
College of Charleston, 131
College of the City of New York, 131
College curriculum, definition of, 129
College of Philadelphia, 112, 117
College *versus* the university, 129, 130
Colleges for Our Land and Time, 118*n.*, 130*n.*
Collins, Ellsworth, 140
Colloquies, 46
Colonial Enlightenment, 110
Colonial period of American education, 109–114; historical background, 109, 110
Colonial Period of American History, 109*n.*
Colorado School of Mines, 131
Columbia College, 112, 132
Columbia University, 139
Columella, 63
Comenius and the Beginnings of Educational Reform, 72*n.*
Comenius, John Amos, 66, 69, 70–74, 101
Commentaries, 35
Commissariat of Education, 157
Committee of Ten, 126
Common School Journal, 122
Community colleges, 137
Communist ideology in education in Soviet Union, 154
Compayré, G., 65*n.*
Comprehensive secondary schools of England, 152
Compte-rendu, 79
Compulsory education: in England, 155; in France, 157; of the Nazi regime, 153; in Soviet Union, 158; in the U.S., 136; under the Weimar Republic, 153
Compulsory school attendance, 98, 124
Conant, James B., 141*n.*
Concerning the Mind (De Anima), 68
Concerning the Teaching of the Arts (De Tradendis Disciplinis), 67
Condillac, Etienne Bonnot de, 80
Condorcet, Marquise de, 80
Condorcet and the Rise of Liberalism, 80*n.*
Conduct of the Schools, 76
Congregational Day Schools, 129
Congress of Vienna, 94
Connecticut Common School Journal, 122
Connectionistic, stimulus-response, psychology, 138
Consolation of Philosophy, 26, 27
Constantine, 16
Constantinople, fall of to the Turks, 39
Constitutional Convention, 109
Constitutional provisions for education in America, 116
Continental realists, 70
Contributions of William T. Harris to Public School Administration, 124*n.*
Controlled schools of England, 151
Cornell University, 130
Cosmopolitan period of Greek education, 9, 10
Council for Basic Education, 140*n.*
Council of National Education, 79
Council of Peoples' Commissars, 153
Council of Trent, 55

Countdown in Segregated Education, 137*n.*
Counter Reformation of the Catholic Church, 55
County schools of England, 151
Cours d'Etudes, 80
Cousin, Victor, 98*n.*, 122
Cranston, Maurice, 74*n.*
Crèches, 154
Cremin, Lawrence A., 120*n.*, 125*n.*, 140*n.*, 143, 144
Crimean War, 94
Crusades, the, 34
Cultural History of Western Education, 40*n.*
Cultural nationalism of the 19th century, 93
Curriculum: of American academies, 117; of American colleges, 129; changes in American schools, 119; based on science, 104; of Boston Latin schools, 112; classical, *versus* subject election, 130; college, 129; of colonial colleges, 112; elective program of, 130; of English charity schools of the 18th century, 87; of English elementary schools, 100; of French secondary schools, 99; of French primary schools, 97–99; of junior high schools, 141; nuclear age effect on, 141, 142; of philosophical schools of Athens, 8; problems in present educational crisis, 141, 142; of Rhetor schools, 16; of schools under Nazi regime, 153; of the Society of Jesus, 56
Curriculum Principles and Social Trends, 142*n.*
Curry, Jabez, 127*n.*
Curtis, S. J., 100*n.*, 101*n.*
Cyclopedia of Education, 51*n.*
Dalton Contract Plan, 140
Dame Schools, 111
Dartmouth, 112, 132
Dartmouth College Case, 130
Darwin, Charles, 104
Daunou Law, 97
Davis, Sheldon E., 122*n.*
Deaf-mute, education of, 129
Debate, training in, 16
Decameron, 42
Declamation, training in, 15, 16
Declaration of Independence, 109
Deerfield Academy, 129
Deferrari, Roy J., 128*n.*
Defoe, Daniel, 83, 86
DeGarmo, Charles, 103
De Institutione Oratoria, 17
Delbos Act, 156
Democracy and Education, 139
Democracy and liberalism, 93
Democracy's College: The Land Grant Movement in the Formative State, 118*n.*
Denominational colleges, 112, 131
Denominational schools, 128, 129
De Oratore, 17
Depression in 1929, 135
Descartes and His School, 67*n.*
Descartes, René, 66, 67
Description of the Famous Kingdom of Macaria, 69
Desegregation: curricular issues involved in, 141; sources of information on, 141*n.*
Desiderius Erasmus, 46*n.*
Developing a Curriculum for Modern Living, 142*n.*
Development and Scope of Higher Education in the United States, 129*n.*
Dewey on Education, 139*n.*
Dewey, John, 139, 140
Dialogues, 7

Dialogus de Oratoribus, 17
Didactica Magna, 71*n.*
Diderot, Denis, 79, 80
Diderot and the Encyclopedists, 79*n.*
Diderot Studies, 79*n.*
Diesterweg, B., 91
Dillworth, Thomas, 113*n.*
Discourse on Method, 67
Discourse on the Moral Effects of the Arts and Sciences, 81
Dock, Christopher, 113
Dominicans, 35, 57
Donatus, 18, 28
Donohue, J. W., 56*n.*
Doric Age, 3
Dorpat, University of, 54
Dream of Descartes, 67*n.*
Drury, John, 69
Dushkin, Alexander M., 129*n.*
Dutch Reformed Church, 110
Dutch School of New Netherland and Colonial New York, 55*n.*, 111*n.*
Dworkin, Martin S., 139*n.*
Dystychs of Cato, 28

Early Christianity and Greek Paideia, 23*n.*
Early Protestant Educators, 76*n.*
Early Quaker Education in Pennsylvania, 111*n.*
Eby, F., 76*n.*
Eckelberry, Roscoe H., 131*n.*
Eddy, Edward D., Jr., 118*n.*, 130*n.*
Edgar, J., 52*n.*
Education: Adult, 122; Athenian, 5, 6; as branch of political science, 8; Committee of postwar German Allied Control Council, 150; of the Christian church, 18, 19; in classical antiquity, 1–20; in classical antiquity, selected references on, 19, 20; at close of the Middle Ages, 35, 36; during early Middle Ages, 23–28; early Roman, 14; in *Émile*, 83; federal support of, 119, 120; function as formulated by Plato, 8; Greek, 2–10; of the Homeric period, 4; influence of the Reformation on, 50, 51; as an intellectual discipline, 31, 32; Jesuit, methodology of, 57; Jewish in America, 129; in the late Middle Ages, 31–36; legal, 132; medical, 131, 132; medieval, 21–37; in the Modern Era (1600–1900), 59–100; naturalism in, during the 18th century, 77–91; professional, 131; progressive, 139, 140, 151; realism in, during the 17th century, 61–76; Roman, 12–19; science of, 138, 139; Spartan, 4, 5; universal, 136; university departments of, 134; vocational, in 19th-century Germany, 96; of women, 5, 8, 68, 83*n.*, 117, 132, 133
Education Act of 1944, 100*n.*, 155
Education for American Democracy, 136*n.*
Education: The Challenges Ahead, 142*n.*
Education of the Clergy, 27
Education in the Forming of American Society, 112*n.*
Education in Great Britain since 1900, 101*n.*
Education in the Junior High School Years, 141*n.*
Education of Man, 103
Education in New Jersey, 111*n.*
Education in Scotland, 52*n.*
Education of Young Children in England, 87*n.*
Educational Act of 1944, 101

Educational aim of Herbart, 101, 102
Educational content of scholasticism, 32
Educational crisis in American schools, 141–143
Educational development during the 17th and 18th centuries, chronological table of, 60
Educational encyclopedism, 71
Educational function of the state, 8
Educational Goals for America, 136*n.*
Educational ideals of chivalry, 34
Educational ideas of Locke, 73, 74
Educational Issues in the Kindergarten, 104*n.*
Educational magazines and journals, 122
Educational opportunity in 20th-century America, 137, 138
Educational Periodicals during the 19th Century, 122*n.*
Educational practice in England in the 18th century, 87–89
Educational psychology, 101
Educational Psychology, 138
Educational purposes of scholasticism, 31, 32
Educational reform in Germany in 18th century, 84–87
Educational Research Bulletin, 142*n.*
Educational significance of the Renaissance, 42–44
Educational theory: of the Colonial period, 113, 114; of the 19th century, 101–104; and the Reformation, 49–57; and the Renaissance, 44–46
Educational Theory of Rousseau, 84*n.*
Educational Views of Benjamin Franklin, 113*n.*
Educational views of Martin Luther, 52
Educational Wastelands, 140*n.*
Educational Work of Thomas Jefferson, 117*n.*
Educational writers: of Imperial Rome, 17; of the Middle Ages, 25
Educational Writings of John Locke, 73*n.*
Educational writings of Pestalozzi, 89, 90
Educational Writings of Richard Mulcaster, 69*n.*
Education of the Reformation, 51–54
Eight-year study of progressive education, 140
Eighteenth century, education in, 60, 77–91
Eisenhower, Dwight D., 135
Elective program of curriculum, 130
Elementarwerk, 85
Elementary Book, 85
Elementary curriculum of English schools, 100
Elementary education: in the middle colonies, 110, 111; in the New England colonies, 111, 112; in the southern colonies, 110
Elementary Education Act of 1870, 100
Elementary schools: in America, 118, 119; of colonial America, 110–112; of early Rome, 14; graded, 124, 125; for the poor in England, 99
Eliot, Charles W., 130
Elyot, Thomas, 45
Émile, 81–83, 86*n.*
Empiricism of John Locke, 73, 74
Encyclopedia, 79

Encyclopedism, educational, 71
Encyclopedists, French, 78
English and American public schools, difference between, 48*n.*
English Classical School in Boston, 125
English education in the 19th century, 99–101
English Education 1789–1902, 99*n.*
English Education under the Test Acts: The History of the Non-Conformist Academies, 75*n.*
English education since World War I, 151, 152
English educational practice in the 18th century, 87–89
English educational theorists of the Renaissance, 45
English Grammar, 119
English Grammar Schools up to 1660, 55*n.*, 70*n.*
English humanists of the Renaissance, 45
English High School in Boston, 125
English Life in the Middle Ages, 34*n.*
English public schools of the Renaissance, 47, 48
English recent developments in education, 155, 156
English Reformation, 40
English Revolution of 1688, 61
English schools in operation, 155, 156
English sense-realism, 69
Enlightenment of the 18th century, 77, 78, 93
Ephebic (cadet education) of Athens, 5
Epic poems of the Homeric period, 4
Epicurus and the Epicureans, 9
Erasmus, 42, 44, 46, 47*n.*, 62*n.*
Erasmus Concerning Education, 62*n.*
Erasmus' Services to Learning, 46*n.*
Erfurt, University of, 47
Eriginia, Joannes Scotus, 27
Essay Concerning Human Understanding, 73
Essay on National Education, 79
Essays of Bacon, 66
Essays on Catholic Education in the United States, 128*n.*
Essays on Education, 104
Essays on Educational Reformers, 43*n.*
Essays in Intellectual History, 67*n.*
Essentialism, 140
Essentials of Method, 103
Ethics, The, 8
Eton (English public school), 48
Etymologies, 26
Euclid, 10
Europe Since Napoleon, 94*n.*
European education, effects of reports about, on American education, 122
European institutions and ideals, transplantation of, to America, 110
European recent developments in education, 153–160; British, 155, 156; French, 156, 157; German, 153, 154; Soviet Union, 157; selected readings on, 160–162
Euthyphro, 7
Everson v. *Board of Education,* 137*n.*
Evolution: of the American Teachers' College, 134*n.*; theories of, 104
Experience and Education, 139
Experiment in Education Made

at the Male Asylum of Madras, 89
Experimental psychology, 138
Experimental stations, agricultural, 130

Factory system, rise of, 93, 94
Farrell, A. P., 56*n.*
Farrington, Frederic E., 98*n.*
Faulkner, Harold U., 136*n.*
Federal aid bill of 1963 (proposed), 142, 143
Federal government and the educational crisis, 142, 143
Federal Internal Improvements Land Act, 121
Federal support of education, 119, 120
Fellenberg, Emanuel, 91
Feltre, Vittorino da, 44, 47
Fenelon, François de Salignac de la Mothe, 76*n.*
Fichte, Johann Gottlieb, 91
First Amendment to the Constitution, 127
First Book of Discipline, 52
First Part of the Elementarie, 68
First Textbooks in American History, 119*n.*
Fischer, E. K. B., 67*n.*
Fisher Act, 100, 155
"Five Formal Steps of the Recitation," 102, 103
Fletcher, C. S., 142*n.*
Fletcher, S. S., and J. Welton, 103*n.*
Flexner, Abraham, 132*n.*
Flexner Report, 132
Florence, University of, 47
Focus on Change: Guide to Better Schools, 142*n.*
Folk-schools, 95
Ford, P. L., 112*n.*
Formal mental discipline, doctrine of, 74
Formalism in education of the Reformation, 50
Foster, Herbert D., 51*n.*, 52*n.*
Foundation of John Dewey's Educational Theory, 139*n.*
Foundations for American Education, 139*n.*
Founding of American Colleges and Universities before the Civil War, 131*n.*
Founding of the American Public School System, 118*n.*
Franciscans, 35, 57
Francke, Hermann, 74, 75, 76, 84
Franklin, Benjamin, 113, 114, 117
Free competition, 94
Free school societies, 122
Freedmen's Bureau, 127
Freehill, Maurice E., 142*n.*
French education since 1918, 156, 157
French education in the 19th century, 97–99
French educational theorists of the Renaissance, 44–45
French educational theory and nationalization, 18th century, 78–84
French Elementary Schools, 98*n.*
French Encyclopedists, 78
French humanists of the Renaissance, 44, 45
French Liberalism and Education in the 18th century, 81*n.*
French national education, 1870–1900, 98, 99
French physiocrats, 78
French recent developments in education, 156, 157
French schools in operation, 153
French Thought in the 18th Century, 84*n.*
French Tradition in Education,

76*n.*
Froebel and Education by Self-Activity, 103*n.*
Froebel, Friedrich, 88, 103, 104; influence of Pestalozzi on, 91, 103; influence of Rousseau on, 103; kindergarten established by, 103, 104
Froebel's Chief Writings on Education, 103*n.*
Froebel's Kindergarten Principles Critically Examined, 104*n.*
"From the Renaissance to the Industrial Revolution," 41*n.*
Fuller, B. A. G., 73*n.*
Fürstenschulen, 47

Galen, 45
Gallaudet, Thomas H., 129
Gargantua, 45, 63
Garragahan, G. J., 57
Gary (Platoon) Plan, 140
Gate to Science, 69
Gay, P., and O. Montreux, 98*n.*
General Committee of the Communist Party, 157
General Idea of the College of Mirania, 113
General Method, 103
General School Regulation of Frederick the Great, 84
Gentlemen of Port Royal, 76*n.*
Geography, "natural method" in, 87
George Peabody College for Teachers, 133
George Peabody Educational Fund, 127
Georgia, University of, 117
Gerberich, J. Raymond, 139*n.*
Gerbert, 28
German Education, Past and Present, 84*n.*, 97*n.*
German education since World War I, 1949, 154; in the German Federal Republic (West Germany), 154; in postwar reorganization, 154; in the Weimar Republic, 153
German Higher Schools, 96*n.*
German humanists of the Renaissance, 45, 46
German 19th-century schools, 95-97
German recent educational developments, 153, 154
German Reformation, 49
German research universities, influence of, on American education, 132
German Teachers and Educators, 47*n.*, 70*n.*
German universities of the 19th century, 96, 97
German Universities and University Study, 53*n.*
Germany, American students in, 132
Germany, educational reform in, in 18th century, 84–87
Germany, unification of, 94
Gibson, W. J., 52*n.*
Gifted Student, The, 142*n.*
Gifted students, problems of, 142
Gilman, Daniel Coit, 132
Glorious Rebellion of 1688 in England, 78
Glory that was Greece: A Survey of Hellenic Culture and Civilization, 3*n.*
Good, H. G., 107*n.*
Goodrich, Samuel G., 119
Graded elementary schools, 124, 125
Graduate education in 19th-century America, 132
Graduate fellowships through federal aid, 142
Grammar Free School in colonial New York, 111

Grammar schools: of the American colonies, 48; of England, 100, 101; of England for the upper classes, 99; of Imperial Rome, 16, 17; of 19th-century America, 124
Grammatical Institute of the English Language, 119
Grammaticus, 15
Gratian, 16
Graves, Frank P., 68*n.*
"Great books" as basis of liberal education, 18
Great Didactic, The, 72
"Great Public Schools," 99
Greek culture, spread of, 9
Greek dominance of Roman education, 14–18
Greek education, 2–10; cosmopolitan period of, 9, 10; fusion with Roman, 9, 10
Greek educational theories, 6–9
Green, F. C., 81*n.*
Green, J. A., 90
Greene, Harry A., 139*n.*
Greenwood, Isaac, 113*n.*
Grizzel, Emit D., 125*n.*
Grocyn, William, 45
Groot, Gerhard, 45
Groton, 129
Growth of American Law, The, 132*n.*
Grundschule, 153, 154
Guarino, Battista, 43*n.*
Guidance counseling and testing, 142
Guild Schools, 35
Guimps, Roger de, 91*n.*
Gwynn, I. Minor, 142*n.*
Gymnasien, 47, 74, 96
Gymnastic school *(palaestra)* of Athens, 5

Hadrian, 16
Hall, Clifton L., and Edgar W. Knight, 126*n.*
Hall, G. Stanley, 138
Hall, Samuel R., 133
Halle, University of, 75, 86
Hansen, Allen Oscar, 116*n.*
Hardy, C. DeWitt, and Richard Hofstadter, 129*n.*
Harris, William T., 123, 124
Harrow (English public school), 48
Hartlib, Drury, and Comenius, 63*n.*
Hartlib, Samuel, 63, 69
Harvard, 112, 130
Harvard College in the 17th Century, 112*n.*
Harvard Law School, 132
Harvard Medical School, 132
Hayes, Cecil B., 122*n.*
Hegius, Alexander, 45
Heidelberg, University of, 47
Hellenistic Civilization, 9*n.*
Hellenized Roman education, 15–18
Helmstadt, University of, 54
Helvetius, Claud Adrien, 78, 79
Henry Barnard: School Administrator, 123*n.*
Henry Barnard's American Journal of Education, 123*n.*
Herbart and the Herbartians, 103*n.*
Herbart, Johann Friedrich, 101–103; educational aim of, 101, 102; influence of Locke on, 74; influence of Pestalozzi on, 91; influence of, in the U.S., 138
Herbartian Psychology, 102*n.*
Herbart's Outlines of Educational Doctrine, 103*n.*
Heritage of the Reformation, 50*n.*
Hexter, J. H., 65*n.*
High School in a New Era, 141*n.*
High schools, 125, 126; function of, 126; standardizing as-

sociations for, 126; tax support for, 125
Higher education: in colonial America, 112; in 19th-century America, 129; for women, 132, 133
Higher Education in Transition, 129*n.*
Hilgard, Ernest R., 138*n.*
Hindshaw, W., and D. Salmon, 88*n.*
Hinsdale, B. A., 123*n.*
Historical and Critical Discussion of College Admission Requirements, 126*n.*
Historical Introduction to Modern Psychology, 102*n.*
Historical Studies of Rhetoric and Rhetoricians, 16*n.*
History of American Education, 107*n.*
History of the British and Foreign School Society, 88*n.*
History of Catholic Education in the United States, 128*n.*
History of Christian Education, 55*n.*
History of Classical Scholarship, 47*n.*
History of Early Scottish Education, 52*n.*
History of Education in Great Britain, 100*n.*
History of Education in Pennsylvania, 111*n.*
History of Elementary Education in England and Wales, 88*n.*
History of the Hornbook, 112*n.*
History of the Municipal University in the United States, 131*n.*
History of Philosophy, 73*n.*
History of Public Permanent Common School Funds in the United States, 121*n.*
History of the Public School Society of the City of New York, 122*n.*
History of the Sciences, 10*n.*
History of Secondary Education, 125*n.*
History of Secondary Education in Pennsylvania, 111*n.*
History of Society of Jesus in North America, 57*n.*
History of Technology, 41*n.*
History of Women's Education in the United States, 133*n.*
Hitler, Adolf, Schools, 154
Hodgson, G., 65*n.*
Hofstadter, Richard, and C. De-Witt Hardy, 129*n.*
Holbrook, Josiah, 122
Holland, Lucy E., 90*n.*
Holmes, P., 112*n.*
Home and Colonial Infant School Society, 91
Homeric period, education of, 4
Honeywell, Roy J., 117*n.*
Hoole, Charles, 69
Horace, 17
Horace Mann and the Common School Revival in the United States, 123*n.*
Horace Mann, Educational Statesman, 123*n.*
Hornbooks, 112*n.*, 113
How Gertrude Teaches Her Children, 90
How We Think, 139
Howe Military School, 129
Howes, Raymond F., 16*n.*
Hughes, T., 56*n.*, 78*n.*
Hughes, Thomas A., 57*n.*
Huguenot wars in France, 40
Huguenots, 49
Human Nature and Conduct, 139
Humanism, 39; in education in Rennaissance, 43, 44
Humanism and Social Order in

Tudor England, 45*n.*
Humanistic contents of education of the Reformation, 50
Humanistic realism, 62–64; in the schools, 64
Humanistic Schools of the Renaissance, types of, 46–48
Humanitarian Movement in the 18th-century France, 78*n.*
Humanities, 43; Cicero's conception of, 17
Hume, David, influence of Locke on, 74
Hurst, William, 132*n.*
Huxley, Thomas Henry, 104
Hyma, A., 45*n.*

Ideal society, Plato's exposition of, 7
Ideals of monasticism, 24
Ignatius of Loyola, 55
Il Cortegiano, 45*n.*
Iliad, 4
Illiteracy: in Russia, prior to 1917, 157; in the U.S., 136
Imperial rivalries, 94
Imperial University, 79
Improvements in Education as It Respects the Industrious Classes, 89
Individual freedom, development of, in age of Pericles, 6
Individualistic aspect of education, 4
Individuality, emphasis on, in teachings of the Sophists, 6
Inductive logic, 66, 71
Industrial capitalism, 94
Industrialism, 93, 94
Infant School Society of New York, 118
Infant schools: of America, 118; of England, 88; of France, 98
Infant Schools: Their History and Theory, 88*n.*
Influence of Reconstruction on Education in the South, 126*n.*
Institute of the Brothers of the Christian Schools, 76
Institutes, 117
Institutes of Oratory, 17–18
Institutio Oratoria of Marcus Fabius Quintilianus, 18*n.*
Institutional effects of education of the Reformation, 51
Institutional and social aspect of education, 4
Integration of schools, 137, 138
Intellectual Life of New England, 112*n.*
Intelligence Quotient, 138, 139
Intercultural education, 141
Intergroup Relations Bibliography, 141*n.*
International relations, 94
Introduction to Divine and Human Readings, 26
Introduction to the Pedagogy of Herbart, 102*n.*
IQ, 138, 139
Irens of Spartan education, 5
Isidore of Seville, 26
Isocrates, 9
Italian universities of the Renaissance, 46, 47
Italy, unification of, 94

Jacobs, Charles M., 51*n.*
Jackson, Sidney L., 120*n.*
Jacksonian democracy, 115
Jaeger, Werner, 23*n.*
James, William, 138
Janelle, P., 55*n.*
Jansenists, 57, 76*n.*
Janua Linguarum, or Gates of Languages Unlocked, 72
Jeannes, Anna T., 127*n.*
Jefferson, Thomas, 116, 117
Jena, University of, 53, 54, 102
Jernegan, M. W., 113*n.*
Jerome, 24
Jesuit Code of Liberal Educa-

tion, 56*n*.
Jesuit Education, 56*n*.
Jesuit education, methodology of, 57
Jesuits: in America, 57*n*.; and French education of the 18th century, 78
Jesuits of the Middle United States, 57*n*.
Jewish education in America, 129
Jewish Education in New York City, 129*n*.
John Amos Comenius, 72*n*.
John Amos Comenius: Selections, 70*n*.
John Baptist de la Salle, 76*n*.
John Calvin, 51*n*.
John Dewey: Master Educator, 139*n*.
John Locke, 74*n*.
Johns Hopkins University, 132
Johns Hopkins University Medical School, 132
Johnson, Alvin W., 127*n*.
Johnson, Clifton, 119*n*.
Johnson, Ernest F., 127*n*.
Johnson, Marrietta, 140
Jones, Lloyd, 88*n*.
Jones, Richard F., 66*n*.
Jorgensen, A. N., 139*n*.
Joseph Lancaster, 89*n*.
Journals, educational, 122
"Juan Luis Vives: His Attitude toward Learning and to Life," 67*n*.
Julian, 17, 18
Julius Rosenwald Fund, 127*n*.
Junior high schools, 137; curriculum of, 141
Justinian, 10
Juvenal, 17

Kandel, I. L., 99*n*., 125*n*., 126*n*.
Kant, Immanuel, influence of Locke on, 74
Keatinge, M. W., 71*n*.
Kelly, Robert L., 131*n*.
Kennedy, John F., 136, 142
Kilpatrick, William H., 55*n*., 104*n*., 111*n*., 139
Kindergarten in American Education, 104*n*.
Kindergartens, 103, 154; first in America, 104
King's College, 112, 132
Knapp, Robert B., 141*n*.
Knight, of chivalry, 34
Knight, Edgar W., 122*n*., 126*n*.
Knight, Edgar W., and Clifton L. Hall, 126*n*.
Knowledge, Socrates' appraisal of, 7
Knox, John, 52
Kohlbrenner, Bernard J., and J. A. Burns, 128*n*.
Kolesnik, Walter B., 74*n*.
Königsberg, University of, 54

Labor conflicts, 94
Laboratory School: at the University of Chicago, 139; at the University of Missouri, 140
Laboring and Dependent Classes in Colonial America, 1607–1783, 113*n*.
La Chalotais, Louis René de Caradeuc de, 79; influence of on Basedow, 85
La Fontainerie, F. de, 76*n*., 81*n*.
Laissez-faire capitalism, 94
Laissez-faire doctrine of economics, 78
Lancaster, Joseph, 88, 89, 118
Lancasterian schools, 88
Lancasterian System of Instruction in the Schools of New York City, 89*n*., 118*n*.
Land-grant colleges, 118, 130, 131
Landjahr, The, 150
Langdell, Christopher C., 132

Lange, A. F., 103*n.*
Langevin Plan, 152
La Reforme de l'Education en Allemagne au dix-huitieme Siècle, 87*n.*
Larkin, Oliver W., 136*n.*
La Salle, John Baptist de, 76
Late Middle Ages, 21; education in, 31–37
Later Roman Education, 26*n.*
Latimer, William, 45
Latin Grammar, 48
Latin Grammar school, 15; collapse of classical, 114
Laurie, S. S., 72*n.*
Lawrence Scientific School at Harvard, 131
Laws of Twelve Tablets, 14
L.E.A., 100, 101, 151
Leach, A. F., 64*n.*
Learning, connectionism's explanation of, 138
Learning-living methodology of progressive education, 139
L'école unique, 156
Lectures on the Republic of Plato, 8*n.*
Lectures on Schoolkeeping, 132
Legal education, 132
Legal Status of Church-State Relationships in the United States, 127*n.*
Lehrer, Stanley, and William W. Brickman, 127*n.*, 129*n.*, 137*n.*, 139*n.*
Lehrfreiheit, 75, 96
Leipzig, University of, 47, 102
Leonard and Gertrude, 89, 90
Lernfreiheit, 75, 96
"Letter to the Mayors and Aldermen of All Cities of Germany in Behalf of Christian Schools," 52
Liberal Arts College, The, 129*n.*
Liberal arts colleges, 118, 132; *versus* the research universities, 130
Liberal education: as formulated by Plato, 8; "great books" as basis of, 18; revival of in the Renaissance, 42, 43
Liberal Education of Boys, 46
Liberal revolutions of 1830–1833, 94
Liberalism and American Education in the 18th Century, 116*n.*
Liberalism and democracy, 93
Libraries of Rome, 16
Life of Rabelais, 63*n.*
Life and Work of Pestalozzi, 90*n.*
Lily, William, 48
Linacre, Thomas, 45
Link, Arthur S., 136*n.*
Literary development in age of Pericles, 6
Literary education and monasticism, 24, 25
Literators, schools of the, 14, 15
Little, C. E., 18*n.*
Lives of Ancient Men, 42
Livingstone, R. W., 7*n.*
Loans: to college students by the federal government, 142; to private schools by federal government, 137*n.*
Lochhead, Jewell, 87*n.*
Locke, John, 45, 63, 66, 73, 74, 74*n.*, 77, 101; education, ideas of, 73, 74; empiricism of, 73, 74
Logic, inductive, 66, 71
Lombard, Peter, 32
London Infant School Society, 88
Lotteries for support of public schools, 121
Louis XIV, wars of, 61
Louisiana Purchase, 130
Louisville, University of, 131
Lowndes, G. A. N., 101*n.*

Loyola and the Educational System of the Jesuits, 56*n.*, 78*n.*
Ludi schools of early Rome, 14
Ludimagister, 15
Ludus Literarius, 69
Luther on Education, 52*n.*
Luther as an Educator, 52*n.*
Luther, Martin, 40, 49, 51–54; educational views of, 52
Lutheran Elementary Schools in the United States, 128*n.*
Lutheran parochial schools, 128
Lutheran State Church, 94
Luther's Correspondence and Other Contemporary Letters, 51*n.*
Lycées, 97
Lyceum, the American, 122
Lycurgus, constitution of, 4; laws of, 14
Lyon, Mary, 132, 133
Lysis, 7

MacDonald County Rural School, Missouri, 140
Macedon, 3
Mack, Edward C., 99*n.*
M.A. degrees, 132
Magazines, educational, 122
Magnus, Albertus, 32
Main Currents in the History of Education, 27*n.*
Making of Our Middle Schools, 117*n.*, 125*n.*
Mann, Charles R., 131*n.*
Mann, Horace, 122, 123
Manual-labor schools, 117
Marburg, University of, 53, 54
Marcus Aurelius, 17
Marique, P. J., 55*n.*
Maritain, Jacques, 67*n.*
Marriage of Philology and Mercury, 25–26
Martial, 17
Mason, S. F., 10*n.*
Masso, Gildo, 66*n.*
Mathematical deductions of the Cartesian method, 67
Mathieson, W. L., 55*n.*
Maurus, Rabanus, 27
Mayo, Charles, 91
McCloy, Shelby T., 78*n.*
McClure, E., and W. C. B. Allen, 87*n.*
McGrath, John J., 137*n.*
McLachlan, H., 75*n.*
McMurry, Charles, 103
McMurry, Frank, 103, 140
Measurement and Evaluation in the Modern School, 139*n.*
Mechanical arts, federal funds for instruction in, 130
Medical education, 131, 132
Medical Education in the United States and Canada, 132*n.*
Medical Education in the United States Before the Civil War, 132*n.*
Medieval education, 21–37; selected references on, 36, 37
Melanchthon, Philip, 51, 53, 54, 55
Memorabilia, 7
Mendicant Orders, 35
Mennonites of Pennsylvania, 114
Mental discipline, formal, doctrine of, 74
Mental Discipline in Modern Education, 74*n.*
Mental testing, 138, 139
Mercantilism, 94
Merchant Taylor's (English public school), 48
Meriam, J. L., 140
Merovingian kings, 21
Merriwether, C., 111*n.*
Method of Recitation, 103
Methodists, 78, 88, 119
Metternich's system, 94
Michigan College of Mining and Technology, 131
Middle Atlantic States Associ-

ation of Secondary Schools and Colleges, 126
Middle-class constitutionalism of Locke, 77
Middle colonies, elementary and secondary schools in, 110, 111
Milan, University of, 47
Military schools, 117
Military service, preparation for, in Athens, 5
Mills, Caleb, 124
Milton on Education, 63*n.*
Milton, John, 62–64
"Milton as Schoolboy and Schoolmaster," 64*n.*
Mines, state schools of, 131
Minor educational writers of the early Middle Ages, 27, 28
Minor Educational Writings of Jean-Jacques Rousseau, 81*n.*
Minority groups, educational opportunities for, 137
Mississippi, University of, 137
Missouri University, Laboratory School of, 140
Mittelschulen, 96, 150
Model lesson plan, 102
Modern Education in America, 136*n.*
Modern era (1600–1900), 59–106; selected references on, 104–106
Mohammedan influence on European education, 35
Monasticism, 24; and literary education, 24, 25
Monitorial schools: in America, 118; in England, 88, 89
Monroe, Paul, 36, 43, 44*n.*, 51*n.*, 62, 118*n.*
Monroe, W. S., 72*n.*
Montaigne, Michel de, 45, 63–65, 74
Montaigne and the Education of Judgment, 65*n.*
Montesquieu, Charles de Secondat, Baron de la Brède et de, 77
Montessori, Maria, 107*n.*
Montessori Method, 104*n.*
Montreux, O., and P. Gay, 98*n.*
Moore, Harry, 136*n.*
Moorish intellectual centers of Spain, 10
Moral teachings of the Sophists, 6
Moravians, 111
More, Thomas, 45
Morison, S. E., 112*n.*
Morley, J., 79*n.*
Morrill Act, 118, 130
Morrill, James L., 130*n.*
Morris, E. A., 63*n.*
Morse, Jedidiah, 119
Mother's Guide, 90
Mount Holyoke, 133
Mulcaster, Richard, 66, 68, 69; educational principles of, 68, 69
Mulhern, J., 111*n.*
Municipal colleges and universities, 131
Municipal schools of the late Middle Ages, 36
Murphy, Gardner, 102*n*
Murray, Lindley, 119*n.*
Music school of Athens, 5
Music, scope of term in Athenian education, 6
Muths, C. F. Guts, 87
My Investigations into the Course of Nature in the Development of the Human Race, 90

Naples, University of, 33
Napoleon: empire of, 77; overthrow of, 94, 97, 98
Napoleonic reform of education, 97
National Defense Educational Act, 142

National Education Act, 137*n.*
National Education Association, 126, 133
National Education Improvement Act, 140*n.*
National Herbartian Society, 103
National higher education of 19th-century America, 130, 131
National ministry of education, 155
National period (1787–1890) of American education, 115–134; historical background of, 115, 116
National revolutions of 1848–1850, 94
National school systems in 19th-century Europe, 94–101; in England, 99–101; in France, 97–99; in Prussia, 94–97
National Society of England, 99
National Society for Sciences and the Arts, 80
National Society for the Study of Education, 103
National systems of education, 78
National Teachers' Association, 133
Nationalism in education in the 19th century, 92–104; historical background, 93, 94; political background, 94
"Natural method" in geography, 87
"Natural selection" theory in biological evolution, 104
Naturalism of Condillac, 80*n.*
Naturalism in education, 18th century, 77–91; historical background, 77, 78
Nature, meaning of, in *Émile,* 82
Naval Academy at Annapolis, 131
Nazi regime, education under, 149, 150
Neef, Joseph, 91
Negative education of *Émile,* 82, 83
Negro education, 127, 137, 138; Phelps Stokes Fund for, 127*n.*, rural, 127*n.*
Nettleship, Richard L., 8*n.*
Nevins, Allan, 118*n.*
New Atlantis, 66
New and Complete System of Arithmetic, 119
New Deal program, 135
New Discovery of the Old Art of Teaching School, 69
New educational ideal, early Middle Ages, 23
New England Association of Colleges and Secondary Schools, 126
New England Primer, 112, 113
New Greek period of education, 4
New Guide to the English Tongue, 113*n.*
New types of schools at close of the Middle Ages, 35, 36
New York Free School Society, 122
New York, University of the State of, 121
Newcastle Commission, 100
Newcomer, Mabel, 133*n.*
Nietz, John A., 113*n.*
Nineteenth century, educational development in, 92–104; historical background of, 93, 94; political history of, 94
Nineteenth-century educational theory, 101–104
Nineteenth-century Europe, education in: national systems, 94–101; of England, 99–101;

of France, 97–99; of Prussia, 94–97
Nineteenth-century German schools, 95
Nineteenth-century public schools in America, 120–127
Noah Webster: Pioneer of Learning, 119*n.*
Noah Webster: Schoolmaster to America, 119*n.*
Nominalism and realism, reconciliation between, 31, 32
Normal School at Oswego, 91
Normal schools, 133
North Carolina Journal of Education, 122
North Carolina, University of, 117
North Central Association, 126
Northwest Association of Secondary and Higher Schools, 126
Northwest Ordinances, 119, 120, 121, 130
Norwood, William F., 132*n.*
Nouvelle Héloïse, 81
Novum Organum, 66
Nuclear age in school curriculum, 141, 142
Nursery schools, 104, 137, 154, 158

Obedience as ideal of monasticism, 24
Oberlin College, 133
Oberschul-collegium, 85*n.*, 86, 94, 96
Objective method of education of Aristotle, 8
Odysseus, 4
Odyssey, 4; translation into Latin, 14
Of the Affection of Fathers to Their Children, 64
Of the Conduct of the Understanding, 73*n.*
Of the Education of Children, 64
Of Pedantry, 64
Ogden Movement, 127
"Old field school" of Virginia, 110
Old Greek education of the historic period, 4–6
Old Textbooks, 113
Old Time Schools and School-books, 119*n.*
Oliphant, James, 69*n.*
On Authography, 27
On the Education of Boys, 44
On the Education of Boys and Their Moral Culture, 44
On the Education of Children, 44, 45
On the Education of Girls, 76*n.*
On the Education of a Prince, 44
On Dialectics, 27
On Going State University, 130*n.*
On Grammar, 27
On the Instruction of a Christian Woman, 67
On Noble Character and Liberal Studies, 43
On Oratory, 14
On the Origin of Inequality Among Men, 81
On a Plan of Studies for Youth, 67
On the Regulation of Study, 46
On Rhetoric, 27
On the Soul (De l'Esprit), 78
Open markets, 94
Opera Didactica Omnia, 72*n.*
Oratorian schools, influence of Descartes on, 67
Oratorians, 57
Oratory of Jesus, 76*n.*
Oratory, training in, 9, 17
Orbis Pictus, 69, 72
Ordensburgen, 150

Origen, 24
Origin and Development of the High School in New England before 1865, 125*n*.
Origin of the First German Universities, 54*n*.
Origin of Species, 104
Origins of Modern Science, 65*n*.
Oswego Normal School, 133
Our Colonial Curriculum, 111*n*.
Our Public Elementary Schools, 100*n*.
Outlines of Educational Doctrine, 101
Owen, Robert, 88, 118
Oxford University, 33, 47, 99*n*.

Padua, University of, 47
Paedonomus of Spartan education, 5
Page, of chivalry, 34
Painter, F. V. N., 52*n*.
Palaestra (gymnastic school) of Athens, 5
Palatium, 72
Pangborn, Jessie M., 134*n*.
Pansophia, 71
Pansophism, 66
Pantaenus, 24
Pantagruel, 45, 63
Paris, University of, 33, 47
Parish Catholic schools, 128
Parker, Francis W., 139
Parkhurst, Helen, 140
Parley, Peter, 119
Parochial schools: bus transportation for pupils of, 137*n*.; Catholic, 128; free textbooks for use in, 137*n*.; Lutheran, 128
Pascoe, C. F., 87*n*.
Passow, A. Harry, 142*n*.
Paternalism of Spartan education, 4
Pauck, Wilhelm, 50*n*.
Paulsen, Friedrich, 53*n*., 84*n*., 97*n*.
Paulus Aemilius, 16
Peabody, George, 127
Peace of Augsburg, 49
Peace of Paris, 109
Peace of Utrecht, 61
Peace of Westphalia, 40, 49, 61
Peaceful coexistence, 136
Peasants' War, 49
Pedagogy, first chair of, 86
Peloponnesian war, 3
Pennsylvania, University of, 113
Periclean Age, 4
Periods: of American education, 107; of Greek education, 4; of Roman education, 14, 15
Peripatetic professors-at-large, 6
Peripatetic school (Aristotle's), 9
Perry, William F., 124
Persian Empire, 3
Pestalozzi, 87*n*., 91*n*.
Pestalozzi and His Educational System, 91*n*.
Pestalozzi: His Life and Work, 91*n*.
Pestalozzi, Johann Heinrich, 78, 89–91, 101; educational writings of, 89, 90; influence of Locke on, 74; influence of Rousseau on, 89
Pestalozzi's Educational Writings, 90*n*.
Peter Ramus and the Educational Reformation of the Sixteenth Century, 68*n*.
Petrarch, 42
Petty, Sir William, 69
Ph.D. degrees, 97*n*., 132
Phelps Stokes Fund, 127*n*.
Philanthropic effort in education, 99
Philanthropinum, 85, 86, 87*n*.
Philbrick, John D., 124
Philip Melanchthon, The Protes-

tant Preceptor of Germany, 53*n.*
Phillips Academy, 129
Philosophical class of Plato's ideal society, 7
Philosophical education as formulated by Plato, 8
Philosophical position of John Locke, 73
Philosophical schools: of Athens, 8; of New Greek period, 4
Philosophy development in Age of Pericles, 6
Physical sciences of the 19th century, 104
Physiocrats, French, 78
Piaget, Jean, 70*n.*, 73*n.*
Piarists, 57
Piccolomini, 44
Pickett, Albert, 122, 123
Pierce et al. v. *Society of Sisters,* 137
Pierce, John D., 124
Pietistic movement of Hermann Francke, 74
Pietistic schools, 75, 76, 84
Pike, Nicholas, 119
Pinloche, Auguste, 87*n.*
Pioneers of Modern Education, 62*n.*, 70*n.*
Place of Education in Utopias, 66*n.*
Plan of Education, 79
Plan of a University, 80
Planta, Martin, 87*n.*
Plataea, Greek victory at, 3
Plato, 6–9, 26, 31; ideal society, exposition of, 7
Platoon Plan of Gary, 140
Plattard, Jean, 63*n*
Pliny the Younger, 17
Plutarch, 5, 44, 45
Polis, 3, 4
Political changes in Age of Pericles, 6
Political liberalism of John Locke, 77
Political nationalism of the 19th century, 93
Political schools of the Nazi regime, 154
Political Writings of Jean-Jacques Rousseau, 81*n.*
Politics, The, 8
Pope Pius II, 44
Pope Sylvester II, 28
Population: school age, increase in, 142; of the U.S. in 1962, 136
Port Royal school, influence of Descartes on, 67
Portrait of Socrates, 7*n.*
Positions, 68, 69*n.*
Poverty as ideal of monasticism, 24
Power, Edward J., 27*n.*, 136*n.*
Practical Parts of Lancaster's Improvements and Bell's Experiment, 89*n.*
Praeceptor Germaniae, 53
Presbyterians of Scotland, 49
"Present State of Educational Theory in the United States," 140*n.*
Primary department, 118
Primary school law of France of 1833, 97, 98
Princeton College, 112
Principles of Psychology, 138
Printing, invention of, 39
Priscian, 18, 28
Private ownership of property, 94
Private schools: of Athens, 5; of France, 98; in 19th-century America, 127–129; prohibited in Rome, 17; role of in America, 136, 137
Private versus state control of colleges, 129
Proceedings of the British

Academy, 64*n.*
Professional education, 131
Progressive education, 139, 140, 151; eight-year study of, 140; learning-living methodology of, 139
Progressive Education Association, 139
Progymnasium, 96
Proposals Relating to the Education of Youth in Pennsylvania, 113, 114
Proposed: The University of the United States, 117*n.*
Protagoras, 6
Protagoras, 7
Protestant elementary and secondary schools of the Reformation, 54, 55
Prussia under Frederick the Great, 77
Prussian Elementary Schools, 95*n.*
Prussian-Pestalozzian school system, 91
Prussian school systems, 94–97
Prussian secondary education of the 19th century, 95, 96
Psalter, 113
Psychologizing education, 78, 89, 90
Psychology: child, as base of education, 78; development in Age of Pericles, 6; educational, 101; experimental, 138; of Herbart, 102; stimulus-response, 138
Ptolemaic theory of the universe, 10
Public Education Under Criticism, 141*n.*
Public education in the South, 1860–1900, 126, 127
Public Education in the South, 126*n.*
Public high schools, American, 125, 126; standardizing associations for, 126; tax support for, 125
Public Primary System of France, 98*n.*
Public school movement in America, 121–123; leaders in, 123, 124
Public School Society of New York, 122
Public schools: of America, criticism and problems of, 141, 142; American and English, difference between, 48*n.*; of colonial Maryland, 110; of England, 100, 101; of England in the Renaissance, 47, 48; in 19th-century America, 120–127; religious educational program in, 127
Public Schools and British Opinion, 99*n.*
Puritans, 61, 109

Quadrivium, the, 25
Quaker Education in the Colony and State of New Jersey, 111*n.*
Quaker Education in Theory and Practice, 128*n.*
Quakers, 109–111; schools operated by, 128
Queen's College, 112
Question of Jean-Jacques Rousseau, 81*n.*
Quick, Robert H., 43*n.*, 69*n.*
Quincy Grammar School in Boston, 124
Quintilian, 17, 42

Rabelais, François, 45, 62, 63
Radcliffe College, 133
Raikes, Robert, 88, 119
Ramus, Peter, 44, 66, 68
Rashdall, Hastings, 33*n.*
Ratich, Wolfgang, 70*n.*
Ratichius, Wolfgang, 70*n.*

Ratio studiorum, 56
Rationalism, 78
Ratke, Wolfgang, 70; educational recommendations of, 70
Reading schools, 124
Readings in American Educational History, 126*n.*
Realgymnasium, 96
Realism: in education, definition of, 62; in education in the 17th century, 61–76; historical background of realism in education in the 17th century, 61; humanistic, 62–64; of John Locke, 73, 74; and nominalism, reconciliation between, 31, 32
Realprogymnasium, 96
Realschulen, 74, 75, 96, 97
Reappraisals in History, 65*n.*
Reconstruction, 115, 127
Reform of Secondary Education in France, 99*n.*
Reformation, 49–57 authoritarianism of, 77; educators, 51–54; humanistic contents of education of, 50; influence on education, 50, 51; Protestant elementary and secondary schools of, 54, 55; religious schools of, 54, 55; selected references on, 57, 58; universities of, 54
Reformed Church, 50
Reformed Schools, 69
Reigart, John F., 89*n.*, 118*n.*
Religion, Government, and Education, 127*n.*, 137*n.*
Religious education in the 17th century, 75, 76
Religious instruction, 98, 151, 153
Religious schools: in 19th-century America, 127–129; of the Reformation, 54, 55
Religious wars: between Catholicism and Protestantism, 55; of the 17th century, 61
Rein, Wilhelm, 102
Renaissance: educational significance of, 42–44; educational theorists of, 44–46; English humanists of, 45; English public schools of, 47, 48; Humanism in education in, 43, 44; and humanistic education, 41–48; humanistic schools of, 46–48; ideals of, 41; in Italy, 41, 42; Italian universities of, 46, 47; revival of liberal education, 42, 43; schools of the court and nobility, 47; selected references on, 57, 58; universities of, 46, 47.
Rensselaer Polytechnic Institute, 131
Report on Public Instruction in Germany, 98*n.*
Reports on Elementary Schools, 100*n.*
Reports on European Education, 122*n.*
Republic, The, 7
Research university *versus* the liberal arts college, 130
Restoration of Learning, 140n.
Reuchlin, Jacob, 46
Revolt against the Catholic Church, 49
Revolutions of 1830–1833, 1848–1850, 94
Rhetor, school of the, 15–16
Rhetorical schools, 9
Ribot Commission, 99
Richard, J. W., 53*n.*
Richards, Ellen H., 132
Right Method of Instruction, 46
Rise of American Civilization, 116*n.*
Ritter, Karl, 87
Ritterakademien, 74
Robert Owen, 88

Robinson Crusoe, 83, 86*n.*
Robinson the Younger, 86
Rolland, Barthelemy, D'Erceville, 79
Rolland, Romain, 84*n.*
Roman Catholic Church, revolt against, 49
Roman Catholic Counter Reformation, 50
Roman Conquest of Greece, 3, 10
Roman education, 12–19; decline of, 18, 19; Greek dominance of, 14–18; historical background, 13; periods of, 14, 15
Roman empire support of schools, 16–17
Romanticism and the Modern Ego, 82*n.*
Romanticism of Rousseau, 82*n.*
Rome: libraries of, 16; *Ludi* schools of early, 14; University of, 16, 47
Roosevelt, Franklin D., 135
Roosevelt, Theodore, 135
Roscellinus, 31
Rosenwald Fund, 127*n.*
Ross, Earle D., 116*n.*
Rousseau, 81*n.*
Rousseau, Jean-Jacques, 45, 63, 78, 80–84, 86*n.*, 87*n.*, 89, 101; influence of Locke on, 74
Rousseau and Romanticism, 82*n.*
Rousseau's Émile, 81*n.*
Rudolph, Frederick, 112*n.*, 129*n.*
Rudy, Willis, and John S. Brubacher, 129*n.*
Rugby (English public school), 48
Rugg, Harold O., 139
Rush, Benjamin, 117
Russell, James E., 96*n.*
Russell, William, 122
Rutgers College, 112
Ryan, W. Carson, 132*n.*

Sadler, M., 100*n.*
St. Augustine, 23
St. Benedict, 24
St. Jerome, 23
St. John's College, 123
St. Paul's (English public school), 48
St. Thomas Aquinas, 32
Salamanca, University of, 33
Salmon, D., and W. Hindshaw, 88*n.*
Salmon, David, 89*n.*
Salzman, L. F., 34*n.*
Salzmann, Christian G., 86
Sandys, J. E., 47*n.*
Saxony church-school ordinance, 53
Schaupp, Zora, 80*n.*
Schmidt, George, 129*n.*
Scholarship: aid under Weimar Republic, 149; rise in the early Middle Ages, 25
Scholasticism: 28; educational content of, 32; educational purposes of, 31, 32; of the late Middle Ages, 31, 32; limitations of, 32
Scholastics and their textbooks, 32
School leaving age, 151
School of Organic Education, Fairhope, Alabama 140
School and Society, 139, 140*n.*
School year, length of, 136
Schoolmaster, The, 45, 64*n.*
"Schoolmaster of America," 119
Schoolmaster's Assistant, 113*n.*
Schoolmen, the, 32
Schools; of Comenius, 72, 73; of the court and nobility of the Renaissance, 47; integration of, 137, 138; new types

of, at close of the Middle Ages, 35, 36; of the Pietists, 75, 76
Schulordnung, 113
Schulpflichtigkeit, 51
Schurz, Mrs. Carl, 104
Science: in the curriculum, 104, 112, 114, 130; of education, 138, 139; in education in the 19th century, 93–104; of the 19th century, 104.
Science of Education, 101
Science and Religion in Seventeenth Century England, 66*n.*
Scientific education as formulated by Plato, 8
Scientific method of education of Aristotle, 8
Scotch Reformation, 52
Scott, C. W., 141*n.*
Scriptorium, of the monastery, 24–25
Secondary education: developments of, in England, 100; in 19th-century France, 97; of 19th-century Prussia, 95, 96
Secondary Education in the 19th Century, 101*n.*
Secondary schools, comprehensive, of England, 152
Secondary schools: in the middle colonies, 110, 111; in the New England colonies, 111, 112; in the southern colonies, 110; standardizing associations for, 126; of the Weimar Republic, 149
Selden, William K., 126*n.*
Selected references on: American education, 145–149; American education, general works, 145, 146; American education, readings and collection of sources, 147, 148; American education, recent specialized studies, 148, 149; education in classical antiquity, 19, 20; the Medieval world, 36, 37; the modern era, 104–106; recent European developments, 161–162; the Renaissance and Reformation, 57, 58
Self-observation of the Cartesian method, 67
Seminaries, 117
Seminarium Praeceptorum, 75
Seneca, 17
Sense-realism: 62, 65–70; early representatives of, 67–69; of 17th-century England, 69, 70; representatives of, 66, 67; in the schools, 74, 75
Sententiae, the, 32
Separation of church and state, 127
Sermon On the Duty of Sending Children to School, 52
Seven liberal arts, the, 25
Seventeenth century, educational development in, 60–76
Shapiro, J. S., 80*n.*
Sheffield Scientific School at Yale, 131
Sheldon, Edward A., 91, 133
Shoemaker, Don, 137*n.*
Shoemaker, Ervin S., 119*n.*
Short History of American Life, 116*n.*
Shrewsbury (English public school), 48
Simon, Theodore, 138
Singer, Charles, 41*n.*
Slums and Suburbs, 141*n.*
Smith, Adam, 78
Smith College, 133
Smith, Preserved, 50*n.*, 51*n.*
Smith, William, 113
Social Contract, 81
Social and institutional aspect of education, 4

Social Integration in Urban Communities, 141*n.*
Social-realism, 64, 65
Social trends of the 19th century, 93, 94
Society of Friends, 128
Society of Jesus and the Catholic Reformation, 55–57
Society for the Promotion of Christian Knowledge, 87; *Annual Reports* of, 87*n.*
Society for the Propagation of the Gospel in Foreign Parts, 87
Society and Thought in Early America, 110*n.*
Socrates, 6, 7
Socratic Method, 7
Soldier class of Plato's ideal society, 7
Some Famous American Schools, 129*n.*
Some Thoughts Concerning Education, 73
Sophists: 6; basal principle of, 7; emphasis on individuality in teachings of the, 6; moral teachings of the, 6; negative attitude of the, 7
South Dakota State School of Mines, 131
Southern colonies, elementary and secondary schools in, 110
Southern, R. W., 35*n.*
Southern School News, 141*n.*
Soviet Union, education in, 153, 154
Spain, Moorish intellectual centers of, 10
Spanish-American War, 116
Spanish Armada, defeat of, 61
Spartan education, 4, 5; paternalism of, 4
Spaulding, Bishop John L., 128
S.P.C.K., 87, 89
Spencer, Herbert, 104
Spener, Philip Jacob, 75
Speyer School of Teachers College, 140
S.P.G., 87, 110, 111
Spieske, Alice W., 119*n*
Spinka, Matthew, 72*n.*
Spirit of Laws, 77
Squire, of chivalry, 34
Standardizing associations for secondary schools, 126
State aid for religious educational programs, 127
State boards of education, 120, 121
State colleges and universities of 19th-century America, 130, 131
State higher education of 19th-century America, 130, 131
State normal schools, 133
State Planning Commission, 153
State schools of mines, 131
State universities, 117, 118
State Universities and Democracy, 118*n.*
State *versus* private control of colleges, 129
Stern, John, 50*n.*
Stobart, J. C., 3
Stoics and Stoicism, 9
Stories for Children, 87
Storr, Richard J., 132*n.*
Story of the Eight Year Study, 140*n.*
Stowe, Calvin E., 122
Stratemeyer, F. B., 142*n.*
Studies in Early Graduate Education, 132*n.*
Studies in French Education from Rabelais to Rousseau, 65*n.*
Study of Engineering Education, 131*n.*
Study of words differentiated from study of things, 62*n.*
Sturm, John, 47

Subject election *versus* classical curriculum, 130
Suetonius, 17
Sulla, 16
Sulzer, John George, 87*n.*
Summa Theologica, 32
Sunday School movement, 88, 89; in America, 119
Sunday School Society of Philadelphia, 119
Sunday Schools of Reform Jews, 129
Supreme Council of Public Instruction *(Oberschul-collegium),* 86
Surplus Revenue Act, 121
Swamp Land Grant Act, 121
Swett, John, 124
Swift, F. H., 121*n.*
Switzerland: agricultural schools in, 91; Pestalozzi schools in, 89
System of Studies, 62*n.*
Systematic Refutation of the Book of Helvetius on Man, 80

Tabula rasa theory, 73
Tacitus, 17, 42
Taft, William H., 135
Talented students, problems of, 142
"Talented Youth Project: A Report on Research Under Way," 142*n.*
Tarn, W. W., 9*n.*
Taxation for school support, 121, 125, 126
Teacher education, 103, 133, 134; under the Weimar Republic, 153
Teacher-training institutions in America, 103, 133
Teachers College, Columbia University, 133
Teachers of the Society of Jesus, 56
"Teaching of Modern Languages," 159
Technical education in 19th-century America, 131
Technicums, 158
Tercentenary History of the Boston Latin School, 112*n.*
Terman, Lewis B., 138
Tertullian, 23
Testament, the, 113
Testing, mental, 138, 139
Textbooks: of American schools, 119; of the Colonial period, 113, 114; of Comenius, 72, 74; of the scholastics, 32
Thacher School, 129
Tharp, Louise Hall, 123*n.*
Theocracy of New England, 109, 111
Theodosius, 17
Theological academies, 131
Theological Education in America, 131*n.*
Theories of Learning, 138*n.*
Thesaurus, 72
Thirty-nine Articles of the Church of England, 50
Thirty Years' War, 40, 61, 74, 75
Thomas, Milton H., 139*n.*
Thomson, David, 94*n.*
Thorndike, Edward L., 138
Thorndike, Lynn, 67*n.*
Thursfield, Richard E., 123*n.*
Thwing, Charles, 97*n.*
Toleration Act of 1689, 75
Torrey, N. L., 79*n.*
"Total depravity," theory of, 52
Tractate on Education, 63
Transformation of the School: Progressivism in American Education, 125*n.*, 140*n.*
Transition to modern era: Renaissance and Reformation, 39–58; historical background of, 39, 40

Transitional period, New Greek education, 6–9
Trapp, E. C., 86
Treatise on Man, 79
Trivium, the, 25
Trotzendorf, Valentin, 54*n.*
Truman, Harry S., 135
Trump, J. Lloyd, and Dorsey Baynham, 142*n.*
Tudor School Boy Life: The Dialogues of Juan Luis Vives, 68*n.*
Tuer, A. W., 112*n.*
Turgot, Aune Robert Jacques, 79
Turnbull, G. H., 63*n.*
Turner, F. C., 90*n.*
Tewksbury, Donald G., 131*n.*
Twentieth-century American education, 135–145; growth, 1900–1960, 136, 137; historical background of, 135, 136; opportunities for, 137, 138
Two Hundred Years: The History of the Society for Promoting Christian Knowledge, 87*n.*
Two Treatises on Government, 73

Ufer, Christian, 102*n.*
UNESCO and world education, 159–160
United Nations, 136
United States Commissioner of Education, the first, 123
United States Military Academy at West Point, 131
United States population in 1962, 136
Universal education, 136
Universal Geography, 119
Universities (*see also* under specific name of University): of Europe in the Middle Ages, 33*n.;* of the Greek world, 9; of the late Middle Ages, 32–34; in 19th-century Germany, 96, 97; of the Reformation, 54; of Rome, 16; state, of America, 117, 118
University departments of education, 134
University *versus* college, 129, 130
Until Victory: Horace Mann and Mary Peabody, 123*n.*
Urbanization, 94
Urquahart, Thomas, 63*n.*
Utilitarian educational aims of the Sophists, 6
Utopia, 45
Utopia: of *Christian City,* 66*n.;* of *The City of the Sun,* 66*n.;* of *New Atlantis,* 66

Valentinian, 17
Vandwalker, Nina C., 104*n.*
Varro, Marcus, 63
Vassar College, 133
Vaughan, C. E., 81*n.*
Vegius, Mapheus, 44
Vergerius, Paulus, 43
Verona, Guarino da, 44
Vespasian, 16
Vestibulum (Entrance Hall), 72
Virginia, University of, 116, 117
Visitation Articles of Saxony, 53
"Vives: the Father of Modern Psychology," 68*n.*
Vives, Juan Luis, 66–68; educational aims of, 68
Vocational education in 19th-century Germany, 96
Vocational schools of France, 98
Volksschulen, 95, 96
Volk-State idea dominant in Nazi education, 149, 150
Voltaire, François Marie Arouet de, 77
Von Zedlitz, Baron, 86

Walker, W., 51*n.*
War of 1812, 115
Warfel, H. R., 119*n.*
Warriors of Spartan state, 5
Wars of Louis XIV, 61
Washburne, Carleton, 140
Washington, George, recommendation of, for national university, 117
Watson, Foster, 55*n.*, 67, 68*n.*, 70*n.*
Wayland, Francis, 130
Wealth of Nations, 78
Webster, Noah, 119
Weimar Republic, educational developments in, 149
Wellesley College, 133
Welton, J., and S. S. Fletcher, 103*n.*
Wesley, Edgar B., 117
West Germany, education in, 150
Western Academic Institute and Board of Education, 122, 123
Western Literary Institute and College of Professional Teachers, 123
Western Views of Islam in the Middle Ages, 35*n.*
Westfall, Richard S., 66*n.*
Westminster Catechism, 113
Westminster (English public school), 48
White, Andrew D., 130
Wickersham, J. P., 111*n.*
Wilderspin, Samuel, 88, 118
Wiley, Calvin H., 122, 124
Willard, Emma, 132, 133
William and Mary, College of, 112, 116, 132
William of Occam, 32
William Penn Charter School, 111
Williams, E. I. F., 123*n.*
Wilson, Woodrow, 135
Wimpheling, Jacob, 46
Winchester (English public school), 48
Winnetka Plan, 140
Wirt, William, 140
Wisconsin, University of, 123
Wish, Harvey, 110*n.*
With All Deliberate Speed, 137*n.*
Woelfel, Norman, 136*n.*
Wolke, C. H., 86
Women, education of, 5, 8, 68, 83*n.*, 117, 132, 133
Woods, W. H., 62*n.*
Woodward, Hezekiah, 69
Woodward, W. H., 46*n.*
Woody, Thomas, 111*n.*, 113*n.*, 133*n.*
Work programs integrated into junior high school, 142
World War I, 116, 135
World War II, 135
Writing schools, 124
Wundt, Wilhelm, 138

Xenophon, 7

Yale, 112, 132
Yale Report of 1825, 130
Yeshivah, 129
Yverdun, institute at, 89, 91

Zeno, 9
Ziller, Tuiskon, 102
Zorach v. *Clauson,* 137*n.*
Zwingli, Ulrich, 52